THE HOW TO GROW AND CAN IT BOOK

of Vegetables, Fruits, and Herbs

Other books by Jacqueline Hériteau

The How to Grow and Cook It Book of
  Vegetables, Herbs, Fruits, and Nuts

Oriental Cooking the Fast Wok Way

Take-It-Along Cookbook

THE HOW TO GROW AND CAN IT BOOK

of Vegetables, Fruits, and Herbs

Jacqueline Hériteau

Illustrated by Peter Kalberkamp

Hawthorn Books, Inc.
Publishers/New York

THE HOW TO GROW IT AND CAN IT BOOK OF VEGETABLES,
FRUITS, AND HERBS

Library of Congress Catalog Card Number: 75–10431
ISBN: 0–8015–3718–5

1 2 3 4 5 6 7 8 9 10

For my friends Francesca and John Morris,
and to our children, and your children,
and all those who find joy in growing
the plants that feed us

Contents

Acknowledgments

A finished book always leaves the author in debt to the friends and advisors who enrich it. Many of the recipes in this book are updated heirlooms of Sally Larkin Erath, Francesca Bosseti Morris, Gay Matteson, and other friends too numerous to mention. I also wish to thank the W. Atlee Burpee Seed Company for advice in selecting varieties most suited to growing for canning and preserving; the United States Department of Agriculture, in particular Robert Wearne and Kate Alfriend; Walter W. Washko, agronomist; David A. Kollas, pomologist of the Cooperative Extension Service; Elvin McDonald, editor of the *Hearst Good Housekeeping Illustrated Encylopedia of Gardening*, for counsel in the growing departments; and Gretchen Viesmer of the Mirro Aluminum Company in Manitowac, Wisconsin, makers of canning equipment. I am much indebted for advice and technical information to the Food and Nutrition Extension Service in Washington, D.C.; and to my friend Anne Lemoine for using her head so well as she typed.

ix

Introduction:
The Practical Romantic

There are romantic aspects to growing and putting up your own food supplies—and there are practical aspects. A dollar bill can be beautiful when it is the dollar you didn't spend on a recent rise in food costs. Growing and putting up your own food can save $200 to $500 or more from the annual food budget for a family of four. As long as the cost of energy fuels that make our lives comfortable is climbing, we have an interest in using a little extra personal energy to offset the rises.

But there's more to growing and putting up your own food than the practical advantages of penny pinching.

In Connecticut near Long Island Sound there still are standing some of the mammoth farmhouses built in the last century, farmhouses as big as Grand Hotel, barns bigger than hippodromes, set in cultivated fields rolling away over hills that seem to stretch to Never-Never Land. Those are the Jeffersonian farmhouses of my dreams, nineteenth-century structures that housed men and boys who grew the food that fed the women and girls who put food up. In my dreams they all sang as they worked and lived happily ever after, lives fulfilled, serene and crowned with an old age whose wisdom was as clear as noonday.

Well, by now I know that in the days when Thomas Jefferson plumped for an agrarian economy and a rural society, there was exactly as much romance around the family farm as there is today, and a lot more work. If Jeffersonian ways had been perfect, they would have survived. Our distant view fogs the edges of yesterday's sharp experiences. The labor involved in keeping an enormous agrarian family self-sufficient in all things is not in itself fulfilling. Hard work can be a bore.

What is fulfilling about growing your own food is the sense it gives the gardener of oneness with the earth and the seasons. What is fulfilling about serving your own canned or frozen fruits and jams and jellies and preserves is the sense of personal pride you can take in very special foods that are the work of your own hands. Breakfast pancakes, dripping with melted butter and blueberry jam you made yourself last summer—that's a nice thing to share on a cold winter morning.

New ways to have some of the wonderful homemade foods of the past is what this book is about.

1

Time, Space, and Economics

A joke among suburban householders a few years ago was the twenty-dollar tomato: the tomato that cost twenty dollars to grow when you totted up the bill for rototilling, soil improvement, fertilizer, and garden tools. It can cost that much to grow a tomato (if you try hard), but for the same twenty dollars you can create a garden that can save $250 a year on food bills for a family of four. Invest a little more, put in fruit trees and bramble fruits, work your garden for the highest possible yield, plan to can and freeze the produce from your garden, and you can double the savings. And have a lot of fun while you are at it.

To prove that vegetable gardens save money, the National Garden Bureau, the educational division of the garden-seed industry, headquartered near Gardenville, Pennsylvania, in 1974 experimented with a garden 15 feet by 25 feet, the WIN (Whip Inflation Now) garden (see Planting Plan 1). In it were grown eighteen varieties of vegetables that give a yield from April to December. The garden yield was enough for a family of four to use fresh with leftovers in good supply for canning, freezing, and storing against the months when there is no local fresh produce.

The WIN garden saved over $250 on food bills. The cost of putting in the garden came to a little over the cost of the suburbanite tomato, $20. That figure included seeds, sets, fertilizing, and some money spent

1

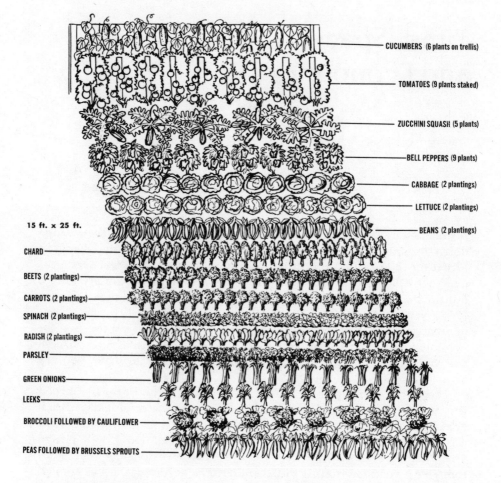

CUCUMBERS (6 plants on trellis)

TOMATOES (9 plants staked)

ZUCCHINI SQUASH (5 plants)

BELL PEPPERS (9 plants)

CABBAGE (2 plantings)

LETTUCE (2 plantings)

15 ft. x 25 ft.

BEANS (2 plantings)

CHARD

BEETS (2 plantings)

CARROTS (2 plantings)

SPINACH (2 plantings)

RADISH (2 plantings)

PARSLEY

GREEN ONIONS

LEEKS

BROCCOLI FOLLOWED BY CAULIFLOWER

PEAS FOLLOWED BY BRUSSELS SPROUTS

Planting Plan 1

on pest control. If the garden had been rototilled, the cost might have risen another $5 to $10.

The table below is the National Garden Bureau table of yields and savings for the WIN garden. They are based on 1974–1975 food prices.

SAVINGS FOR THE 15-BY-25-FOOT "WIN" GARDEN

VEGETABLE	YIELD	COST (per unit)	SAVINGS
Cucumbers	60	25¢ each	$15.00
Tomatoes	100 pounds	$1 for 3 pounds	33.33
Zucchini	40 pounds	39¢ a pound	15.60
Peppers	40 pounds	39¢ a pound	15.60
Cabbage	24 heads	39¢ a head	9.36
Lettuce	48 heads	49¢ a head	23.52
Beans	25 pounds	39¢ a pound	9.75
Chard	48 pounds	59¢ a pound	28.32
Beets	36 pounds	29¢ a pound	10.44
Carrots	36 pounds	29¢ a pound	10.44
Spinach	12 pounds	59¢ a pound	7.08
Radishes	24 bushels	29¢ a bushel	6.96
Parsley	48 bushels	29¢ a bushel	13.92
Green onions	24 bushels	25¢ a bushel	6.00
Leeks	28 bushels	59¢ a bushel	16.52
Broccoli	24 heads	49¢ a head	11.76
Peas	15 pounds	39¢ a pound	5.85
Brussels sprouts	60 pints	59¢ a pint	35.40
		Total	$274.85

A GARDEN FOR CANNING AND FREEZING

There are two big differences between an ordinary vegetable garden and a garden for putting up—for canning and freezing. The main difference lies in the varieties planted; a secondary difference is in the application of gardening practices meant to produce the highest possible yield for the garden space invested.

A garden big enough to give you fresh produce for summer use and for making jams, jellies, relishes, and all those nice homemades can be as small as 25 by 25 feet or as large as 50 by 100 feet, a big garden indeed. But you can grow crops for canning and freezing in a container garden, too. You'll have smaller crops and fewer varieties —that's the difference between a small garden and a big one.

CONTAINER GARDENS FOR CANNING

Food plants flourish in containers as well as in the open garden provided there is sun most of the day. On my New York rooftop, in redwood containers, I am growing dwarf apples, peaches, pears, and rhubarb; at their feet I have strawberries; and in the flower boxes along with geraniums and petunias I have tomatoes, large and small, and peppers. A whole window box full of herbs grows there, and in half-bushel baskets lined with ripped-open garbage bags I am growing eggplants, which climb the fencing along the parapet, and cherry tomatoes and cabbages. I have personally met some carrots (short varieties) that grow in window boxes, and the United States Department of Agriculture (USDA) has grown tomatoes such as Pixie Hybrid and Patio Hybrid in hanging baskets and in bushel baskets. Beets, cabbage, carrots, chives, cucumbers, eggplant, kale, leeks, leaf lettuce, mustard greens, onions, parsley, peppers, radishes, summer squash, Swiss chard, tomatoes, and turnips are the vegetables the USDA lists in its pamphlet on minigardens (Home and Garden Bulletin No. 63).

Can a container garden whose produce is used for canning and freezing save money? Depends: If you go out and invest a fortune in expensive redwood containers—the kind that can withstand the humidity of damp soil—it will take some years before you bank your food savings. If you already have containers or use available old boards (creosoted outside and inside) to make them, or if you recycle old buckets, garbage containers, and other receptacles, then the cost of your installation is minimal, and the profits will come in sooner. Go out and price a jar of pickled tomatoes or gherkins or eggplants, and you will begin to see how the yield of a well-managed container garden can leave you with a pleasant feeling of accomplishment when you confront the food budget.

If you are considering a container food garden, check Tables 1 and 2 for a notion of the yields you can expect from the gardening spaces available.

Vertical Crops in Container Gardens

The highest yield for the smallest space investment comes from crops that grow vertically. Grapes will climb an arbor or a sunny wall with only a few feet of dirt to contain their roots. Strawberries, tomatoes, cucumbers, squashes, pole beans, peas, eggplant, zucchini, and pumpkins can go up arbors, mailboxes, trellises, clothesline poles—anything that has a rough surface on which wooden lath strips or wires or strings can be affixed. Vertical crops can grow down as well as up, from planters set on wall tops, from hanging baskets. Small-fruited tomatoes grow well in hanging baskets (try them in topless plastic gallon containers). Big-fruited vines—pumpkins and squashes—can't support the weight of their crops when grown vertically, and must have shelves or net bags for support as the fruit matures.

Container crops needn't grow in expensive containers: Unused indoor plant pots, large coffee or tomato juice cans, five-gallon trash cans with broken bottoms, plastic laundry baskets, or bushel baskets, lined with plastic trash bags, old pails, old tubs, as well as any of the standard homes for ornamentals—window boxes, wooden planters, or urns of plastic, ceramic, cement, or wood—can be used to grow vegetables successfully. However, remember to puncture plastic bag and other containers' bottoms to create drainage.

If you are going to grow your canning garden in containers, use the space for high-yield or else for luxury crops. Fruits of all kinds, including everything from the dwarf orchard trees to grapes to strawberries, vertical crops (baby eggplants for pickling, cucumbers, tomatoes, pole beans for freezing, baby peas for canning, Bermuda onions, leeks, chives), and herbs and sweet peppers for freezing are all good investments for limited spaces. If you are growing vegetables for economy, use container space to grow family favorites that are costly. Or else use containers to grow varieties hard to find locally—your favorite variety of prune, or berry, or bean, or tomato.

Be sure to use your container space on a season-long basis. While you are waiting for warm enough weather to put out tomatoes and eggplants, you can grow early spring crops, such as pepper cress and the leaf lettuces in the container space. After the summer crops are out, plant quick-to-mature leaf crops like lettuce, late crops of peas and cabbage, and other cold-weather vegetables.

Potting Soils and Watering Needs of Container Gardens

Vegetables and fruit trees generally prefer slightly acid soils, but purchased potting soil for ornamentals is apt to be on the alkaline side. Mix your own in the following proportions: one part peat moss, two parts garden soil or ordinary potting soil, two parts sand or vermiculite or perlite, and one part dried cattle manure. For each bushel, add 9 level tablespoons superphosphate, 8 level tablespoons cottonseed meal, 4 level tablespoons sulfate of potash, and 2 level tablespoons ground limestone. If you are filling a lot of containers on an entire rooftop, lighten the weight by using vermiculite or perlite or even kitty litter (the plain kind) instead of sand. For my rooftop garden, I use bagged potting soil in the bottoms of the containers, topped with a commercially prepared soil for growing tomatoes. It is very light and ideal for the vegetables I grow.

Attention to watering is a must with container gardens. Check the humidity of your container plants daily, particularly in droughts. Outdoor plants, especially those growing high up in the sky, are subject to drying winds, and the limited amounts of soil in their pots dry out quickly. Expect to water container plants every day or two in the high heat of summer. A mulch of moss, wood chips, or plastic will help to keep the soil in the containers from drying out. If you go away for more than a few days in summer, you probably will need a plant tender to water your container garden.

NOOK-AND-CRANNY GARDENS

In the smallest of urban home lots there is a surprising amount of space for a canning garden if you combine container gardening with gardening in nooks and crannies. The stepped container garden illustrated here is another approach. Or you can set railroad ties into a sloping hillside and create terraces for your vegetables and fruits. You can combine ornamentals, vegetables, and herbs in your soil borders just as readily as you can in a window box. Sweet and hot peppers, herbs, cherry tomatoes, rhubarb, and asparagus (which grows into graceful feathery ferns after the early spring cutting season) are excellent choices for the ornamental border. Gherkin cucumbers (the tiny prickly cucumbers meant for pickling), eggplants, and pole beans can climb fences backdropping ornamental borders; or they can be set to grow vertically up any supports the small lot affords. Planting fruit trees instead of the ornamental flowering fruits brings fresh fruits as well as beauty to the landscape. A grape arbor that will yield bushels of grapes takes no more space than a rose arbor and in its own way is lovely to look at as well as generous in its yield.

COORDINATED CANNING IS FUN

Before you start planning a garden, big or small, for canning and freezing, it is helpful to have an overview of how gardening and putting up food can be coordinated.

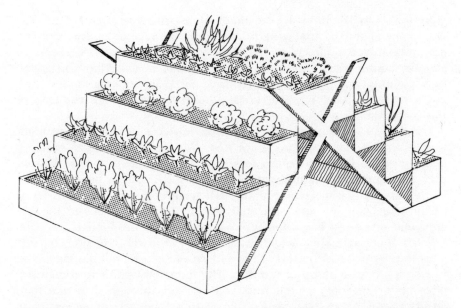

Stepped garden for a patio grows a surprising assortment of herbs and salad greens. A larger version of this staircase of planter boxes could grow enough luxury vegetables to make canning possible—asparagus, strawberries and tomatoes, for instance.

Gardening and canning are, and should be, fun. Fun, as long as you don't undertake more than you have time to do well. Plan a garden that you can handle easily. In order to get the biggest yield for the smallest amount of space and time, select your varieties carefully. Use interplanting and succession planting. Be sure to mulch, and use modern soil-improvement techniques and fertilizers. Plan the harvest dates so that canning and freezing can be done in small batches and are pleasant pastimes rather than demanding chores. Chapter 2 describes garden plans, but first, a word about canning.

You can spend days and weeks canning and preserving, but you don't have to. The most time-consuming part of canning and freezing is in preparing the foods to be processed—shelling the peas, snipping off bean ends, coring and peeling fruits and tomatoes. Once the vegetables have been prepared, putting them into canning jars is not a big job. Processing the foods is simply a matter of watching the clock as the pressure canner or boiling-water bath does its work. Freezing is even easier; the prepared foods are blanched and popped into freezing containers—the freezer does the rest.

What it comes down to is this: Canning or freezing everything your family will eat in a year takes about the amount of time you would spend during that year preparing fresh vegetables for cooking, and probably a quarter of the time you would normally spend in actually cooking the vegetables for individual meals. What you spend now canning and freezing, you'll save later in cooking hours. And you'll save on fuel for those cooking hours as well as on the cost of the foods themselves.

I enjoy my canning and preserving projects because I never get involved with huge batches to process. My pressure canner holds 8-quart jars—so I can in 8-quart lots. I like to have help, too, so I often plan to can on an evening when the family will watch television. It's fairly easy to get the children to shell peas and snip beans in front of the television set, and once that is done I take my loot to the kitchen and process it in an hour or so. Painless and productive.

Often enough when I find myself canning in the morning, friends who stop by work as we talk. I have often exchanged canning days and preserving days with other families. The important point to remember is to undertake only as much as you can get through in a morning, an afternoon, or an evening. Contemplating 5 bushels of beans to be canned is like standing at the foot of the Himalayas: discouraging—unless there is a crowd and you make it a party. If you have to do the job alone, try canning and preserving in small batches; like handling a small garden, it can be fun rather than drudgery.

TABLE 1

Yield Chart for the Vegetable Garden

Figures for the Yield Chart for the Vegetable Garden are based on extrapolations of USDA charts and charts from commercial sources, and on my own experience. Because the row yield depends on many variables, these figures can only be considered informed guesses. If your garden gets little attention and the climate is against it, the yield can be half. If conditions are optimum, the yield could be double.

VEGETABLE OR FRUIT	PLANTS 50′ ROW	YIELD	PINTS AFTER CANNING
Asparagus	35 plants	25 lbs.	15–22
Beans, Pole Shell Type	¼ lb.	2 bu.	70–80
Bush Snap Type	¼ lb.	25 qts.	30–45
Beets	½ oz.	1 bu.	35–40
Broccoli	1 pk.	25–30	30–50

VEGETABLE OR FRUIT	PLANTS 50' ROW	YIELD	PINTS AFTER CANNING
Brussels Sprouts	1 pk.	1–2 bu.	40–50
Cabbage	1 pk.	25 heads	35–40
Carrots	¼ oz.	1 bu.	32–40
Cauliflower	1 pk.	25 heads	35–40
Celeriac	¼ pk.	100 roots	cold store
Chard	½ oz.	3 bu.	24–40
Corn	¼ lb.	75 ears	14 pints
Cucumbers	½ pk.	75 lbs.	50–100
Eggplant	½ pk.	150 fruit	50–60
Garlic (cloves)	½ lb.	¾ bu.	dry store
Horseradish (perennial)	25 roots	too much	
Kale	½ pk.	125 lbs.	70–80
Leeks	2 pk.	100 plants	cold store
Melons	½ pk.	40–60 fruit	30–50
New Zealand, Malabar, and Tampala	½ oz.	2 bu.	24–40
Okra	2 pk.	30 qts.	60–70
Onions (sets)	½ lb.	1 bu.	dry store
Parsnips	1 pk.	1½ bu.	row store
Peas	½ lb.	1 bu.	24–30
Peppers	35 plants	2 bu.	50 pints
Potatoes, White	2–3 lb.	2 bu.	dry store
Potatoes, Sweet	2–3 lb.	2 bu.	40–60
Pumpkins	½ pk.	150 lb.	90–100
Radishes	2 pk.	50–70	use fresh
Rhubarb	17 roots	40–50 lb.	40–50
Rutabaga	1 pk.	1 bu.	dry store
Salsify	2 pk.	1–2 bu.	row store
Spinach	½ oz.	1 bu.	12–18
Squash, Summer Type	½ pk.	60–70	40–50
Squash, Winter Type	½ pk.	150 lbs.	100
Strawberries	35 plants	17–35 qts.	11–22
Tomatoes	17 plants	75 lbs.	40–60
Turnips	1 pk.	1 bu.	35–40
Zucchini	½ pk.	60–70	40–55

TABLE 2

Yield Chart for the Fruit Garden

Figures for the Yield Chart for the Fruit Garden are based on USDA charts and figures from commercial sources, and on my own experience and that of my friends. These figures can only be considered as informed guesses, since the plant itself, the season, the soil, and even the birds, can dramatically affect the yield from a fruit plant.

FRUIT	PER PLANT YIELD	PINTS AFTER CANNING
Apples, Dwarf	1–2 bu.	32–40
Semi-Dwarf	2–3 bu.	60–80
Apricots, Semi-Dwarf	2–3 bu.	70–90
Berries	½–1 qt.	⅓–1
Cherries, Semi-Dwarf	1–2 bu.	35–70
Crabapples, Standard	2–4 bu.	40–70
Grapes	15–30 lb.	15–30
Peaches, Dwarf	1–2 bu.	30–60
Pears, Dwarf	1–2 bu.	32–40
Plums, Semi-Dwarf	1–2 bu.	30–60

TABLE 3
Weekly Food Guide

Use this table, based on the U.S. Department of Agriculture's Daily Food Guide, to develop a view of how much you might need in the way of canned or frozen goods for your family if you decided to grow it all yourself and can it. The 36-week time period it covers would be those months of the year when the fresh product isn't available from the garden.

FOOD	TIMES SERVED IN ONE WEEK	AMOUNT NEEDED PER PERSON FOR 36 WEEKS
Citrus Fruit	7 1-cup portions	63 quarts
Citrus Fruit Juices		
Tomatoes and Tomato Juice		
Dark Green and Dark Yellow Vegetables (such as spinach, chard, and broccoli, carrots, pumpkins, squashes)	4 ½-cup portions	18 quarts
Other Fruits and Vegetables (such as apples, green peas, summer squash, asparagus)	17 ½-cup portions	76 quarts

2

Planting Plans
for a Canning Garden

To make canning fun, you have got to have a well-thought-out plan. Sow bean seed so that all the beans are ripe in the same two weeks, and you'll find canning and freezing the beans a great big chore. Plan the garden so the beans ripen over the eight or twelve weeks of summer, and you'll eat fresh beans as often as you like. And on the days when you don't want to serve beans, you can freeze that day's bean harvest while you cook dinner. It's that simple. If you want to can in 8-quart lots, you don't necessarily have to have 8 quarts of beans ripe at the same time. Each vegetable has a specific processing time. Beans in quart jars are processed in 25 minutes, but so are beets in pint jars. Beets are root crops that can be dug at any point over many weeks, unlike beans, which must be harvested as soon as they are 6 to 8 inches long and still young to get the best flavor and to keep the bushes producing.

HOW MUCH TIME DOES IT TAKE?

An experienced gardener can rototill a garden 15 by 25 feet or much larger in an hour or so. He can lime it, fertilize it, and rake it smooth for planting in a short afternoon. He can plant it in less than a day. If he puts a protective blanket of mulch over the soil, there should be

11

no weeding and very little in the way of watering chores, since the mulch keeps the soil moist between rains unless you hit a stretch of drought.

Hilling soil around the maturing plants, scratching or watering in fertilizer once during the summer months to encourage production, thinning as soon as newly planted seedlings begin to crowd each other—these are chores that absorb a couple of hours now and again. Removing crops that are finished and replacing them with new plantings takes a few hours per row. All told, a few hours every weekend is as much time as the garden will demand, as long as it gets regular attention and as long as it is put in properly in the first place in well-dug and enriched soil.

A vegetable garden is no more work than a flower garden, and it is easier to plant and maintain because it doesn't have to be an ornament in the landscape.

PLANNING A GARDEN FOR LARGE-BATCH CANNING, PRESERVING, AND FREEZING

If you are going to go into canning and preserving in a big way and have lots of potential helpers, planning a garden that will give you all you need is fairly simple. Use Table 3 to figure out how many quarts or pints you want of each vegetable or fruit. Use Table 1 to figure out how many seed packets and how long a garden row you need to provide the yields necessary to make the desired number of quarts. Use Table 2 to figure out how much fruit you want to grow and put up. Make it easier for yourself by planning to plant vegetables and fruits that will mature in succession, not all at once. There are early, mid-season, and late vegetable and fruit varieties in each species. Lay out your garden plan on graph paper, then use the tables at the back of the book to figure out when you must plant which item in order to have it mature at a time that you aren't already involved with canning whatever has matured in the nearby rows.

Of course, the best laid plans of mice and men are subject to weather, so it may not all unfold like clockwork. A late spring can get the beans off the ground at the wrong time and ripen them just when the squashes are booming. However, some effort to time your canning and preserving chores will stand you in better stead than no plan at all. Table 1 will give you some notion of what you might expect from plantings in 50-foot rows. Let me stress, however, that this yield section cannot be taken too literally: No one can accurately predict how many pounds or bushels you will harvest. Harvests depend on the weather, the soil, and other factors we could sum up as "luck." They also depend on seed. Many of the hybrid seeds can yield twice as much crop as ordinary seed. It is also true that how much row your seed packet will plant depends on seed-company packaging, and that isn't uniform.

The table, then, is an informed guess as to what you can expect. It should keep you from planting twice as much—or twice as little— as you can possibly want to put up.

Before you start working out a carefully timed planting plan, look at Planting Plan 2 for a big garden 50 by 90 feet. Around it could be dwarf fruit trees, which need about 10 feet of space all around, and bramble fruit bushes, which need about 4 feet of space all around. I'm not suggesting you follow it exactly; instead, choose from it only those vegetables and fruits you especially would like to put up or on which you normally spend a lot. I have included in this planting plan everything I would like to put up in the way of vegetables and fruit, including some things that normally don't grow in my area but may grow well in yours. The garden will yield plenty of fresh produce for use all summer long as well as all you will want to put up for winter use. Here are some of my favorite uses, canned and frozen, for the crops from this garden:

Apple rings, spiced for serving with meat dishes
Apple slices, frozen for pies
Applesauce, canned
Asparagus, frozen
Lima beans, frozen for succotash and frozen baby lima beans
Snap green beans, frozen (beans are almost my favorite vegetable,
    so the plan shows beans everywhere there is free space)
Blackberries, blueberries, and raspberries, preserved in jellies and
    jams or frozen for pies, muffins, and pancakes, and thawed
    to serve with ice cream
Beets, canned or pickled
Broccoli, frozen
Brussels sprouts, frozen
Carrots, made and frozen in carrot cake, frozen with mixed
    vegetables to serve with stews, or preserved in carrot jam
Cauliflower, which I pickle
Chard, frozen
Sour cherries, frozen or canned for pies
Corn, canned—creamed or whole kernel—or preserved in relishes

Cucumbers, pickled or made into relishes
Herbs, dried or frozen
Kale, left in the row for winter use
Melons, cantaloupes, frozen in balls
Okra, frozen for gumbos
Onions, big ones, chipped for winter use and frozen, or dried and
    stored
Green onions, frozen
Peaches; canned, halved or sliced; preserved into jams; or frozen,
    sliced, for pies
Peas, canned with baby onions or frozen
Peppers, frozen in chips for winter use and to make meat sauces
Pumpkins, canned or frozen for pies
Rhubarb, frozen for pies, canned for desserts, or preserved into
    jams
Strawberries, preserved into jams or frozen
Spinach, frozen
Summer squash, frozen
Fall and winter squash; stored; or canned or frozen, mashed
Tomatoes; made into juice, paste, or purée; or canned or frozen
    whole
Green tomatoes, made into relishes and piccalilli
Zucchini, frozen or pickled

PLANTING PLAN 2
The Big Canning Garden (50 by 90 feet)
(Raspberries, apples, blackberries, and sour cherries
can be grown outside the garden.)

PLANTS	SPACE BETWEEN 50-FOOT ROWS (in feet)
Turnips, early, followed by rutabaga	1½
Parsnips	1
Leeks	1
Herbs	1
Horseradish	1
Salsify	1
Garlic	1
Strawberries	4
Strawberries	4
Asparagus	4
Asparagus	4
Peas, followed by cucumbers	2½
Peas, followed by green beans	2½

PLANTS	SPACE BETWEEN 50-FOOT ROWS (in feet)
Snap green beans, successive plantings	2½
Lima beans	3
Beets	1½
Broccoli, early and late; followed by Romaine lettuce	2
Brussels sprouts, followed by cucumbers for pickles	2
Cauliflower, followed by mid-season carrots	2½
Chard	1½
Corn, pumpkin at its feet	3
Corn, pumpkin at its feet	3
Green onions	1
Kale	1½
Cucumbers, for pickles and to eat fresh, started with early radishes	4
Melons, cantaloupes or early watermelons, started with early cress	4
Okra	2
Early lettuce, followed by sweet peppers	2
Rhubarb	3
Spinach, followed by New Zealand spinach	1½
Summer squash	3
Winter and fall squash	4
Zucchini	3
Tomatoes, staked, following early lettuce	3
Tomatoes, preceded by radishes	3
Carrots, early, followed by late Brussels sprouts	2

PLANTING PLAN 3
The High-Yield Garden (25 by 28 feet)

PLANTS (in double rows)	SPACE BETWEEN 25-FOOT ROWS (in feet)
Tomatoes, preceded by spring lettuce	3
Snap beans, preceded by radishes	2½
Zucchini, preceded by early bush peas	3
Carrots, followed by late garden cress	2
Beets, followed by late parsnips	1½
Onions	1
Garlic	1

Planting Plan 3 for a high-yield garden is an entirely different approach to a canning garden. A small garden, it includes only those vegetables that give the highest yield for the space and effort involved. Here are bush snap beans, tomatoes, zucchini, carrots, beets, and onion and garlic sets. Except for the onion and garlic sets, which must occupy the rows from early spring until very late summer, you can follow and precede the rows of produce for canning with vegetables to serve fresh. The tomatoes can be preceded by early lettuce, which will be out of the row by the time the tomatoes go in in midspring; the snap green beans can be preceded by radishes and the zucchini by peas, since both radishes and peas can be planted almost before the snow is gone. The carrots can be followed by a late crop of peppers or by garden cress, a salad green that matures in just about ten days. The beets can go in early, come out fairly early in summer, and can be followed by a crop of late parsnips, which will mature in fall and can stay in the rows and be harvested at will until the rows freeze. The following spring the unharvested parsnips will still be good.

This plan is designed for a garden space 25 by 28 feet. However, it could be used for a space 14 by 50 feet, if you plant quadruple rows of everything. A glance at Table 2 will give you some idea of how much you can expect to put up from this garden.

Planting Plan 4 for a double-harvest garden takes yet another tack. It begins with crops that mature in the cool weather of early spring. Once the rows are free, these crops are followed by crops to be used fresh in summer or fall or to be put up, and some can stay in their rows through the winter for cold-weather harvests.

PLANTING PLAN 4
The Double-Harvest Garden (50 by 22½ feet)

PLANTS	SPACE BETWEEN 50-FOOT ROWS (in feet)
Garden cress, followed by broccoli (for fall)	2
Radishes, followed by green snap beans (use fresh in summer)	2½
Mustard greens, followed by kale (to stay in rows all winter)	1½
Scallions, followed by lettuce (for fall)	1½
Loosehead lettuce, followed by endive (for fall)	1
Spinach, followed by radishes (for fall)	1½
Early turnips, followed by spinach (for fall)	1½
Bush snap beans, followed by turnips (for fall)	2½
Summer squash, followed by peas (for fall)	3
Early peas, followed by parsnips (to stay in rows all winter)	2½

Kohlrabi, followed by horseradish
  (to stay in rows all winter)   1½
Swiss chard, followed by salsify
  (to stay in rows all winter)   1½

PLANTING PLAN 5
The Small Canning Garden (50 by 25 feet)

PLANTS	SPACE BETWEEN 50-FOOT ROWS (in feet)
Radishes, followed by tomatoes (with herbs in between)	3
Early lettuce, followed by cucumbers	4
Early peas, followed by cucumbers	4
Early peas, followed by snap green beans	2½
Early broccoli, followed by late carrots	2
Early broccoli, followed by beets (long season)	1½
Asparagus (perennial)	4
Strawberries (perennial)	4

Planting Plan 5 for the small canning garden includes only produce that is very popular for putting up—tomatoes, cucumbers for pickles, bush snap green beans in quantity, asparagus, strawberries, beets, broccoli, peas. Here, early radishes are followed by tomatoes with a few herb plants such as dill and parsley at their feet. Early lettuce is followed by cucumbers. Early peas are followed by cucumbers in one row; in another row they are followed by snap bush green beans planted in succession every ten days. Early broccoli is followed by long-standing carrots and beets. Asparagus and strawberries, both perennials, occupy their rows all year round.

Planting Plan 6, a 25-by-16½-foot garden of favorite vegetables, herbs, and flowers, includes America's favorite garden plants for eating—tomatoes, cucumbers, lettuce, sweet green peppers, snap green beans—along with a handful of herbs and a lot of flowers.

Early bush peas are followed by tomatoes, interplanted with dill, parsley, sage, and chives. Early lettuce is followed by cucumbers. Early peas are followed by sweet green peppers in one row and by cos lettuce for fresh summer use in the other row. Early radishes are followed by snap green beans. On one side of the garden, after their foliage has yellowed in late spring, spring-flowering daffodils are overplanted with quick-to-bloom Lady marigolds, twenty inches high. On the other side, early tulips are followed by Cut-and-Come-Again zinnias, twenty-four inches high. Both the zinnias and the marigolds make super cut flowers, and they bloom early and stay in bloom all summer long.

PLANTING PLAN 6
Favorite Vegetables, Herbs, and Flowers (25 by 16½ feet)

PLANTS	SPACE BETWEEN 25-FOOT ROWS (in feet)
Spring flowering bulbs, followed by Lady marigolds (20 inches high)	2
Early peas, followed by tomatoes (interplanted with dill, parsley, sage, chives)	3
Early lettuce, followed by cucumbers	4
Early peas, followed by sweet peppers	2
Early peas, followed by cos lettuce (for summer use)	1
Radishes, followed by snap green beans (succession planting)	2½
Tulips, followed by Cut-and-Come-Again zinnias (24 inches high)	2

PLANTING PLAN 7
Urban Garden Against a Fence (50 by 30 feet)

PLANT	SPACE BETWEEN 50-FOOT ROWS (in feet)
Pole lima beans	3
Asparagus	4
Asparagus	4
Tomatoes	3
Cucumbers	4
Strawberries	4
Melons	4
Lettuce	1½
Herbs	1½
Wild strawberries (as edge)	1

Planting Plan 7, a 50-by-30-foot urban garden against a fence, includes only luxury items to put up or freeze and utilizes every spare bit of soil in a small city lot 70 feet wide. At the back of the lot, a 50-foot row of pole lima beans climbs the fence; in front of that are two 50-foot rows of asparagus; in front of the asparagus are tomatoes in pink and yellow varieties for canning; strawberries are in the next row; melons come next; then a narrow row of lettuce, fronted by herbs, in particular parsley, which makes a pretty edging, chives, and some dill plants; and in front of that, *fraises des bois*, wild strawberries, which produce white starlike blooms and tiny sparkling red fruits all summer long, have been placed as an edge. What about the 20 feet left over? On either side of the vegetable row is walking space of about 10 feet, planted with two dwarf apple trees, two tiny Bonanza peach trees, four raspberry bushes, and two blueberry bushes.

The only caution with this garden is that the south must be the side on which the wild strawberries are growing. If it is anywhere else, the vegetables may get too much shade to produce properly.

There are many other approaches to planning your garden for putting up. Plan a garden for crops that store well in a cool place, or plan one that includes only easy-to-grow vegetables, or plan one that includes all your favorites for eating fresh plus the few crops that can be left in the garden all winter.

Vegetables to Store in a Cool Place

Beets	Pumpkins
Cabbage	Winter radishes
Carrots	Rutabaga
Celery	Fall and winter squash
Onions	Turnips
Parsnips	

Easy-to-Grow Vegetables

Bush snap beans	Kale
Beets	Lettuce
Carrots	Pumpkins
Chard	Radishes
Collards	Rutabaga
Corn	Squash
Cucumbers	Turnips

Vegetables That Can Winter Over in Their Rows

Parsnips	Kale
Horseradish	Salsify

Carrots, beets, and turnips can't winter over in areas where there are hard frosts, but they can stay in their rows until then.

3

If You Have No Space, Start a Community Garden

Cooperative community gardens are as old as time and can be more fun than a private vegetable garden—a kind of participation sport. When my grandfather was a young father, he bought a big plot of land outside his village in France and marked it out with a gardening plot for each child born. It proved to be a great investment because, as the town grew, the land became very valuable. Until they had land of their own, my uncles and aunts and their families all shared this big gardening space, and my cousins grew up picking peas together.

The most famous community gardening system in the world is probably in England where thousands and thousands of people rent garden lots from local authorities, corporations, and nationalized industries. These are called "allotments." Some are very simple gardening setups, but others (which can rent for as high as $20 per plot) have everything from running water to greenhouses and community centers with toilet facilities.

On the home scene, many corporations—including Dow Chemicals in Midland, Michigan; Hercules, Inc. in Wilmington, Delaware, and the RCA Laboratories at the David Sarnoff Research Center, Princeton, New Jersey—have made garden lots available to employees, lands once used for ornamental or recreational purposes. If you don't have gardening space of your own, land may be made available to you by your employer or you may find suitable space for rent by a community group.

20

There are several approaches to community gardening. In Appleton, Wisconsin, at the Papal Gardens, families rent land from farmers who do all the soil preparation (the biggest and hardest part of the job) as well as much of the planting and cultivation. The farmers receive rent for their land plus an hourly wage for their work and payment for the use of their machinery. The community gardeners do the details of cultivating and handle the gardens from the thinning of seedlings to the harvest.

In Ann Arbor, Michigan, at the Ecology Center Community Organic Garden, the land has been made into one giant garden, and all the members of the community share all the aspects of soil preparation, planting, and harvesting. As the crops come in, they share harvests and offer, free, anything left over (crop excesses) to anyone who wants it.

In New York City, at the project called the Greening of Ruppert, a community group salvaged a one-third-acre paper-strewn site by planting sixty private vegetable gardens, along with trees and shrubs, and set up a playground for youngsters to use while their parents garden.

GETTING ORGANIZED AND FINDING LAND

If your employer offers land, you have a head start. Whether land is made available on this basis or you have to go out and find it, you need a leader, preferably someone who knows food gardening and who is enthusiastic about your project. Someone has to organize. While all members of the project can help find land and help work, one person or two should negotiate the lease once the land is located, should contract for any facilities you build, and handle the group buying of seeds and equipment.

Here are some places to look for land: farmland on the edge of town; empty urban lots; corporation land; town lands, such as filled dump sites; church lands; and private land owned by public-minded citizens. The best locations should be within easy reach of the majority of the members. Access to water or land where water from town pipes can be made accessible at not too great a cost is a must. More community gardens have gone down the leafy path to the land of weeds because they couldn't be watered in time than for any other reason.

Make sure before you sign that the land will be available for several years. A lease is necessary if you plan to plant perennials such as fruit trees and asparagus or if you hope to take advantage next year of your land-taming efforts of this year. It is heartbreaking to get the soil into good condition and then to lose your garden to a new owner.

Before you rent the land, make sure it isn't going to be too small, or too large, for your purposes. If only a few lots are left over after all members have been given a share, you probably can find additional gardeners to join you. But there's no point in leasing a much larger piece than you know your current needs call for.

SOIL PREPARATION

If the lot is open space, free of interior walls, trees, shrubs, fences, or other obstructions, the easiest way to prepare for planting is to hire a farmer to till the land the previous fall and to plow and harrow it early in the spring. At the same time he can add soil conditioners, manure, and other fertilizers. Chapter 4 describes soil improvement for the home garden. The principles there apply to large gardens as well.

Soil preparation, though common to the whole community garden, is a special area of expertise, so assign the responsibility to one member or family team. Working with your assistant farmer or with the local Government Extension Service, arrange for a conditioning and soil-improvement program for the entire garden. Individual gardeners can take it from there, adding special conditioners or fertilizers to their private lots. But make sure they start with a good basic product.

LAND ALLOTMENT

Divide the land into equal-sized garden lots. Though Joe may insist he only wants half a lot this year, next year he may want more. If only half a lot is to be used this year, its "owner" can leave the other half fallow until he wants to use it, covering it with mulch to keep weeds from seeding neighboring land.

Try to plan the lots so each is equally close to watering facilities. If this is impossible, look for ways to compensate those distant from the water source for whatever hardships the distance creates.

Lots can be divided and set apart in any number of ways. String and peg markings that can come out once the plants have grown enough to define the garden lot is the only way if the land is to be plowed or rototilled as a single piece of ground. Fencing, stone outlines, or the planting of perennials to outline each area makes it impossible to plow or rototill the piece as a single lot.

Chapter 2 has plans for high-yield gardens both large and small. Study these and the yields in Table 2 in order to decide what size lots your community group should undertake.

WATER SOURCE

The water source for a community garden can be an underground system of sprinklers that will water the whole section. Underground systems present some problems, however. They are costly, and unless the installation is deep, the land can't be rototilled or plowed. Best for most community gardens only a few acres in size are water pipes with hose connections set around the outer edges of the land. You will also need some connections in one or two central sections. These shouldn't interfere with plowing or rototilling of the acre as a single tract.

Make sure the watering system is such that if individual hoses are to be run from water pipes, there will be enough pipes for each member to attach his hose when he wants rather than waiting in line or waiting to water every other day. If your lettuce has wilted because you went away for a week and you are desperate for water, it can cause bad feelings if you can't have water that instant because it is the turn of six other people at the pipe.

Make sure the water pressure will be enough to allow many gardeners to water at once. Though you won't all want to water simultaneously, gardeners tend to garden between the end of work and dinnertime, and in most communities most people have dinner at about the same time.

BUYING AS A COMMUNITY

For community gardens, rental plus the investments to be made in equipment should turn out to be less divided among individual members than if each were buying equipment for his private garden. A rototiller, a shredder for turning garden refuse into compost, a watering system, extra hose lengths, and a distributor cart for lime and fertilizers can be shared.

Unless you live within walking distance of the garden, you will want a shed sturdy enough so that it can be locked for sheltering equipment and protecting it from vandals. This can be a major item of expense, but if the labor of building the shed is undertaken by the gardeners, costs come down.

If you are not within walking distance of your home, then some form of toilet facilities will be necessary. Have it installed when the water system is installed.

Seeds, started plants, orchard trees, and rhubarb, strawberries, and asparagus can all be bought at less cost from seed companies that sell to farmers in quantity lots.

Seed packets of some of the less popular vegetables, such as celeriac, can be shared by two or more gardeners. A few flowers brighten the look of the community garden, and their seeds can be shared as well, since it is unlikely you'll want a whole row of sunflowers for instance.

Fruit plants, orchard trees, and bramble fruits are perennials. Many community groups plant these in a single section of the gardening area, maintain them as a group, and share the harvests equally. Since these are items of major expense, sharing the cost makes them more readily available. Be sure before you plant your community orchard that you have the right from the owner of the land. Since the trees may have to come out when you give up the land or he finds another use for it, he should be consulted, and your agreement on the subject should appear in the lease you sign.

KEEPING THE WEEDS DOWN AND THE CROPS PICKED

You can't start quibbling with your neighbors about each weed that grows among the carrots, but you should not allow any member of the group to let weeds get to the point where they are going to cause problems for the rest of you. Weeds such as dandelions and crabgrass are spread by the wind after the seeds have ripened. Others, such as quack- or quickgrass, spread by means of underground runners; when land is rototilled or plowed, these weeds' root systems are cut into tiny pieces, each of which is distributed through the garden ready to grow vigorously next year.

Beware of letting your own land go to weeds, and make sure all the members of the group understand their responsibility in this area.

Many garden crops continue producing over several weeks as long as the fruits are picked as they mature. Summer squash, snap beans, tomatoes, and peppers are among them. If you are going to be absent for a week or two just as the beans are coming in, offer your crop to a neighbor gardener in exchange for keeping it picked; then when you get back from vacation, the plants should still be producing.

The general gardening information in this book applies to community gardens, which are really only home gardens a little distance from home.

P.S.: In my grandfather's family community garden, the hard work, weeding, staking, pruning, was done early in the day. My aunts and uncles took picnic dinners to their gardens Saturdays and Sundays. My uncles played *boule* after the meal, which was shared toward sundown, while the ladies sewed and the children fished in the stream nearby or gathered wild blackberries from the bushes that grew along the dirt road. Just before it was time to leave, everybody went to work picking the garden clear of all the ready crops so that they were still absolutely fresh when they were brought home.

Except for occasional hassles over who wasn't being responsible for his weeds, it was a very pleasant way to grow food and get to know one another.

4

How to Double the Yield

Whether you are gardening in a big or a small space, when you are gardening for canning and freezing, you really want bumper crops. Soil will produce bumper crops only if it is well prepared. This is one place where I take no shortcuts.

There are three qualities good soils have—the structure that is called "good garden loam," fertility, and a pH balance correct for the plants intended to grow in it.

SOIL STRUCTURE

When we talk about "soil structure," we are talking about the elements that compose it. Loam is composed of about one-third soil, one-third sand, and one-third humus. Potting soils for indoor plants are such a composition. The soil in your backyard may not be, and if it isn't, it will be more than worth your time to make it so.

That portion of soil that I refer to as "soil" is the portion that has the nutrients necessary for plant growth. It is composed largely of very fine clay particles. When soil is solid clay, you can make statues with it, but you can't grow food plants in it. Plant rootlets are covered with very fine hairlike cells which draw moisture and nutrients from the soil to feed the rest of the plant. In clay, the rootlets can't grow.

26

Furthermore, even if they could, there is neither air nor moisture in hard-packed clay, so growing wouldn't do them any good. Sand mixed with soil makes a growing medium that lets air and water in. Humus lightens the soil and holds moisture. Loam soils hold lots of air and moisture. In moist soils (not wet, but damp) the nutrients plants require for unchecked growth are held in a somewhat soluble state. That means that the little hairlike cells on the rootlets can absorb nutrients and water and carry them through the plant system. In airy, light soils, the cells can expand quickly and operate at maximum efficiency. Good loam is worth all the effort it may take to create it because it will give you a lush garden and bumper crops with a minimum effort on your part once the garden is in.

Soil Testing

Test your garden soil this way: Pick up a handful of damp, not soggy, soil and pack it with both hands to make a snowball. Then, with a slight pressure from your thumb, crumble it in your palm. If it won't crumble under slight pressure, chances are it has too high a clay content. If it won't ball, it may have too much sand.

The other way to test your soil for the garden is to send a sample to the local Extension Service. Extension Services are maintained, usually at state universities, by the United States Department of Agriculture. There's a list of these in the back of this book. For nothing or for very little the Extension Service will test your soil and report on the elements needed to make it suitable for the growing of food plants.

Improving Soil Composition

The way to turn soil into good garden loam is to add the missing elements. If the soil is too high in clay, add a balanced mixture of sand and humus. If it contains too much sand, add humus and a rich soil. Actually, it is rare, except at the seashore, to find yourself dealing with soil that is short of earth as well as humus.

The sand required to improve soil composition is called in my area "sharp sand," and sometimes "builder's sand." Under a magnifying glass, you can see that sharp sand has uneven edges that create air spaces when closely packed. Sea sand usually has salt in it and won't do. Gravel yards sell very fine inert sands that pack closely, and these won't do either. Many garden-supply centers sell the right kind of sand in small quantities. Construction suppliers sell it by the "yard," a measure resembling a small truckful.

Humus, which is simply decomposed organic matter, is sold in many forms. If there's a forest in your area, the surface soil there is probably humusy. Well-rotted manures are humus, and the preferred form, for the manures also contain nutrients valuable to the plants. Compost—which is discussed below—and decomposed seaweed are other forms of fertile humus. You can buy almost everywhere bagged, dried cow manure, bagged peat moss, ground peat moss, and other types of humus.

How much of which to add? Mark out a patch of the garden area 2 feet square, strip away the sod, and add to the soil a 1-inch layer of the element you believe is missing. Or add 1 inch of each of the elements you think are missing. With a trowel or a spading fork mix the soil thoroughly to a depth of 18 inches, and try the snowball test again. If the soil balls, then you know that adding a 1-inch layer of each of the missing elements throughout the entire garden will develop good friable loam. If the soil still won't ball, add more of whatever you think is missing until it does ball. Keep a record of each addition so that when you get the composition exactly right, you'll know how you did it. Good soil has an almost silky feeling, and it is light. Some time before you begin improving your garden soil, play with a handful or two of purchased potting soil in a damp state. It will give you a clearer picture than printed words can of the texture you are looking for in your garden soil.

Once you have established just what your soil needs, order the missing elements and add them. Determine the total number of cubic inches of each element to be added in your planned garden, and let the supplier tell you how many cubic yards you want. Dig the delivered materials into the soil to a depth of 18 to 24 inches, and mix the soil almost as thoroughly as a batch of pie dough. Then your garden is ready to fertilize, and it's time to check the pH of the soil.

A word of caution: Don't toss sand and humus onto the sod overlaying a potential garden site. Sod in a great many areas of the United States contains quackgrass (quickgrass) and other weeds that propagate by underground runners. Once you finely chop these underground runners with a rototiller, you have added literally thousands of sturdy new weeds to the garden, weeds that will be very hard to get rid of. I did just that in my Westport, Connecticut, garden, and it took me five years to get the quackgrass out. Instead, strip the sod from the garden site by hand. It's a bore, but the day you spend doing that now will save you days and days and days of weeding in the years to come.

There are other ways to go about preparing a garden, but they aren't suitable in all cases, and they sometimes sound better on paper than they really are.

If you are going to establish a great big garden and you have terrible soil, the best way out (though not the cheapest) is to import —buy, beg, borrow, or steal—as many yards of really good, fertile loam as you need to create an 18-inch toplayer of soil over the garden site. Brace the sides of your mound of soil with cinder blocks or with railroad ties if you can get them. In my area, prices of loam per yard resemble prices of a cord of wood. Spreading a big area with that much loam can be expensive, so make sure the loam you are buying is really beautiful garden soil. If it takes you a week to locate the right supply of loam, spend the week doing it. Test the soil you are buying to make sure its composition is right. I would even go to the trouble of getting an Extension Service analysis of the pH if I were buying from a stranger rather than from a farmer whose word I could trust.

If you have imported a whole gardenful of soil, by the way, don't walk on it, and try to keep pets and children away from it. It will be so loose the first year or two that it will compact easily. In fact, you can expect the surface level of the soil to sink two or more inches during the first few seasons.

FERTILITY

The color of soil doesn't tell you whether or not it is fertile. Nor will the feel of soil. You can tell more about the soil by the things growing wild on it than by the way it looks when held in your hand. If the growth it supports is richly green, and composed primarily of deciduous (leaf-losing) plants with strong, sturdy, compact growth, chances are it is very good soil. If the growth it supports is primarily evergreen, it is probably quite acid, and acidity tends to make nutrients unavailable to plants, or if the plants on the soil are pale green, leggy, spindly, or sparse, it may be very infertile.

The three basic elements in fertile soil are nitrogen, phosphorus, and potash. When you buy a fertilizer described as "complete," it should contain all three in various ratios to each other. Labels such as 5-10-5 or 1-5-5 refer to the proportions of nitrogen, phosphorus, and potash in that order.

Nitrogen is called the leaf maker; plants short of nitrogen are stunted and have small, pale leaves. Phosphorus (phosphates) is called the root maker; shortages of phosphorus cause plants to be stunted and to have poorly developed roots, and it also helps increase the yield of food crops. Potash is called the fruit or flower maker, and when the crop is a fruit, the potash content of the soil will affect the size of the harvest. Plants short of potash have weak stems, and they are also susceptible to disease.

To find out which of these major nutrients exists plentifully already in your garden soil, and in what balance, avail yourself of Extension Service assistance, or buy one of those home soil-testing kits sold by garden-supply centers. The service or your kit can tell which of what must be added.

In the days when manure was a by-product of horse-and-buggy transportation and farmyard animals, rotted manure was everybody's soil improver and nutrient supplier. Today, we more often must use chemical fertilizers, and the Extension Service and your soil-testing kit will both recommend nutrients in that form. To fertilize soil for a vegetable garden, dig in your complete fertilizer at the rate of 50 pounds for each 2,500 square feet of soil.

If, thanks to a miracle, you have available from a local riding stable or farm well-rotted manure, use that as both the humus to improve the soil and as the fertilizer.

Once you have established a suitable soil fertility level, on subsequent years adding a bag or two of dried sheep manure (which I prefer for vegetables to cow manure) or cow manure will go a long way toward maintaining a fertile soil.

Don't overfertilize. You wouldn't add 5 cups of salt to a recipe calling for a tablespoonful, would you?

ACIDITY IN SOILS, AND pH LEVELS

The symbol pH stands for "potential of hydrogen," and it is the password of the organic gardener. I've always thought it would be wonderful to have a garden in which each row had exactly the right pH for the plant growing in it. However, you don't have to go that far to get good crops. Most food plants are most successful in soils with readings between pH 6 and pH 6.8. That's on the acid side. A few need soils that are distinctly acid—blueberries come to mind. They need a pH between 4.4 and 5.1. The natural point is pH 7.

Most American soils have a pH between 6 and 7, so most backyard soils are probably in good balance for most food plants. However, you should test the soil, because it is the pH reaction of the soil that determines to an important degree the availability of many plant nutrients. In other words, fertile loams can starve the plants growing in them if the acidity range is unfavorable to the plants.

The Agricultural Extension Service can give you a sure reading on your soil acidity, or you can test it yourself with a home testing kit.

If you established a garden three years ago and the acidity reading was fine for vegetables, test it again this year. Soil that grows crops year after year—lawn soil for instance—becomes increasingly acid. That's why we lime lawns periodically. Lime "sweetens" soil, and most vegetable gardens require liming every three or four years, just as do lawn soils.

Soils that are too "sweet" or alkaline for the plants to be grown in them can be acidified by the addition of careful doses of ammonium sulfate. Follow container directions carefully.

Once your garden is established, test the pH reaction before the start of each gardening year. If you can, check it several weeks before you begin planting, so that whatever additions you make to correct pH balances will have a chance to combine with the soil before your seeds or seedlings go into the garden.

CONTROLLING PESTS AND DISEASES

Organic gardening, I often think, is simply a modern term for the old-fashioned garden practices. The organic gardener uses natural vegetable and mineral materials and their derivatives to improve soil structure and fertility, and he encourages natural allies, such as birds and beneficial insects, to stick around his plot of land to protect his crops from pests.

Supporters of the organic way claim foods grown in soils that have been free of all chemical additives for seven whole years are higher in nutrient content and larger in size, and they seem to have proved that diseases and insects stay away from their doors.

In my various efforts at organic gardening I have found that plants growing in rich, well-balanced garden loam are far less susceptible to the depredations of insects and disease than plants growing in poorer soil. On the other hand, the promises of organic advocates are sometimes not fulfilled. I tried cultivating roses in Cape Cod, Massachusetts, for several years the organic way, and the Japanese beetles won in spades.

So now I spray my fruit trees (as little as possible) and use USDA-recommended solutions for plant pests and diseases when they threaten to wipe out my crops. See the tables at the back of the book for information on disease and pest control for both fruits and vegetables. But I do follow the organic way of gardening wherever I can, and above all when it comes to keeping the soil in good condition by the addition of humus and natural fertilizers and lime.

THE COMPOST PILE

The compost pile is not the creation of the organic gardener, but it is his favorite way of keeping garden refuse disposed of and supplying humus for the garden.

Compost is fluffy black stuff that looks like soil and feels like a cross between fine soil and ground peat moss. It is the result of the decomposition of all sorts of organic matter—leaves, seaweed, grass clippings, soft prunings from shrubs and trees, straw, hay, sawdust, weeds, dead plants from the garden, and vegetable refuse from the kitchen.

The basic method for making compost is to combine alternate layers of organic matter and soil, with or without lime and fertilizers, and to leave the pile to time and weather. Composting can be as complicated as building the Brooklyn Bridge if you like, or you can do it in several much simpler ways. Given one to three or four years, heaped-up leaves and garden debris exposed to the weather will become compost. In a warm, humid climate, vegetation will compost sooner; in a cool, dry climate, composting takes longer.

One of the great things about composting, in addition to the fact that you get compost for the garden, is that it is a way of handling garden debris. Everything vegetative, excepting diseased plant parts and tough, young tree branches, can go into the compost pile—sod, weeds, carrot tops and peels. Putting it on a compost pile is much easier than piling it into the garbage can or burning it.

The popularity of composting has spread, and today there are many types of equipment on the market intended to help the gardener make quick compost. Many manufacturers in their lines of debris disposers include shredders meant to reduce the bulk of the debris and ready it for quick composting. Some leaf blowers include shredding equipment, and in the future we can expect new and better lawn vacuums with improved shredding capabilities. The smaller the materials piled in the compost heap, the sooner they decompose.

The easiest way to compost is to create a container—it can be a structure or a pit—3 to 4 feet square. In it put alternate layers of organic refuse and soil. If you are building the heap directly onto sod, first cut the sod into small squares and turn them dirt-side up. Heap a 6-inch layer of refuse—whole or shredded leaves, weeds, dead sod, and/or coffee grounds and other kitchen discards—on the bottom. Cover this with a 3-inch layer of manure (it can be fresh) or with a 3-inch layer of soil (any kind) and mix in 1 pound of your garden fertilizer. Build the layers in such a way that the center is concave enough to catch and hold rainwater. Water the pile. Repeat the layers until the pile is 5 feet high or until the cold weather arrives.

Hurry-up composters turn the compost pile every few weeks, and they add magical products that increase the decomposition. If you are in a hurry for compost, buy a book on the subject. If you are a gardener who likes to be as lazy as possible, start a new compost heap each spring and let the previous season's compost piles ripen and decompose with the weather instead of with chemicals or your own elbow grease.

City gardeners are turning to mini-composting, composting of available materials in large garbage bags or in lidded garbage cans. These are easy to turn often and moisten. Buy a starter product that speeds up decomposition. Seedsmen sell them as "compost makers." There are on the market small composting kits including heavy-duty plastic-mesh bins with support posts. Burpee's is about 28 inches high and 4 feet in diameter. It holds 50 or 60 bushels of leaves.

PREPARATIONS FOR PLANTING

You can prepare the garden for planting either in the fall or in the spring. If the garden is brand new, just unearthed from under thick sod and never before used, I'm in favor of preparing it for planting in the fall. But, if you decide in January you want a garden this year, you don't have to wait until next fall to prepare the soil.

The first step in preparing a new garden for planting is to mark out the gardening area with strings attached to pegs. Whether it's to be a square, a rectangle, or some form of curve (I once planted a garden in half circles down the side of a hill, but I wasn't very happy with it), it will look better if the lines are straight. Strip away the sod—preferably by hand, as noted above—and place it on the compost pile. Add sand, soil, or humus, as noted above, to improve the soil structure; then add fertilizers and lime. When I am preparing

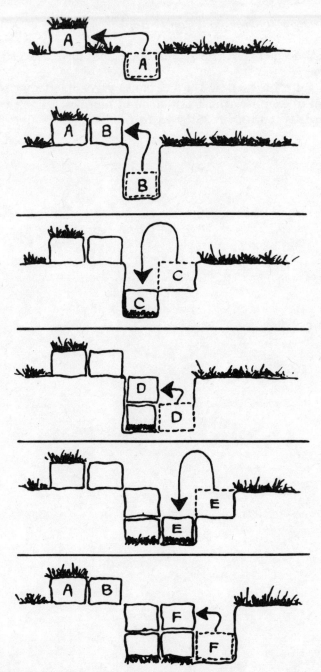

Double-digging fluffs soil to 18 inches. Remove sod first, "spank" it to loosen earth, then bury at the bottom of the hole. Spread a layer of sand, humus, or soil to be added to the area and mix well into the top 18 inches.

humus as needed, fertilizers, and lime and turn the soil over one more time.

You get a nice tan and a nice fluffy garden soil that way. And a great deal of exercise. And fresh air. And muscles. I don't recommend it for gardens more than 25 by 25 feet.

5

Easy-Does-It Planting and Maintenance for Vegetables and Fruits

From the beginning of time, gardeners have been trying to find ways around the weather. In very cool regions, you can start seedlings for your food crops indoors or buy started seedlings at garden-supply centers. Not all the food plants react well to transplanting, but most do. The drawback to this approach is the work involved. If you are planting a tiny food garden, setting out a few started lettuce seedlings along with tomato, sweet pepper, and cucumber seedlings makes perfectly good sense and will result in earlier crops. To set out enough started seedlings to fill a garden meant for canning and freezing is a lot of work.

Another route to an early garden is to plant the seeds outdoors several weeks early under individual greenhouses. Suppliers offer various types from mound-shaped plastic hats for individual plants to row-length plastic tents or covers. As long as the weather and the soil are really cold and there is little sun, the plastic covers don't seem to build up enough heat inside to speed growth in any very dramatic fashion. And they do blow around in wind storms. In really cold areas, they may be worth the effort and cost of installation; in moderate climates I don't think the earlier crops you may or may not get are worth the effort involved. I personally would rather wait till the weather gives my plants the nod, because then they grow quickly and easily.

37

TIMELY PLANTING

The right planting date for vegetables and fruits depends on the individual plant. There are three principal planting times—early spring, mid-spring, and late spring. See the tables at the back of the book. Cool-weather vegetables are planted in earliest spring or early to mid-spring and are usually harvested before the really hot weather sets in. Broccoli is one of these.

The crops planted in mid-spring won't stand up to late frosts but do survive heat. Tomatoes, beans, and corn are mid-spring crops.

Late spring can be defined as the period that begins when temperatures reach and stay at 70 degrees. One of the food crops to be put in at this time is eggplant, another is the melons. They are warm-weather crops.

Early Spring

A gardener's definition of early spring is "as soon as the ground can be worked." It is the period that begins when the mucky wetness of winter freezing has left the soil and a handful of loam balls in your hand and breaks easily under slight pressure. There may still be late freezes, but severe winter weather has gone for good. The earliest of the cool-weather crops will stand up to some frost.

Although you can plant early peas, lettuce, onion sets, and a few other crops before the last frost, you should not work the earth before it has dried enough to pass the snowball test described above. To turn over wet, half-frozen soil compacts it and spoils its texture. If your garden has been dug and prepared for planting in the late fall, you can sow pea seeds, lettuce seeds, onion sets, and a few other plants even before the last frosts.

Mid-Spring

Mid-spring is the season between the last frost and the time when the temperature steadies at 70 degrees. The crops for mid-spring planting don't stand up to frosts. You can set out seed for plants meant for mid-spring planting in early spring, but they generally just sulk, and they sometimes never come up at all.

To get a head start on a few of the most popular food plants in this category, sow seeds indoors so you will have seedlings to set out when the weather is right. Plants that bear heavily over a long season are those I consider worthwhile for starting indoors. For a minimum of house space, they give the largest crops. Tomatoes, cucumbers, and sweet peppers are in this category.

Late Spring

Since late spring is that time when the temperature has reached 70 degrees and is staying there, we really are talking about early summer weather. There are only a few crops that can't go in before this. Okra, melons, eggplant, and sweet potatoes are the most commonly grown of the late-spring food plants. I don't think any of these is included in the category of food plants best for putting up, either in canning jars or in the freezer, though you may. The average food garden for putting up doesn't include them. If you want to include them, start them indoors and set them out as seedlings for an earlier crop. If they are set out as seed in cool regions of the country, few of these will ripen before the first of the fall frosts.

There are early-fruiting eggplants and small melons that are ready for harvest before standard types; they are indicated for cool areas.

Outdoor Planting Times for Individual Crops

Since the planting time for food plants is divided into three distinct periods, plan the sowing of your garden accordingly. The lists below include only plants that go into the vegetable garden—that is, all the vegetables, plus strawberries, melons, and rhubarb, which grow in the garden along with vegetables. The other fruit plants—orchard fruits and bramble fruits, such as raspberries—are set out in late fall in warm regions, and in cool areas in early spring while the plants are still dormant.

Plant These in Early Spring

Asparagus	Kale
Beets	Leeks
Broccoli	Lettuce
Brussels sprouts	New Zealand spinach
Cabbage	Onion sets
Carrots	Parsnips
Cauliflower	Peas
Chard	Potatoes
Chicory	Radishes
Cress	Rhubarb
Dandelions	Strawberries
Jerusalem artichokes	Turnips

Plant These in Mid-Spring

Artichokes	Peppers
Beans	Pumpkins
Celeriac	Rutabaga
Celery	Salsify
Corn	Shallots
Cucumbers	Spinach
Gourds	Squash
Kohlrabi	Tomatoes
Parsley and other herbs	

Plant These in Late Spring

Eggplant	Okra
Melons and watermelons	Peanuts

These lists include a number of vegetables that most of us don't can or freeze. However, you may want to grow them for eating fresh, and knowing when to schedule the planting is helpful when you are working out the overall garden planting plan for spring.

SEEDLINGS FOR TRANSPLANTING

Starting Seedlings Indoors

If you have a sunny window or fluorescent lighting fixtures known as "growing lights," you can start your own vegetable seedlings indoors rather than buying started seedlings from the garden-supply center. One advantage in starting your own is that you can select a variety particularly suited to canning or freezing. The other advantage is economy.

Most seeds can be started four to eight weeks before setting out the started seedlings in the open garden. Four weeks early is the right time to start seeds indoors for fast-growing plants, and eight weeks is the right time for slow-growing types. Check the number of days each type requires to mature (Chapter 6) to know which are fast and which are slow growers.

For vegetables, flats and peat pots are the best containers for indoor starting. You can substitute refrigerator trays, baking tins, large egg cartons with individul pressed cardboard pockets—anything

Seedlings grow well under fluorescent lights.

large that won't be harmed by soil or disintegrate the minute it gets wet. The containers or flats whose plants are to be left in them until it is time for transplanting should be 4 inches deep. I start a few things in egg cartons, things that I will later want to transplant to individual pots—tomatoes, for instance, and green peppers.

Some plants don't transplant at all well—notably, all the cucumber relatives, gourds and squashes among them. These must be started in individual peat pots. The peat pots can then be set into the garden along with their contents, and the plants in them won't suffer transplant shock.

I have occasionally found that the only cucumber seedlings I could get had been started in flats. Before I knew better, I would cut up the seedlings and plant them. They always either poked along miserably or failed completely. Now when I am confronted by that problem, I buy the smallest flats I can find and plant the whole flat in a single hill. If I can't find a small flat, I cut a big flat in half. Some of the plants won't do well, but most manage since the roots will have faced minimal disturbance.

When you are starting seedlings indoors because you want specific varieties of seedlings for your garden and you can't get them locally, plan to devote a lot of containers and space to the seedlings. A happy alternative to starting your own seedlings when you want lots of them is to make a deal with the local garden center to grow your selected varieties of a number of vegetables in their cold frames or greenhouses. The other alternative is to build a greenhouse, a cold frame,

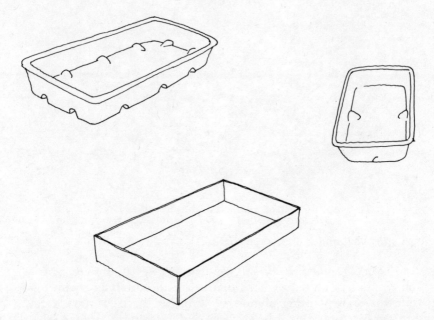

Flats for starting seedlings

or a hot bed of your own. Cold frames and hot beds are very good places to start spring seedlings, and they aren't a lot of work. However, they aren't successful unless you know what you are doing and how to handle them, so investigate what will be required of you before you invest in either.

Bagged potting soil for indoor plants is suitable for starting seedlings. Or, make your own potting soil of one-third garden loam, one-third sand, and one-third fine-ground peat moss or vermiculite. Or, use the recipe in Chapter 1 for container potting soil. If you are going to start seedlings next spring indoors, dig loam before the ground freezes this fall and store it in the garage for spring indoor gardening.

You can also start seedlings in pure vermiculite, perlite, ground peat moss, sphagnum moss, or any other light growing medium available. The catalogs offer all these, as do garden centers.

Fill containers two-thirds full with potting soil or whatever starting medium you are going to use, moisten it by placing the container in a sinkful of tepid water for a moment, allow the water to drain, and sift a little dry growing medium over the containers. With a sharp pencil or a pointed kitchen knife, draw small furrows ¼ inch deep in the soil of the flat and sow the large seeds in the bottoms of the furrows. Before sowing the tiny seeds, fill the furrows with vermiculite and sow the seeds on the vermiculite. Sow large seeds an inch or more apart. Sow small seeds ¼ to ½ inch apart.

Once your seeds are in their tiny furrows, cover them with a thin layer of vermiculite, soil, or sphagnum. Place a plastic film loosely over the container and set it in a room where temperatures are between 62 and 65 degrees. I've found this a good average for vegetables. (Flowers generally are warm-weather crops, and most flower seedlings grow well in temperatures between 65 and 75 degrees.) Keep the soil damp but not wet. When the seedlings are up and showing their first four leaves, remove the plastic cover and place the containers in a sunny window in a warm room.

If you have fluorescent lights, set your seedlings under them to grow. Many gardeners today are growing seedlings in tiered installations in basements, where the combination of cool air, humidity, and grow lights produces very sturdy little plants. Growing seedlings under lights is a subject too lengthy to be dealt with properly here. If you are going to grow vegetable seedlings under lights, you must follow the instructions that come with the fixture. Some plants are most successful in 10 to 12 hours of light per day, and others require 18 to 20 hours. Some plants do best if the lights are right on top of them, and others do best if the lights are far above them. In other words, learn and follow the rules, or the seedlings won't do well.

Seedlings growing in a sunny window can't be controlled as easily as those growing under lights. As a rule of thumb, seedlings that are spindly and have widely spaced leaves and an upreaching, pale look aren't getting enough light. Try to find them a spot where there is more sunlight. Seedlings whose leaves are growing close to the base in a bunch and have a curled, odd look or show purple or brown "burn" spots may be getting too much sun. In a window, it's unlikely with vegetable seedlings, which thrive on sun, but it does happen with foliage plants and flowering plants. Turn your seedling containers often, or they will lean like the Tower of Pisa toward the sun and grow lopsided.

As the seedlings grow, thin them to avoid crowding. Always remove the weakest, not the strongest. If you don't want to discard the thinnings, transplant (I work with tweezers) to new larger containers. The one-pound coffee can with drainage holes punched in the bottom, which is covered with a 1-inch layer of small pebbles or gravel, makes a good container for a single tomato plant. There are many sizes of individual peat pots ideal for the nurturing of seedlings as they become too crowded for flats. Since the peat pots are planted with the plants in them, they won't be available for use again the following year. Providing individual peat pots for a huge amount of seedlings can be expensive, which is one reason I suggest you start indoors only a few of the long-bearing, mid-spring or late-spring vegetables that would be too expensive to buy from the local garden center.

If you find you can't set your seedlings outdoors until later than you expected, as can happen if the weather goes wrong, transplant them to containers filled only with sphagnum moss and don't fertilize.

If the seedlings yellow, let them dry out, then water them with a half-strength solution of ammonium nitrate.

Occasionally, seedlings growing indoors develop fungus diseases. The name given most often is "damping off." As the name suggests, it is associated with too much moisture. If you have had plants killed by damping off, plant seeds in sterile mediums, such as sphagnum moss, instead of in potting soil, or sterilize your potting soil. One of the easiest ways I know to sterilize potting soil is to place it in a 325-degree oven with a large potato and to bake it the time required for the potato to be thoroughly cooked through.

What To Look For in Seedlings Sold at Garden Centers

Seedlings offered at garden centers are professionally grown, and I have always been happy with mine. However, once in a while a shipment comes through of yellowing, splindly little seedlings no one should plant because they are off to a bad start. For that matter, cabbage seedlings, broccoli, Brussels sprouts, cucumbers, and tomatoes offered by centers are sometimes past their planting time. They'll be too spindly, too leggy, and generally they'll have a lot of yellowing leaves at the base. Don't buy these. Instead, go to another garden center. If you really want tomatoes and such tomatoes are the only ones offered, compromise and buy them, but institute a liquid feeding program and repot the plants in good soil as soon as you get them home. Try to improve them by liquid feedings every few days for a week or ten days before you set them out in the open garden. As for cabbages and things cabbagy that have that yellowed look, you can get others for planting in late summer for fall crops—they are cold-weather vegetables grown at the end of the season as well as at the beginning—so bide your time and let the yellow ones go.

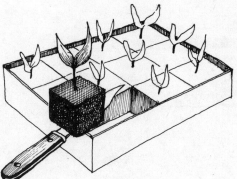

Transplanting seedlings

PLANTING THE GARDEN

Once the garden has been marked out and the soil prepared for planting, as described in the previous chapter, and your planting plan (Chapter 2) is ready, it is time to get down to business—the planting of the garden.

I plant a large garden in four work periods. When I am still expecting some light frosts, I put in the peas (early varieties), early lettuces, onions sets, and radishes. When what I call "early spring" arrives (that is when the frost is out of the ground and it begins to dry) I put in the rest of the early-spring seeds (see page 39). When mid-spring arrives, and all danger of frost is past, I put in seedlings and seeds for the mid-spring vegetables. The few things that are warm-weather plants, late-spring vegetables, go in after the weather reaches a steady 70 degrees. In my area, New England, the planting seasons described above are about six to eight weeks apart.

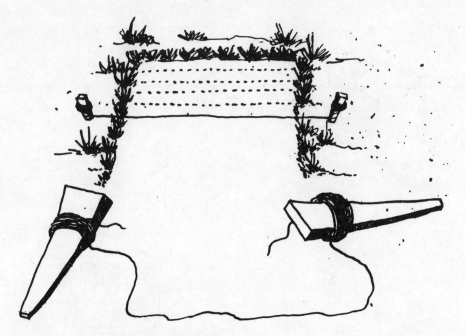

Pegs and string to keep rows straight

Tools and Materials

For working a big garden for canning with the least amount of hard labor, I like to have available a rototiller, a square-ended hoe and a pointed hoe for planting and cultivating, a steel rake for smoothing the soil, a digging fork or a forking spade (with sturdy flat tines that curve upward a little), a wooden plank to place between rows so you can walk on it when planting, two pointed wooden pegs with sturdy cotton string the length of the rows attached to them, a trowel for transplanting, a plastic bucket to hold starter solution for transplanting, and a sharp little kitchen knife for cutting apart seedlings in flats.

A big roll of black sheet plastic for mulch is a very good investment for a new, large vegetable garden. Once your garden has been in and has been kept weed-free for three to five years, you should have far fewer weeds than in the beginning. Unless you let a lot of weeds whose seeds spread by airlift mature next to the vegetable garden, weeds in a well-kept garden really become minimal in time. But in the beginning, the most thorough way to discourage weeds is to lay black plastic between the planting rows. Then the only weeds with any chance of developing well are those right next to the seeds, and you can keep them under control by scratching around the growing vegetable seedlings every few days in spring.

For toting all my tools to the garden, I use a plastic wheelbarrow. The plastic barrow is lighter than the prettier wooden one or the metal barrow. A barrow also is handy for toting away to the compost heap any weeds dug up and, once the garden matures, for removing played-out plants whose harvests are over.

Sowing

With your planting plan in hand and the garden all smooth and ready for planting, measure off the rows you are going to sow. If your garden is on a slope, plan the rows to run horizontally across the slope; otherwise rain will wash down the gulleys between rows and erode the soil. Plan to plant the lowest-growing of the crops at the south end of the garden; you don't want tall crops standing between the sun and the shorter crops. Tomatoes, Cos or Romaine lettuce, fall and winter squashes, and a few other vegetables will mature well if slightly shaded, but the rule of thumb for good food crops is sunlight all day.

Place your wooden plank alongside the center of the row to be planted and place one peg at each end of the row with the string taut between the pegs. You will plant under the string, keeping the row straight. Draw either the end of the pointed hoe or a corner of the square hoe down the row under the string, creating a furrow the depth and width required for the seed you are going to plant there. Chapter 6 gives planting instructions for each vegetable. As a generalization, furrows for seeds are ½ to 1 inch deep and about the same width. A few seeds are better planted in shallow furrows 10 or 12 inches wide, and to create those furrows use the flat back of the steel rake. When you draw the furrow with the hoe, walk down the row to the end. As you walk back up the row, drop seeds into the furrow. Go back down the row again, using the back of the rake or the hoe to draw soil up over the seeds. Use the flat of the tool to tamp the earth gently but firmly over the seeds. A few seeds—radishes come to mind—are sown broadcast; that is, they are just scattered widely over the planting soil, then tamped into the soil.

The system I prefer for sowing seed is to make furrows twice the depth they need be and to half-fill the furrows after the seed has been sown. That way the seeds and roots have a little more protection from the elements than when planted in shallower furrows. In time, the furrows will fill completely. Why not plant them more deeply, rather than half-fill the furrows? Because when planted more deeply in spring, the seeds receive less warmth from the sun and will take longer to sprout. The rule of thumb is to plant the seeds at a depth about three times their height. Chapter 6 tells the correct depth for each seed type.

In Chapter 6, you will see that a number of vegetables are planted in "hills." A hill just means a group. Plants that have viny tendrils are often planted this way—cucumbers, for instance. Seeds are generally sown six to a hill and thinned back to three or four plants when the seedlings are up.

Setting Out Started Seedlings

Seedlings fresh from the indoors need a week to get used to outdoor growing conditions before they can face the open garden with calm and certitude. Set their containers in a sheltered, semisunny spot the first day out, and each day expose them to a little more sun and a little more wind. Don't let the containers dry out; they'll need watering more often than they did indoors if the weather is sunny.

On planting day fill your plastic bucket with water and let it warm in the sun for a few hours, or fill it with lukewarm water. Dissolve in it a starter solution or a liquid fertilizer. Some seedsmen advertize a hormone-vitamin stimulant for use when transplanting seedlings. I've had good luck with seedlings soaked in water containing any of these.

The first step when setting out seedlings is to prepare the row as for planting seeds. Set your pair of pegs at either end of the row and stretch the string between them. Dig planting holes a little larger and deeper than the size of the seedling root balls and at even distances the length of the row. Kneel on the board for planting, with the plastic bucket and the seedling flats beside you. A paper cup is helpful during this maneuver, and a small, sharp kitchen knife. Cut the seedlings apart in their containers. Dip a little water into the hole to be planted, lift a seedling with the soil ball cupped in your hand, dip it quickly into the bucketful of starter solution, then place it upright in the planting hole. Scoop a little soil into the hole, add another half cup of starter solution, add more soil, then firm the soil up around the seedling stem, and tamp it down gently. When tugged on, a properly planted seedling resists uprooting.

To transplant plants growing in individual peat pots, moisten each in starter solution, then tear away the top edge of the pot, and set the pot into its hole. Fill the hole with starter solution, and when it has drained away, fill the hole with soil and firm the plant into place.

MULCHING WITH PLASTIC OR ORGANIC MATERIALS

There are two ways to use plastic sheets with mulch. One is to place the plastic between rows, leaving a very narrow planting space of bare soil in which the furrow for the seed can be drawn. The other way is to place the plastic so that it is centered on the row and to cut X's in the center of the plastic, spaced to accommodate started seedlings. Cut the X with a safety razor and peel back its segments to dig your planting hole. The X system is used for large, started seedlings, for instance, tomato plants.

Hay, straw, or spoiled hay (which costs considerably less than good hay, when you can find it) are preferred mulches among many organic gardeners. Pile any of these in a loose, 2- or 3-foot layer between rows sown with seed. Such mulches discourage weeds, and add humus to the soil as they decompose.

Other organic mulches are seaweed, leaves, peat moss, and buckwheat hulls. If you are going to use seaweed, gather it in after the big early-fall storms on the shore and heap it layered with soil near the garden site. It will have partially decomposed by the time you are ready to use it. If you are going to use leaves, best grind them first after they have been gathered in the fall or, anyway, before you put them on the garden. Spread thickly over the garden during a dry cold winter, they are apt to cake in layers instead of decomposing. Caked layers of mulch just keep the soil cold and wet and delay spring planting. That's why I have never favored year-round mulches. I tried one once (maybe not enough), and it kept the asparagus and rhubarb (perennials) in cold storage well past their usual harvest time.

There is another caution associated with organic mulches: They require nitrogen to decompose, and they will compete with the crops for the supply in the ground. Add a complete fertilizer (10-10-10) at the rate of 3 pounds to each 100 square feet organically mulched. Leaves and wood chips—another suitable mulch—are acid. If you use either of these, keep a check on the soil pH.

Whatever you use, do mulch. A mulch blanket over the garden cuts weeding to almost nil. This alone helps vegetables to thrive, since it frees them from competing with other plants for available supplies of moisture and nutrients in the soil. A mulch also cuts down tremendously on watering chores and helps plants thrive despite mid-summer droughts.

GARDEN MAINTENANCE

Watering

Once your garden is seeded and mulched, water it well with a fine spray. That wetting combined with a few days of warm sunlight will encourage quick sprouting of the seeds. If the garden appears dry and no seeds have sprouted in the days that follow planting, water again thoroughly. It is the combination of moisture and warmth that makes seeds germinate.

The outdoor garden in good soil requires a thorough rainfall or watering once a week. A good watering is one that gets water down to between 12 and 18 inches deep. Dig in your garden some day when the top appears completely dry and measure how far down you must dig before the darker shade of moist soil appears. Usually, soil stays relatively moist below 6 to 8 inches. However, if there's a drought in progress, the garden can dry to 12 or 18 inches, sometimes more. It takes 1½ inches of rainfall or watering to bring moisture down to between 6 and 8 inches deep. To get moisture down 12 to 18 inches requires about 2½ inches of rainfall or watering. To estimate how much water your watering device is bringing to the garden, put a clean, straight-sided jar in the garden, and turn the watering device on in its area. Check the time. When the jar shows 2½ inches of water, check the time again. This will tell you how long your device should be left on to bring that much water to the garden.

Although I prefer a soaker that lies flat on the ground and dribbles water with the soil for my flower borders, I think an overhead watering device is better for vegetables. However, in gardens where there are serious attacks of mildew or other diseases that flourish in moisture, it might be a good investment to provide soakers to lie between the rows alongside the plants.

Thinning Seedlings

Once the first few seeds pop above ground, seedlings will start filling their rows quickly. Pretty soon, they'll start crowding each other. Your next chore, then, becomes thinning the seedlings. Seedlings of greens such as lettuce and spinach are great in salads or treated as boiling greens. The only caution I'd offer is that you be sure before cooking or using that you have removed the root from each and that all the soil is gone from the curly corners of the leaves.

The seedlings of beets and carrots are excellent as vegetables when the roots have swelled a little, so wait as long as you can to thin these.

Thin only enough to provide space for plants on either side. You can thin again if you have to, but you can't replace missing seedlings from overzealous thinning without waiting several weeks for the seed to grow.

When harvesting beets and carrots and other root crops, always remove the largest and most crowded, leaving the small plants to mature in the open spaces you create. This is another way to thin seedlings.

When thinning very small seedlings, such as carrots, remove the extras on a day when the soil is dry enough to be quite loose. If it is very moist and stuck together, each tiny seedling is apt to lift a whole clump of soil and several neighbors with it as it comes up.

What To Do If the Weeds Get a Head Start

I hope it never happens to you. More than once it has happened to me that I have not mulched and not weeded and have come back four or six weeks after planting to find my garden captive of a large, flourishing colony of weeds. What farmers, the professionals, do is to cut all the weeds down just above ground level with a sharp hoe. I've tried pulling the weeds by hand, and I've also tried digging the soil between vegetable rows and turning the weeds over and back into the ground. It is brutal work and not particularly successful. I recommend the sharp hoe, followed by a strong-minded and thick mulching program.

Fertilizing Crops That Are Growing

Chapter 6 suggests which plants and when to fertilize during growth. They generally are either very heavy feeders or else plants that produce a harvest over a long period. Generally speaking, a well-fertilized, well-prepared vegetable garden doesn't require fertilizing once it is in. Some gardeners fertilize crops at mid-season to encourage larger fruit or bigger harvests. Seedsmen do it successfully to create outsize fruit. Try it sometime, and if you find the results worth the extra effort, plan on a mid-season feeding for all the food plants.

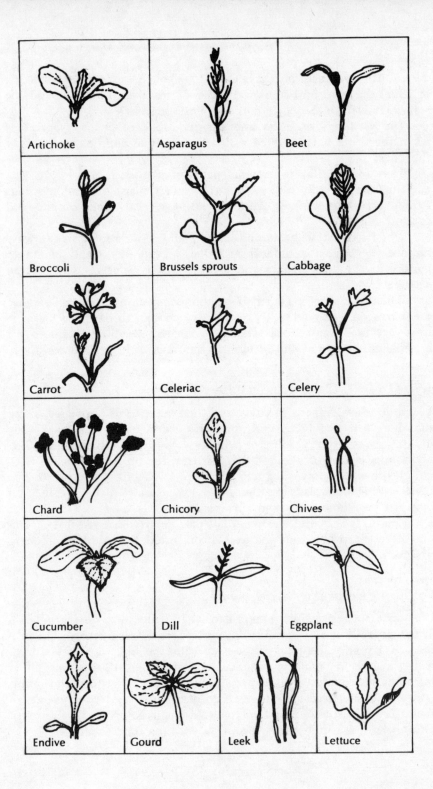

PLANTING SECOND AND THIRD CROPS

Radishes (which aren't canned but do keep soil occupied while the garden is waiting for the proper time to plant canning crops) are one of the first crops out of the ground in spring. Garden cress, an early-spring green, which matures in ten days under ideal conditions and is over in a month, is another good occupant for land in waiting. Chapter 2 describes planting plans where successions of crops will follow each other through the whole summer. When I overplant (follow a first planting with a second vegetable crop), I fertilize the row that has just been cleared and add a little compost. Before planting the new furrow of seeds, turn the soil, breaking all clods, and rake it with the steel rake. It should be as fresh and smooth-looking as when it was originally planted. Don't leave little weedlings to grow up.

PUTTING THE GARDEN TO BED IN THE FALL

The best time to put the garden to bed for the fall is after all the weeds have stopped traveling with fall breezes. If you watch the fields around your town, you will see that as the greens fade to the browns of fall, all the fuzzy things that send seeds through the air are pretty well dried up. The milkweed pods will remain, but the dandelions and wild asters are all out of plumes. A garden put to bed then will have fewer weeds waiting to sprout when it comes to life in spring.

By "put the garden to bed" I mean turn the soil and add any raw organic matter to it that you have handy. If the garden has been mulched with organic material, turn it under—that is, lift clumps of soil and flip them upside down back into the garden. Organic materials turned into the soil in fall will generally have decomposed by spring. Fertilize the garden in fall only with a very slow-release fertilizer; there's no point in having all that fertilizer wash down through the soil with fall, winter, and early-spring rains. And fertilize in the fall only those areas where you plan to put in early-early-spring crops, such as early peas or early lettuce.

I remove the black-plastic mulch from the garden in the fall. It is my theory that the soil beneath such a mulch stays sweeter and more wholesome if it is allowed to breathe at least part of the year.

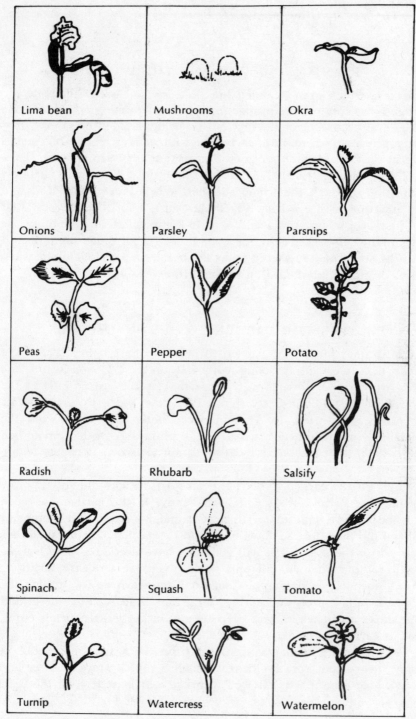

Seedlings of vegetables

SETTING OUT FRUIT PLANTS

There are two principal types of plants that supply us with fruit: the orchard fruits and the bramble fruits. The few fruit plants that grow in the vegetable garden—strawberries, rhubarb, melons—have been discussed above along with the planting of vegetables. Both the orchard and the bramble fruits are set out in fall in warmer regions and in early spring—while still dormant—in cooler regions.

If you plan to add orchard and bramble fruits to the list of foods you want to put up (and I recommend you do—they are very rewarding), you will have to plant pairs of some varieties. Many of the fruits require cross-pollination before they will set fruit. It is surprising how many experienced gardeners don't seem to know this. I worked with a wonderfully talented Italian gardener once who, in his own garden, had cut down a handsome, mature apple tree. He told me that after 10 years of no fruit, he had decided the tree wasn't worth keeping. Well, there wasn't another apple tree in sight, and though I am sure he knew about the importance of cross-pollination, when it came to why his own tree didn't produce, it had slipped his mind as a factor.

Apples and pears are trees that require cross-pollination to produce fruit, with the exceptions noted below. Most but not all peach and nectarine varieties are self-pollinated; they do not require cross-pollination. Plums require cross-pollination. Sour cherries pollinate themselves, but the big, dark sweet cherries do not.

There are exceptions to these rules. Golden Delicious, Jonathan, and Red Rome Beauty apples are self-pollinators, but Snow and Mac-Intosh, which are good for canning, are cross-pollinators. Stark Hal-Herbta Giant, Stark Honeydew Hale, and J. H. Hale peaches do not require cross-pollination. Duchess and Keiffer pears do not require it, but Bartlett—especially good for canning—does. Giant Damson and Green Gage plums and Burbank Grand Prize prunes do not require cross-pollination. There are other exceptions, of course, but these are some of the best-known ones.

Suggested as pollinators for apple trees are any variety except the one planted and except the Winesaps and a few catalog offerings such as Stark Scarlet Styamared. Stark Brothers, seedsmen noted for the development of dwarf and semidwarf varieties, list as the most potent apple pollinators Starkrimson, Starkspur Earliblaze, and Starkspur Golden Delicious. Among the best pollinators for peaches are Burbank July Elberta, Starking Delicious, and Stark Early Elberta; and any variety of peach tree other than the one planted. Pollinators for a pear tree can be any other variety of pear tree except Magness. Good pear pollinators are Starking Delicious and Moonglow. Bartlett and Seckel pears are not compatible and won't pollinate each other. Good pollinators for dark, sweet cherries are Venus, Stark Gold, and Van. Plum trees can be cross-pollinated by any other variety of plum; Redheart is considered one of the best. Good pollinators for other varieties of prunes are BluFre and Stanley.

Whatever fruit tree you are planning to plant, it may be that you won't need to plant a cross-pollinator: One of the advantages to living in a community that gardens, or of planting trees in a community garden is that there are usually enough other types of orchard fruits around so that the cross-pollination needs of your own choices are already taken care of. The cross-pollinator doesn't have to be in your backyard. If it is somewhere in the neighborhood and the bees haven't been decimated by insecticides, they will provide transportation from the neighbor tree to yours of all the pollen your fruit needs. To find out whether there is a pollinator in your neighborhood, ask gardening neighbors when their trees bloom and what types they are. If their trees bloom at the same time as your tree or trees, chances are they are suitable cross-pollinators.

Chapter 1, Table 2 gives yields to be expected from smaller orchard trees and bramble fruits. It will give you a notion of how many trees or bramble fruits your property can accommodate. The Fruit Planting and Spraying Table at the back of the book describes the height of the trees at maturity, spacing required for healthy growth, and pollination requirements.

ORCHARD FRUITS

Planting

Like garden vegetables, fruit trees flourish in good garden loam with a pH on the acid side. Full sun and good drainage are other orchard requirements. Avoid planting orchard fruits, particularly those that will bloom early—as do plums for instance—in low areas where late frosts settle. A sheltered corner protected from north winds is the best place for orchard fruits.

The planting hole for a fruit tree must be large enough to hold the roots comfortably and deep enough to set the trees at the levels at which they grew in the nursery rows. Some dwarfed fruit stock is grafted and has special planting requirements. Follow instructions provided with these plants.

The fruit trees sold by local garden centers are usually "balled and burlapped," that is, the roots are in a compact ball of soil and wrapped in burlap or plastic. Some seedsmen ship by mail trees in a condition called "bareroot." Bareroot shipments are trees whose roots have been stripped of soil to make transportation costs lighter, and these are only shipped in a dormant state.

While you dig the planting hole for stock to be set out, don't leave the plants in burning sunlight. Keep them shaded, out of the wind, and cool.

Fertilize the soil at the bottom of the planting hole for orchard fruits before planting. I add a handful of a slow-release fertilizer, such as bone meal, for each dwarf to be planted, and I use bagged, dried cow manure or fertile compost as the humus.

Set balled-and-burlapped plants into their planting holes in their burlap coverings. Once the plant is in the hole, cut long gashes into the burlap and pull the top of the burlap free, but don't attempt to remove it. It will rot in time, and won't prevent tree roots from growing. Once a balled-and-burlapped tree is in its hole, fill the hole two-thirds full with soil mixed with equal parts of sand and humus (peat moss for instance). Then pour in enough water to fill the hole and let it drain out. Fill the hole completely with improved soil to just below the crown, the point at which the tree trunk meets the roots. Water again. Then make a saucer of soil around the tree so water won't run off when it rains.

Bareroot trees usually transplant well if they are set into the ground before their buds begin to sprout. Soak bareroot trees 2 to 4 hours in a bucket of lukewarm water to which you have added a transplanting hormone or fertilizer. Prepare the hole as you would for a balled-and-burlapped tree. Then make a firmly packed mound of improved soil, high enough so that when the tree roots are spread over it the crown of the tree will be just at or an inch or so below the soil level of the ground. Spread the bare roots over the mound, make sure the tree is sitting straight, then proceed to fill the hole with soil and water as described above.

Maintenance

I mulch with dried cow manure or fertile compost to keep weeds away from the trunk the first year or two. Fertilize newly planted fruit trees at the beginning of their second spring with a 45-percent solution of nitrogen at the rate of ¼ pound per inch of trunk diameter. How do you measure trunk diameter? The only way I ever found prac-

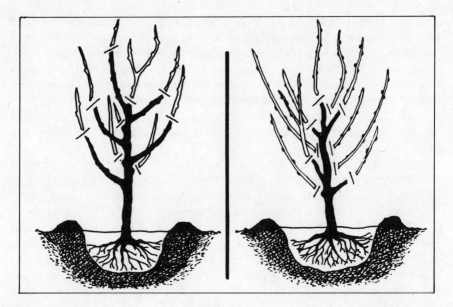

Drawing at left shows how to prune back apple, pear, and cherry trees at planting time. Drawing at right shows planting-time pruning for peach, nectarine, and plum. Circular mound around newly planted trees retains water. Do not plant dwarf or semi-dwarf fruit trees below nursery level unless otherwise instructed, as you may be burying the graft union.

tical was to wrap a dressmaker's measuring tape around the tree to find the circumference, and then divide by π (approximately $3\frac{1}{7}$).

Keep newly planted orchard trees well watered their first season. Check the soil around the tree or trees every day or so. When it is going from damp to dry, water with a bucketful of lukewarm water. More trees are lost or retarded by lack of watering than from any other cause, including bad weather.

Most standard (regular) and some dwarf and semidwarf fruit trees must be pruned before or right after planting. Prune away any crossed or ill-shaped branches, then reduce the number of side branches, and cut those that remain back 8 to 10 inches. Leave the central stem longer than the side branches.

Spray Programs

If you want to go the organic way with your orchard, care for the plants meticulously, water them carefully, and hope you will get fruit without spraying. Orchard fruits, along with roses, are the plants

I have found I must use chemical assistance for. If you don't want to take any chances, at planting time use one of the combination sprays recommended by the local garden center for fruit trees. When new growth is 1 inch long, begin a biweekly (every two weeks) spraying program for eight weeks. When the tree blossoms, follow the spraying schedule listed in the Fruit Planting and Spraying Table at the back of the book.

Thinning

The standard fruit trees often undertake to produce more fruit than they can mature, so growers thin the number of fruits to improve the quality of the crop. This is not usually needed by the semidwarf and dwarf orchard-fruit trees, and cherries don't have to be thinned. The first year, don't let any of your trees set fruit; they need all the strength they have to establish themselves in their new homes. The second and third years and thereafter, if you find your trees are preparing to set just loads of fruit, thin to only one fruit about every 6 inches. Thinning also offsets the every-two-year syndrome, a pattern of productivity that gives you lots of fruit one year, followed by very little or almost no fruit the next year.

Planting Bramble Fruits

Raspberries, blackberries, and blueberries are the preferred bramble fruits for putting up. The raspberries and blueberries thrive as far north as the colder areas of Canada, depending on the variety. The blackberries prefer a milder climate. All three species are successful in well-drained loam with a pH between 5.1 and 6.5. (Actually, the blueberries do well in loams between 4.4 and 5.1 and won't do well in sweeter soils.)

In areas north of Philadelphia, plant raspberries and blackberries in spring as soon as the soil can be worked. In warmer areas plant them in late winter or in very early spring. Planting during these cold periods is easier if you have prepared the soil in the fall before it becomes stiff, wet, and hard to handle without compacting.

Prepare the soil as described for orchard fruits. Plant in trenches deep enough to bring the crowns of the plants level with or just an inch or so below the level of the soil around them. Set the plants 3 to 4 feet apart. Check Table 3 for specifics about the spacing of bramble fruits. Cover the soil around with mulch to keep weeds down. Early every spring, work a small handful of 5-10-5 into the soil around each bush.

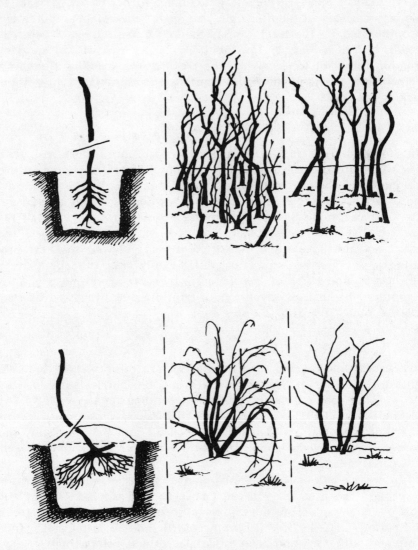

Top strip of drawings shows how to plant red raspberry bushes. Prune back to 2 inches at planting time. Center top shows red raspberry patch before spring pruning; top right shows patch after spring pruning.

Bottom strip shows how to plant blackberry and black and purple raspberry bushes. Mound soil 2 inches high, cut back cane as indicated, and spread mound to ground level as the season progresses. Center bottom shows blackberry and black and purple raspberry patch after spring pruning.

Pruning

Some gardeners stake red raspberries. That's fairly hard work and not necessary as long as you prune the raspberries and keep the bed clean of played-out wood. Canes that have just produced must be cut back almost to the ground to assure the next crop will be fruit of the best quality. At the time of planting, prune canes back to within 6 to 8 inches of the ground, and for the first season, remove all blossoms (except for the everbearer varieties) to prevent the canes from setting fruit. Allow the canes to set fruit the second year, and right after the harvest cut the canes the fruit grew on back to almost ground level. The following spring, cut last summer's new growth back by one-third, leaving canes 24 to 36 inches tall.

Everbearer varieties—varieties that produce a scattering of fruit throughout the growing season rather than a single large crop at one time—should be pruned in the following manner: In the spring cut back to live wood the canes that bore last season's crop. These canes will bear a mid-season crop, and after that they can be cut back to the ground. The new canes will then produce.

Black raspberries are handled somewhat differently. Blackberries and black raspberries look alike, and the only way I know to distinguish between them is by examining the fruit: The core of the blackberry is part of the fruit, while black raspberries come away from the twig leaving behind a little white core so that the fruit itself is hollow after picking. When planting blackberries and black (and purple) raspberries, mound the soil in the planting trench 2 inches high over the crown of the plants and cut the lead cane back to the top of the mound. This induces branching. As the canes grow up, level the soil mounding the trench. After the harvest the second season, shorten the new canes by about one-third to induce branching and remove most of the lateral (side) branches that have borne the season's crop. Cut away all weak wood and all dead wood. After-harvest pruning of blackberries and black raspberries should reduce the shrub by about one-third of its main branches and two-thirds of the twiggy side branches.

Spraying

Raspberries and blackberries growing in well-drained garden loam and properly fertilized every spring will have few problems. Unlike the orchard fruits, a spraying program isn't necessary. You will have a problem, however—the competition with the local bird population to get the fruit at harvest time. Cover the bushes with mosquito netting. Catalogs offer lightweight, long-lasting nylon netting. It is most successful when held just a little above the bushes by tall stakes. Make sure it goes all the way to the ground; birds do seem to be able to get inside.

Handling Blueberries

Blueberries seem to yield more fruit when cross-pollinated. Any two varieties will cross-pollinate each other. Since blueberries, like the other bramble fruits, are grown in early, mid-season, and late varieties —that is, varieties that flower and bear fruit at different seasons— when choosing a pair to ensure cross-pollination, make sure the pair will bloom at the same time. Earliblue and Blueray are early blueberries and can cross-pollinate. Berkeley and Pemberton are late mid-season varieties and can cross-pollinate each other.

Plant blueberry bushes in about the same manner as the blackberries and raspberries, in trenches or planting holes 8 to 10 feet apart, with 4 to 5 feet between plants. The depth of the trench should be enough to bring the crowns of the plants to ground level or an inch or two below. Prepare the soil in the bottoms of the trenches or holes as for planting orchard trees. The one significant difference is that you must cater to the blueberries' need for acid soil. Unless you know your soil has a pH between 4.4 and 5.1, add 1 ounce of ammonium sulfate (sulfate of ammonia) to the soil around each plant. As the plants mature, early each spring add an increased amount of ammonium sulfate until you are feeding mature blueberry bushes 4 ounces. Every three years apply 2 to 8 ounces of 10-10-10, according to the size of the bush, and that year reduce the amount of ammonium sulfate by half.

When you set out blueberry bushes, cut the upper branches back by one-half their length. In subsequent years prune only to remove excessive small growth and the dead ends of branches. The blueberry crop ripens over a period of six weeks, and it will need careful netting to protect it from the birds.

Handling Grapes

Grapes yield a very high return for a small amount of space invested, because they will grow vertically, right up to the top of the garage if you like. That makes them a good candidate for the gardener who has little space and wants lots of fruit to put up. Unfortunately,

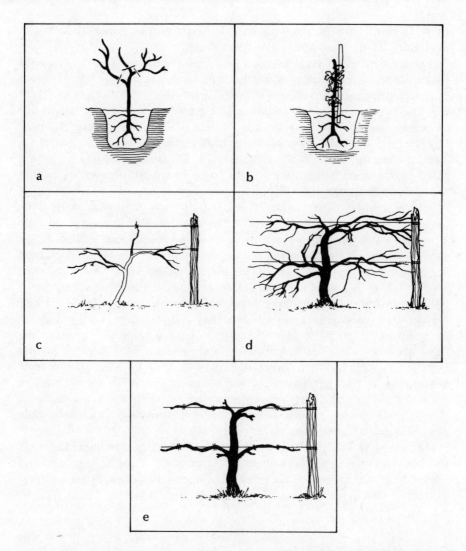

Drawings *a* and *b* show newly planted grapevine pruned and staked for its first season. Drawing *c* shows vine in its second season, with longest vertical shoot trained to the top wire of a two-wire trellis and one cane selected to grow right and left along bottom wire. Drawings *d* and *e* show mature grapevine before and after pruning, using the Four-Arm Kniffin system. Prune in late winter before buds swell, leaving only year-old canes, from ¼- to ⅜-inch diameter, which has 5 to 8 inches between the fifth and sixth buds. Make cuts at least 1 inch beyond the buds. Short spurs near the main stem have been pruned back to 2 buds each to provide wood for renewal of growth. Four-year-old vine should have a total of 40 buds after pruning.

there isn't all that much you can do with grapes other than make jam, jelly, and juice—and serve them fresh.

Grapes are also easy in their soil requirements. They'll grow on rocky slopes other fruits would balk at, and, except for some rather exacting pruning, they demand little attention.

The best varieties for jelly are the acidulous Concords, which are extremely hardy. If you want to go into wine making, you can now buy French hybrids crossed with hardy disease-resistant American species. Aurora, Baco Noir, Cascade, De Chaunac, and Foch—highly rated by the New York Agricultural Experiment Station—are suitable for making a variety of wines.

If you have grapes, one of the fun things to do is to use the leaves to garnish and enhance the flavor of pickled cucumbers; 2 or 3 medium-size leaves per quart jar is the usual ratio. The large, tender leaves of the Seedless Thompson grape is the type preferred for making dolmas—stuffed grape leaves, Greek style.

Buy 2- to 3-year-old grape plants and set them in equal parts of light, well-drained soil, coarse sand, and coarse humus. The best site for grapes is a slight slope, though they will grow perfectly well on flat land as long as the soil isn't soggy. In a community garden, the most economical space for growing grapes is on wire leaders strung between fence posts. In the home garden they can be grown over arbors, up a wall trellis, or along a fence. Some varieties require cross-pollination and are generally noted as such by growers.

In some areas, grapes seem to require spraying. The fruit table gives suggested spraying times.

Pruning is vital in the production of good grape harvests. Left to their own devices, the grapes will put out lots of foliage and set only very small grapes or very few. The most commonly used pruning system is the Kniffin system, illustrated here.

6

Choosing and
Growing the Vegetables

Finding your way around the seed catalogs can be confusing. There are so many varieties offered of each species, and often the little legends under the big beautiful pictures don't give me any notion. of why I should choose that variety rather than another.

When selecting a perennial, a plant meant to come back year after year—like strawberries, asparagus, rhubarb, artichokes, and any of the orchard or bramble fruits—the first consideration is, is this variety hardy in my area? Will it survive cold winters or hot summers, whichever may be your problem? The U.S. Department of Agriculture has printed a map of the United States and Canada and marked it off into hardiness zones. Zone 1 includes the Hudson Bay area and Zone 2 the colder reaches of Canada. Zone 3 includes the northern strip of southern Canada and cold areas of North Dakota, Minnesota, and some portions of New England where temperatures drop to 40 and 30 degrees below zero. Zone 10 at the other end of the scale includes the southern tip of Florida and California where temperatures do not go below 30 to 40 degrees. The map illustrated here gives a clearer picture of relative hardiness zoning in North America. Among perennial plants, select only those you are sure will survive the extremes of weather in your area.

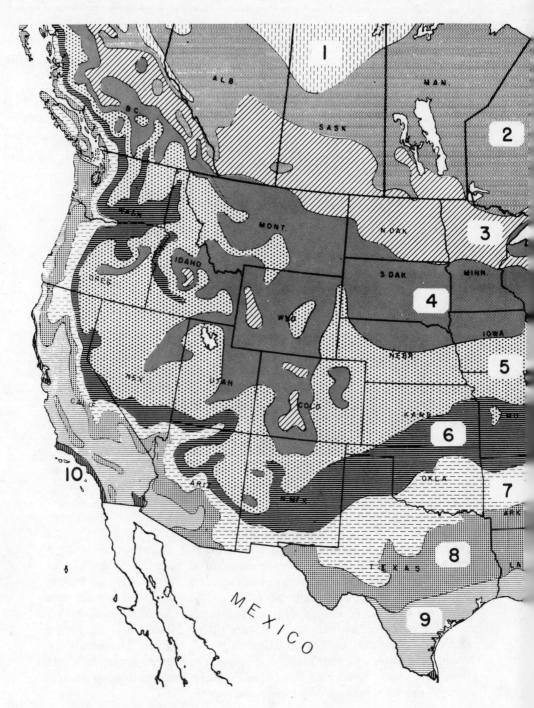

Plant Hardiness Zones

APPROXIMATE RANGE OF
AVERAGE ANNUAL MINIMUM
TEMPERATURES FOR EACH ZONE

ZONE 1	BELOW -50° F	
ZONE 2	-50° TO -40°	
ZONE 3	-40° TO -30°	
ZONE 4	-30° TO -20°	
ZONE 5	-20° TO -10°	
ZONE 6	-10° TO 0°	
ZONE 7	0° TO 10°	
ZONE 8	10° TO 20°	
ZONE 9	20° TO 30°	
ZONE 10	30° TO 40°	

EARLY, MID-SEASON, AND LATE VARIETIES

Among the food plants that are annual, seeds are offered for several varieties of each species. Each variety has specially desirable characteristics. There are varieties noted as exceptionally good for making pies or jams, freezing, preserving, or canning. These will stand up to processing better than will more tender varieties described as best for the "home garden," which are better used fresh. Some plants—those not often canned, jammed, or frozen, or those usually put in cold or dry storage, root crops for instance—usually aren't offered in varieties noted as especially good for canning.

The other important consideration when you are planting a garden and intend to put up a lot of its produce is the dates that the crops will ripen. Varieties noted as "early" withstand cold weather in spring and at the end of summer better than do "mid-season" varieties. Mid-season varieties, however, are apt to stand up to hot weather better than varieties noted as best for either "early" or "late" growing. The varieties offered as "late" usually take longer to mature, can withstand some frost at the end of the growing season, and often have an especially full flavor.

There's another type of "late" crop. Among cold-weather or early-spring vegetables, those noted as "late" are often those that will stand up to the increasingly intense heat of approaching summer.

The varieties I have suggested below are those grown successfully in most temperate regions of the country. If you have a special climate problem in your area, it would be well worth your while to talk over selections of perennial plants—orchard and other fruits, for instance—with the local garden center and to get recommendations from the Agricultural Extension Service before making selections.

Seeds for annual varieties of food plants are sold in all sorts of places from supermarkets to hardware stores, dime stores, garden-supply centers, and supply centers for farmers. Prices in supply centers for farmers are sometimes lower than they are on the shelves of other suppliers, and the seeds are offered in larger quantities. The quality generally is very good. I have often joined with a handful of neighbors to buy large packets of seeds from farm-supply centers, enough seeds to supply all our gardens. Buying great big packets for your own small garden can lure the gardener into planting far too many seeds per square foot. Harvests in crowded gardens are poor, so don't you succumb to that temptation. Garden supply catalogs are among the best sources for unusual varieties and very good new hybrid plants and seeds. I buy vegetable seeds from catalogs that devote more space to vegetables than to fruit or flowers (and flower seeds from catalogs that devote more space to flowers than to vegetables or fruit).

ARTICHOKES (PERENNIAL)

Set out plants in mid-spring. Plant 5 to 6 inches deep in trenches 3 feet apart, with 3 feet between plants. Crop matures the second season —in spring in warmer areas, in summer or late summer in cooler regions.

Canning notes. Baby artichokes, halved and canned or frozen, make good cocktail tidbits and luxury material for pies, salads, and gourmet cookery. Artichokes grow well in mild seashore climates but don't winter well in cool areas. Grow them in containers and bring them indoors for winter. They are attractive plants.

Varieties. Large Green Globe artichoke is the one I've grown. Today few catalogs supply the northern half of the country, probably because they proved to be more tender than seedsmen offering them a few years ago supposed. You can order Large Green Globe from southern growers, such as Robert Nichols Seed Company, 2700 Logan, P.O. Box 15487, Dallas, Texas 75215.

Tips. Plant artichokes in trenches and line the bottoms of the trenches with 1 inch of rotted manure, compost, dried cow manure, or with a handful of 5-10-5. When the plants are 4 inches tall, mulch the soil well. When plants are 8 inches tall, remove all but six of the suckers that develop at the base. Transplanted suckers will make a new row. Cut plants back to the ground in fall and mulch to protect against winter weather. Fertilize halfway through the growing season with a handful of compost or 5-10-5 per plant. Harvest artichokes before the bracts begin to open.

Companion plants. In early spring or late summer, plant lettuce, radishes, or early turnips around your artichokes.

ASPARAGUS (PERENNIAL)

Set out plants in early spring. Plant 5 to 6 inches deep in trenches 4 feet apart, with 18 inches between plants. Crop matures second or third season in mid-spring.

Canning notes. Because asparagus out of season is very expensive, this is one of the most advantageous of all crops to grow for freezing and/or canning.

Varieties. Asparagus is subject to asparagus rust, so select resistant varieties such as Mary Washington. Buy 2- or 3-year-old roots: They can be harvested the second and third year. The 1-year-old roots offered are less expensive but take a year longer to produce a picking crop. Asparagus started from seed won't be ready to harvest for 4 or 5 years.

Tips. Sandy loam is best. Mix the bottom of the trench for asparagus with one-third its volume in sand, line it with 1 inch of rotted or dried manure or compost, and cover it with 4 inches of sandy soil. Spread the roots 18 inches apart on humps in the trench floor and cover with 2 inches of soil. As the roots develop shoots, fill in the trench. In August, or in early spring, transplant asparagus volunteers. In early spring the next year, work a handful of compost or garden fertilizer around each plant. Before spear growth starts, work in ½ ounce of nitrate of soda per plant. After the cutting season, rake 1 pound of nitrate of soda in for each 40 plants. As asparagus spears appear in spring the second season and reach 6 to 8 inches in height, break them close to the ground or slice them off just below the soil level. (If you fail to keep the bed picked, the spears will reach for the sky, and production will slow and come to an end.) When production begins to slow six or so weeks after it begins, let the remaining spears grow up. At the end of the summer, cut all the spears to the ground and burn them.

Companion plants. Sow viny vegetables—such as cucumbers, fall squash, or pumpkins—in the asparagus patch.

BUSH SNAP BEANS

Sow seed in mid-spring, in succession plantings for continuous crops, 1 to 1½ inches deep, gradually thin to 3 to 5 inches apart, in rows 20 to 30 inches apart. Crops begin to mature in about 50 days.

Canning notes. Snap green beans are the most popular for freezing. Harvests last a period of weeks only. To have enough for freezing, sow successive plantings of bush snap-bean seeds every 10 days through late spring and early summer to keep crops coming all season long.

Varieties. Burpee's Tenderpod (50 days to maturity) is that famous seedsman's most popular bean. Canyon (52 days) is recommended for canning and freezing. It is resistant to mosaic and curly-top virus. Greensleeves (56 days) is another recommended variety for canning and freezing. If you want to grow green snap beans up a trellis or along a fence, select White Half Runner (60 days). It produces 3- to

4-foot runners that need no staking. A good variety for putting up. Brittle Wax (52 days) and Goldencrop Wax (54 days) are two varieties of yellow snap beans recommended for freezing and for canning.

POLE BEANS

Sow seed in mid-spring 1 inch deep, 4 to 6 seeds per pole, poles 30 to 36 inches apart. Crops begin to mature in about 60 days.

Canning notes. Because pole beans grow straight up, they are a good choice for the canner whose only space is vertical. Though they begin to bear later than bush beans, they yield heavily over a longer period. They are an all-summer crop. The vines grow 6 to 8 feet tall and will climb a trellis or a fence. For the community garden, easiest staking is a rough pole.

Varieties. Some of the best for canning or freezing are Burpee Golden (60 days to maturity), a tender, stringless, butter-yellow type. Kentucky Wonder (65 days) has an especially distinctive flavor and is excellent for freezing. The pods when small are served as snap beans; when larger they can be dried and split for a harvest of shell beans. Blue Lake, White Seeded (60 days) is popular for canning and freezing. Its small white seeds are good as dried shell beans. There's a rust-resistant variety of Kentucky Wonder for areas where rust is a problem.

Tips. When pole-bean blossoms appear, work 1 tablespoonful of 4-8-4 or a handful of compost into the soil of each hill. Pick pole beans to be eaten as snap beans when still thin and before they begin to swell out—then they are stringless. Or let the pods swell and shell the beans, then freeze or dry them.

Companion plants. Grow radishes, lettuce, and other quick crops in the bean row in early spring, then follow with beans.

SHELL BEANS

Sow seed in mid-spring 1 inch deep, 4 to 6 per pole, poles 30 to 36 inches apart. Crops begin to mature in about 95 days.

Canning notes. These are handled in all respects like the pole beans described above. Leave shell-bean pods on the plants until they have swelled and yellowed. Then let the bushes dry, pick off the pods, shell the beans, and dry them on screens in a dry, airy place before storing.

Varieties. Red Kidney (95 days to maturity) is a popular shell bean for Spanish and Mexican cookery; it grows to about 2 feet tall. White Marrowfat (100 days) is a popular "navy" (white) bean, considered best for baking.

Companion plants. See above. Also sow long-growing flowers, such as dwarf marigolds, at the foot of the pole vegetables.

BUSH LIMA BEANS

Sow seed in mid to late spring 1 to 1½ inches deep, gradually thin to 4 inches apart, with 30 to 36 inches between rows. Crops begin to mature in about 75 days.

Canning notes. These are easier to grow than the pole limas since they need no support; they also mature earlier.

Varieties. There are several types of lima beans—some are fatter and mealier, others are flatter and greener, like the baby limas we buy frozen. A package of the large-seeded type is apt to sow a shorter row than a packet of the small-seeded type. Fordhook (75 days to maturity) is a potato lima, growing on plants 24 inches across and about 20 inches tall. Excellent for canning and freezing. Don't plant seeds until the soil warms. Burpee's Improved Bush Lima (75 days) is a flat bean, easier to shell than the others. Fordhook No. 242 (75 days) stands droughty summers; a very good lima for canning or freezing. Baby Fordhook Bush Lima (70 days) is a small potato type that grows on plants only 14 inches tall. Henderson Bush Lima (65 days) is a buttery baby lima for canning, freezing, or drying.

Tips. When lima-bean blossoms appear, work 1 tablespoonful of 4-8-4 or a handful of compost into each hill.

Companion plants. See above.

POLE LIMA BEANS

Sow seed in mid-spring 1 inch deep, 4 to 6 per pole, poles 30 to 36 inches apart. Crops begin to mature in about 90 days.

Canning notes. Pole limas are the limas to plant if your garden space is limited. They grow straight up and can be trained on strings to climb almost any kind of wall or fence. They give a high yield over a long period. In the open or community garden, where there are no walls, plant them in rows with rough poles in the center of each hill as support.

Varieties. Prizetaker (90 days to maturity) has exceptionally large beans excellent for freezing. There are more large beans per pod to this variety than to others, so there is less shelling involved per pound of produce you put up. Since limas are sometimes hard to shell, it is a quality worth considering. Burpee's Best (92 days) gives a higher yield per plant than most other limas. It is a strong climber that will grow to 10 or 12 feet. Its beans are of the mealy potato type.

Tips and companion plants. See Pole Beans.

BEETS

Sow seeds in early spring ½ inch deep, gradually thin to 2 to 3 inches apart, in rows 12 to 18 inches apart. Crops begin to mature 55 to 60 days later.

Canning notes. You can can beets, pickle them, or store them in a dry, cool place for winter. Which you plan to do will govern the variety you choose. Beets are an advantageous crop, since you can harvest and cook the greens while the roots are reaching maturity. Beet greens can be frozen like spinach.

Varieties. Red Ball (60 days to maturity), harvested at 3 inches in diameter, is a sweet little beet for canning or pickling. Burpee's Golden (55 days) is a newcomer to the market whose unique contribution is that it doesn't bleed and is a color you never expect a beet to be. Harvest these for canning or freezing while still quite small. The tops make excellent cooking greens. Lutz Green Lead, Winter Keeper (80 days) can be harvested small for canning and pickling or left in the row through late fall to be harvested for winter storage in a cool, dry place. Tops make excellent greens to freeze. Fire Chief (70 days) is another excellent small canning beet.

Tips. Work loam 6 to 8 inches deep for this root crop, and don't make the soil sandy or roots will be fibrous. When seedlings are large enough to become crowded, thin them to stand 2 inches apart and wash and cook the thinnings. Pull crisp young beet leaves from plants as needed, but don't ever strip a plant of more than one-third of its leaves. Harvest beets, unless intended for winter storage, when they are 3 inches around. Leave winter beets in their rows until hard frosts are expected; then dig and layer them in damp sand in a cool place.

Companion plants. After the beets have been harvested, fill the row with a mid-summer crop such as snap beans.

BROCCOLI

Sow seed ½ inch deep in flats indoors, and set out seedlings in early spring. Keep 18 inches between plants, 20 to 24 inches between rows. Crops begin to mature in about 40 days after being set out.

Canning notes. Broccoli plants can go into the ground about 30 days before the date of the last frost. You can plant a second batch of broccoli seedlings in mid-summer for early fall harvests. Broccoli is one of the best vegetables for freezing.

Varieties. There are two types of broccoli—the type that makes a big central head like cauliflower and also gives secondary crops of side shoots and the type that gives only one head. De Cicco (60 day to maturity) and Calabrese (85 days) yield heads and side shoots. The quick variety, Green Comet Hybrid, matures 40 days after plants are set out and produces single heads weighing as much as one pound, but it has no side shoots. Spartan Early (55 days) is a fast broccoli that does give small side shoots after the main head has been picked. If you want to follow an early crop of broccoli by a second mid-spring crop in the same row, sow Green Comet Hybrid for the early crop, and try Early Green Scouting for the second or fall crop.

Tips. Start seeds indoors 4 to 6 weeks before planting time. About 25 plants will fill a 50-foot row. Fertilize with a tablespoonful of 4-8-4 for each plant just before the broccoli head matures to encourage a second crop. Dr. Robert Wearne of the Agricultural Extension Service in Washington, D.C., reports that his spring broccoli, cut back after the major crop in late spring, will continue producing side sprouts all summer long. That's never happened to me, but, if you feel lazy about digging up the broccoli row, leave it in and see if you can duplicate his results. Harvest broccoli heads when the buds are still tightly curled. Cut the heads along with about 5 inches of stem.

Companion plants. Follow this early-spring crop with a late-spring vegetable, such as snap beans, or a summer lettuce, such as Cos.

Caution: It is a good garden practice not to let broccoli follow or precede any of the other cabbagy vegetables in the garden row —cabbage, Brussels sprouts, cauliflower, for instance.

BRUSSELS SPROUTS

Sow seed ½ inch deep in flats indoors, and set out seedlings in early spring. Keep 18 inches between plants, 20 to 24 inches between rows. Crops begin to mature in 85 to 90 days after being set out.

Canning notes. Brussels sprouts are excellent frozen and one of the easiest vegetables to prepare for freezing.

Varieties. Jade Cross Hybrid is a popular variety, a deep blue-green Brussels sprout that matures in about 85 days. Long Island Improved (90 days) is planted in many areas and is the suggested seed for late sowings.

Tips. Start seeds indoors 4 to 6 weeks before planting time and set plants out about 30 days before the date of the last expected frost. You can plant a crop of seedlings for fall harvests about 90 days before the date of the first expected frost. The sprout buds develop in the leaf axis growing along the main stem. Pick sprouts as they reach 1 to 1½ inches across and are still tightly curled. Pick the lowest maturing sprouts first and remove the leaf in whose axil each picked sprout grew. Do not remove the top leaves. Brussels sprouts stand up to light frosts.

Companion plants. See Broccoli.

Caution: see Caution note under Broccoli.

CABBAGE

Sow seed ½ inch deep in flats indoors, and set out seedlings in early spring. Keep 18 inches between plants, 20 to 24 inches between rows. Crop begins to mature in about 72 days after being set out.

Canning notes. Though we neither can nor freeze cabbage, it makes good sauerkraut, and the big heads of late cabbage will store well in a cool place.

Varieties. Stein's Flat Dutch (83 days to maturity) is recommended for both early and late planting. It keeps well and makes good sauerkraut. Danish Roundhead (105 days) is a good fall or winter cabbage. Penn State Ballhead (110 days) is another good kraut and winter-keeping cabbage.

Tips. Start seeds indoors 4 to 6 weeks before the date the last frost is expected, and set plants out about 30 days before that date. Start a second set of seedlings indoors about 3 months before the date the first frost is expected, and set these seedlings out 60 days before that date. Space early cabbage 18 inches apart in rows; set the large late varieties 24 inches apart in rows, which are 2½ to 3 feet apart. When the heads are solid, harvest the cabbage; they may burst if left too long on the plant. Cabbages you aren't ready to harvest can be yanked hard enough to break the roots, then left upright in the row for a week or so. If the winter is not severe, you can store cabbages layered in hay in their rows.

Companion plants. See Broccoli.

Caution: See Caution note under Broccoli.

CARROTS

Sow seed in early spring ¼ inch deep, gradually thin to 1 to 2 inches apart, in rows 20 inches apart. Crops begin to mature about 68 days after sowing.

Canning notes. Baby carrots, canned or pickled, are popular, and larger carrots, mixed with peas and/or beans, are often canned as a mixed vegetable. Carrot cake can be frozen, and carrots make a good marmalade.

Varieties. Depth of available planting soil affects the way carrots grow and their texture. For shallow or heavy soil choose Oxheart (75 days to maturity) and Short 'n Sweet (68 days). In deep soils Imperator and Gold Pak (75 days) are good types. The gourmet carrot for using in the baby stage is Little Finger (65 days). For average soil depths, Goldinhart (70 days) is recommended for its heavy yield. Danvers Half Long (75 days) gives a big crop and is recommended for putting up. Carrot seeds can go into the ground any time after 30 days before the date of the last frost; a second crop can go into the ground in summer, 90 to 60 days before the date the first freeze is expected.

Tips. Soil for carrots must be deeply worked loam. Get your carrots in early, before the crabgrass begins to sprout; carrots take a long time to germinate and the fine little seedlings are easily crowded out by fast-growing weeds. Then it becomes hard to dispose of the weeds without uprooting the carrot seedlings. Sow the carrots broadcast over a 12-inch-wide furrow ¼ inch deep, cover them with just a little fine soil, and tamp firmly into place. Water the newly sown seeds with the finest spray on your hose. Pull the largest carrots as needed to leave space for the smaller ones to develop. Mature crops can stay in the ground with mulch for protection until just before hard frosts. If you decide not to can your carrots, you can store them in a cool place, layered in damp sand and minus their tops. Moisten the top layer of sand monthly to keep the carrots from drying out.

Companion plants. Sow radishes with your carrots; they'll mark the row and will be up and out by the time the slow-to-germinate carrot seeds begin to grow.

CAULIFLOWER

Sow seed ½ inch deep in flats indoors, and set seedlings out in early spring. Keep 18 inches between plants, 20 to 30 inches between rows. Crops begin to mature in about 50 days.

Canning notes. Grow cauliflower to pickle or freeze, broken into florets, or to cool-store as whole heads.

Varieties. Many growers give days to maturity for cauliflower as the average from the time plants—not seeds—are set out in the garden. Snow King Hybrid, which matures 50 days after plants are set out, is the earliest of the cauliflowers to mature and is a good choice.

Tips. Start seed of the earliest cauliflower variety you can find indoors 60 to 75 days before the expected date of the last freeze, and set cauliflower seedlings out about 30 days before that date. Sow a second crop of cauliflower seed about 3 months before the date of the first real frost in your area. Cauliflower is grown by most gardeners as a late crop. Pure white cauliflowers heads, which are the prettiest for pickles and relishes, or frozen, are the result of "blanching." When the heads begin to form on a plant, tie the outside leaves over the head with raffia or soft rags. The heads are ready 2 to 3 weeks after they have been covered. Don't let mature heads stay on the plant—the flavor and texture will deteriorate. If you aren't ready to put up cauliflower when the crop is ready, pull up the plants and hang them upside down in a cool, dark place until canning day.

Companion plants. See Broccoli. Or make cauliflower a late crop, following rows left empty by carrots, beans, or early tomatoes.

Caution: See Caution note under Broccoli.

CELERIAC

Sow seed in mid-spring ¼ inch deep, gradually thin to 4 inches apart, in rows 30 to 36 inches apart. Crops begin to mature in about 120 days.

Canning notes. This usually isn't canned or frozen but, instead, is stored for winter use in a cool, dark place like other root vegetables. Don't plant a whole row unless you know celeriac and want to have lots. It is a root vegetable with a celery flavor and won't appeal to everyone.

Varieties. Alabaster matures in about 120 days from seed.

Tips. Sow celeriac seed about 30 days before the average date of the last frost in rows moistened for speedy germination. Make the furrows 2 inches deep but cover the seed with only ¼ inch of soil. As the seedlings grow, draw the soil up around the plants. When the seedlings are 2 inches high, thin to stand 4 inches apart. As the plants mature, rake the soil up around them until they are mounded 2 inches high. After thinning, work a handful of 4-8-4 into the row. Roots are best when 2 inches around. Pull the celeriac up by the roots on a day when the soil is moist enough so that the roots pull easily. Twist off the tops and store the roots layered in moist sand in a cool place.

Companion plants. Celeriac can follow a row left empty by early lettuce or peas.

CHARD

Sow seed in early spring ¼ deep, gradually thin to 4 to 6 inches apart, in rows 18 inches apart. Crops begin to mature in about 60 days.

Canning notes. I prefer frozen spinach to frozen chard; but where spinach is hard to grow, I plant chard or kale instead for a boiling green and a green to freeze. Actually, chard is a good plant to invest space in for canning in small batches because it produces all summer long until frosts. After you've pulled off the green leafy part, you can cook the central rib as you would asparagus for eating fresh.

Varieties. Fordhook Giant, which matures in 60 days and goes on producing all summer in the row, is the most popular strain in many areas.

Tips. You can plant chard as soon as the ground can be worked— about 30 days before the last expected frost. In areas where the last frost is expected January 31, chard can be planted up to April 1. Sow the seed in furrows 2 inches deep, cover with ¼ inch of soil, and tamp. When the plants are 3 inches high, thin to stand 4 inches apart. Thin again to 7 inches when the plants are 7 inches high. Cook the thinnings to eat fresh. At mid-season, work a handful of 4-8-4 into the soil in the row. When harvesting, give the outer leaves a sharp twist to break them free. Don't tug at the plant.

Companion plants. Early radishes or early lettuce can precede chard.

CORN

Sow seed in mid-spring 1 inch deep, with 4 inches between seeds, in hills of 5 seeds each, in double rows 3 feet apart. Crop begins to mature in about 70 days.

Canning notes. Canned corn kernels, creamed corn, corn relish, frozen whole corn, or corn kernels are all well worth the effort it takes to put them up. Because you need a lot of those very tall corn plants to produce enough corn for canning, corn is best suited for the very large canning garden. Mini corn grows small and makes a nice cocktail pickle; it's a suitable choice for the container canning garden. Because corn sugar turns to starch very quickly, this is one canning item that should be processed almost the minute it is picked. Corn for putting up should be fully mature; very young ears have less flavor.

Varieties. Gold Cross Bantam (86 days to maturity) is one of the sweetest for canning and freezing. Early Extra-Sweet (71 days) is one of sweetest early corns. Illini Xtra-Sweet (85 days) does not turn its sugar content to starch as quickly as do other corn and is very sweet. My preferences for corn to put up on the cob are Butter and Sugar Hybrid (73 days) or Sugar and Gold Hybrid ((67 days). Silver Queen (late white variety, 92 days) with an exquisite flavor is one of my favorites for eating fresh, but it's not quite as good for canning as the yellow and white corns. If you want to grow your own popcorn, Creme Puff Hybrid (105 days) is a good one. In areas where summers are short, there are early white hull-less popcorns that mature in 95 days—Pepper Popcorn Hybrid and White Cloud are two. We string popcorn for our Christmas tree, and I have found the yellow popping corns better for that purpose than the whites.

Tips. There's time for only one crop of corn. Sow seed in mid-spring about when the apple blossoms fall. Corn requires cross-pollination, so always sow it in double rows, even if they must be short rows. Cover the seeds with ½ inch fine soil and tamp into place. Water well after sowing. When the corn is 4 inches tall, thin to 3 plants per hill. At thinning time, add a tablespoon of 4-8-4 per corn hill; when the tassels appear at the tops of the plants, add another. Harvest corn when the silk begins to turn dark brown. Ripe ears are usually plumped out. Pick only ripe ears for canning.

Companion plants. You can save garden space by planting pumpkins, squash, or cucumbers at the feet of the tall-standing corn plants.

CUCUMBERS

Sow seed in mid-spring ½ inch deep, gradually thin to 4 to 6 inches apart, in rows 4 feet apart. Crops begin to mature in about 53 days.

Canning notes. You can pickle regular cucumbers when they are quite small. And you can eat pickling cucumbers when they are young. However, there are cucumbers developed especially for pickling, and these are best for putting up. Start one crop of cucumber seeds indoors about 4 weeks before planting time, and when you set these out, sow seed for a second crop that will come in when the first crop is harvested. Cucumbers are prone to a number of diseases. Disease-resistant varieties go on yielding after more vulnerable varieties have succumbed to disease and stopped producing. If you've ever had problems with cucumbers or their relatives, the squashes and melons, be sure to plant resistant varieties for canning.

Varieties. If you want some cucumbers to eat and some to pickle, plant Burpee Hybrid or M & M Hybrid (60 days to maturity). These are disease resistant and produce heavy crops of eating cucumbers that can also be used for pickling. For pickling, the popular cucumbers are Burpee Pickler (53 days), and an F2 hybrid pickling cucumber, Ohio MR 17 (57 days). Pioneer (51 days) is disease resistant and high yielding. Wisconsin SMR 18 (54 days) is a good cucumber for brining, the process that makes dill pickles. West India Gherkin (60 days) produces small 2- to 3-inch fruits covered with fleshy prickles and is the type to use for tiny pickles or sweet gherkins. An interesting variety is 180 Lemon (65 days); it is ready to pick when yellow markings first appear on the skin. These are lemon-shaped cucumbers, rather fun to use for dill pickles. Tastygreen Burpless Hybrid and Sweet Slice Hybrid (56 days) are "burpless" pickles, very mild. Tastygreen makes good pickles. Salty Hybrid (50 days) is another good variety for putting up fresh pack or for brining. For small gardens, Patio Pik Hybrid, is a compact plant used for pickling or for table.

Tips. Sow cucumber seed indoors in individual peat pots in sphagnum moss or vermiculite 4 weeks before planting time. About

10 days after the last frost, set the seedlings 4 to 6 inches apart in hills, 4 plants to a hill, in hills 4 feet apart. Cucumbers grow on vines that should be trained outward. Between plants sow cucumber seeds for a second crop later in the season. Or plant cucumbers at the outer edges of the garden and lead the runners out onto the grass. If you want a cucumber to grow up a wire-mesh fence or other support, plant the tiny gherkins. The fruit is so light it can ripen on the vine without pulling the vine down. If you train larger cucumbers to grow down or up, support the fruits as they begin to enlarge on small shelves or in mesh bags tacked to the support. Mulch planted cucumbers to preserve moisture, always water under the foliage, and never touch the foliage when it is wet. Soil for cucumbers should be well drained and contain lots of humus to keep the plants moist. Make your last sowing of cucumbers no later than 4 months before the average date of the first real frost.

Cucumbers are heavy feeders, so add an extra handful of compost or fertilizer to the soil in each hill. After planting mulch well. Water the cucumbers thoroughly when fruits are beginning to mature. If you keep cucumber vines picked, they'll keep producing for a long time.

Companion plants. Early-spring lettuce, radishes, and peas can precede cucumbers, or plant your cucumbers at the feet of tall plants such as corn or tomatoes.

EGGPLANT

Sow seed ½ inch deep in flats indoors, and set out plants in late spring. Keep 18 inches between plants, 20 to 30 inches between rows. Plants begin to mature 62 days after setting out.

Canning notes. This isn't the most useful vegetable for canning, but baby eggplants do make nice cocktail appetizers, and you can can or freeze a number of vegetable mélanges that include eggplant.

Varieties. There usually is only one eggplant crop, set out as plants in the spring. Early Beauty Hybrid (62 days to maturity) is a good variety for northern gardens. Even then, in cool regions you can expect to gather only a few eggplants before frosts arrive. Black Beauty (72 days) produces fruit of excellent quality but is a little too late for northern sections. T. S. Cross Hybrid (72 days) is a good selection in areas where eggplants are subject to disease.

Tips. Start seeds indoors 8 to 9 weeks before the last expected frost, and set out 18 inches apart after the soil has warmed. Harvest when fruits are 4 inches in diameter and a glossy purple-black. When the weather begins to cool, protect the plants with a plastic canopy. You can store fruit, wrapped loosely in newspapers, in a cool, dark place for a week or two at least before processing.

Companion plants. Precede eggplants with peas, early radish, beets, or lettuces.

Caution: A member of the tomato-potato family, so don't follow or precede eggplant with either tomatoes or potatoes.

GARLIC

Plant garlic sets in early spring ½ inch deep, 3 inches apart, in rows 8 inches apart. Crop begins to mature about 125 days after planting.

Canning notes. You can "put up" garlic by braiding the stems of dried roots (heads) and storing in a cool, dry, dark place. They'll be good through winter and until spring when, like onions, they begin to sprout.

Varieties. Not all catalogs offer garlic sets. Burpee offers the variety Extra Select. The sets are mother bulbs just like those you buy in the store, composed of several cloves each. A pound of garlic sets plants a row about 20 feet long and yields about 200 heads—more than you are likely to use over one season. Garlic offered as Elephant Garlic is larger than other varieties and a little less potent in flavor.

Tips. Garlic thrives in a soil that is rich and well drained. Plant cloves 3 inches apart, broad end down, in furrows ½ inch deep. Cover with ½ inch of soil and tamp. When the stems begin to fall over, dig the crop. Allow the garlic heads and stems to dry in the garden for two or three days, brush away the soil, braid the stems together to make a rope of garlic, and hang for the winter in a cool, dry, dark place.

Companion plants. Garlic fends off beetles and other pests. Plant it with vulnerable ornamentals such as roses or among members of the cabbage family.

HORSERADISH (PERENNIAL)

Plant roots in early spring 12 inches deep, 15 inches apart, in rows 2 feet apart. Crop is harvested in the fall.

Canning notes. This isn't the most important of all plants to the canner. But you might like sometimes to make your own horseradish sauce, fresh or bottled. Horseradish is a perennial; leave some of the roots in the row every fall, and you'll have horseradish forever —and ever—and ever.

Varieties. Horseradish is propagated by small sets or roots, which are planted in early spring. Maliner Kren is the standard variety planted.

Tips. Half a dozen roots should provide as much as you can use. You might fill the row with garlic or other herbs if the garden is wider than 9 or 10 feet. Horseradish tends to go wild; if you rototill forgotten roots into the garden, you'll have horseradish coming out of your ears in time.

Companion plants. Plant shallow-rooted early crops, such as radish or lettuce, over the horseradish roots.

KALE

Sow seed in early spring ½ inch deep, gradually thin to 10 inches apart, in rows 18 inches apart. Crops begin to mature in about 60 days.

Canning notes. Kale can be frozen like spinach and it makes a tasty summer boiling green used fresh. Because you can pick kale leaves at will all summer, it is one of the crops you should plant to freeze in small batches. When the season is drawing to a close, harvest all the tender leaves remaining and freeze.

Varieties. Dwarf Blue Curled Vates (60 days to maturity) is an early variety that withstands cold, either as an early-spring planting or as a summer planting for harvesting in fall or winter. In areas south of Philadelphia, kale often winters over in the rows and can be picked after the first frosts, which seems to improve the flavor. Blue Curled Scotch kale (55 days) is attractive in ornamental borders.

Tips. Start kale seeds indoors and set plants out in early spring, or sow seeds in the rows a month before the last average frost. Or use kale to fill a row emptied in midsummer—two and a half months before the scheduled date of the first frost. Thin plants to stand 18 inches apart in the row when they are 3 inches high. To encourage a long season, scratch a little garden fertilizer in around each plant as it begins to mature. Harvest kale leaves as they become bright green. Leaves left on the plant too long become dark and bitter. Cover kale with hay if it is to be left in the row for harvesting through winter.

Companion plants. An early crop of radish or garden cress can be planted along with kale.

Caution: This is a member of the cabbage family, so don't precede or follow kale in soil where cabbage, broccoli, Brussels sprouts, or cauliflowers were or will be crops.

LEEKS

Sow seed in early spring ¼ inch deep, gradually thin to 2 to 3 inches apart, in rows 12 inches apart. Crops mature in the fall.

Canning notes. Leeks are an exquisitely flavored onion type of vegetable that look a little like giant green onions. They're hard to find in local markets and worth growing for that reason. You may or may not want to put up leek soup, though it is excellent frozen, but you can store leeks in a cool, dark, moist pile of sand in fall and have fresh leeks for use in soups and stews all winter long.

Varieties. Broad London (sometimes called Large American Flag) is a commonly available variety of leek. Set out as seed a month before the date of the last frost, and transplant when 6 to 8 inches tall so they'll be ready for harvesting before the first frost.

Tips. You can start leeks from seed in a cold frame, set them out in early spring, and get crops by summer's end—about 130 days. My method has been to sow the seed before the spring frost under plastic tents in well-drained, well-fertilized soil. They are going to be in the ground a long time and need lots of food. Make the furrows 4 to 6 inches deep if you want well-blanched leeks, and cover the seed with soil of a depth of ¼ inch. Hill the soil around the plants as they develop. When the leeks are 6 to 8 inches tall, lift and transplant 8 inches deep in other rows 12 inches apart. As the roots grow, hill the soil around them until the trench is almost filled; the hilling blanches the bottom portion of the leeks. At the end of the growing season when the leeks are about 2 inches in diameter, or even if they aren't, dig the leeks, going well under the plants with the spading fork to avoid slicing them. Store them in damp sand in a cool, dark place for winter, or wash well and use for freezing or canning. In areas south of Philadelphia, leeks will winter over relatively well in the garden if covered with hay and can be dug when the ground is soft in winter, or else they can be harvested in spring.

Companion plants. Plant early lettuce along the edge of the row.

LETTUCE AND SALAD GREENS

Sow seed in early spring ¼ inch deep, 2 to 3 inches apart, in rows 12 inches apart. Crops begin to mature in 10 days in some varieties.

Canning notes. Salad greens aren't canned or frozen for themselves, but they are used in some canning recipes. Lettuce leaves can be included with canned garden peas, for instance, and I have mixed lettuce and spinach as freezing greens with nice results; cooked lettuce is sweet and combines nicely with a sharp taste of kale for freezing. Early lettuce is a good companion plant for all mid- and late-spring vegetables, since it will be up and out before they go in.

Varieties. The lettuce divide into three major types—butterheads, such as Bibb, Boston, and Fordhook (which has heavier, fleshier leaves than Bibb or Boston); crispheads or heading lettuces, which include Iceberg lettuce; and loosehead or leaf lettuces, such as oakleaf green and red varieties. The butterheads mature in 75 to 80 days, the looseheading types in about 45 days. Sow seeds of both these in early spring, and by the time the leaf lettuce is played out, the butterheads will begin to be ready. For an early, early crop, sow seeds of garden cress, sometimes called pepper cress, a sharp-tasting relative of watercress. For summer crops, in early spring sow seed of Cos or Romaine. When the earlier types are played out, these will be ready to harvest—83 days after seeding—and will provide greens that will stand up to summer heat. Second sowings of any of the early types 90 to 60 days before the freeze frost will provide you with salad greens for the fall season.

Tips and Companion plants. Lettuce can go anywhere. It grows well in containers, and the small garden cress fits well in a window box. Larger lettuces fit comfortably at the feet of tall plants, such as cauliflower, broccoli, corn, pole beans and other climbers, and in among flowers in ornamental beds. If you are intercropping (planting lettuces with taller-growing plants), just broadcast the seeds over well-prepared beds after the big plants are in. Otherwise, sow seed thickly ¼ inch deep in furrows 4 inches wide and ½ inch deep. Cover with ¼ inch of fine soil, tamp and water. Thin the seedlings as often as necessary and use the thinnings, well-washed, in salads. Pick side leaves from looseheads or leaf lettuces at will. Cut heading varieties from the stalks, close to the ground, and dig and discard the roots.

MELONS

Plant seedlings in late spring in individual peat pots, 1 inch deep, 8 to 10 inches between plants, in rows 4 feet apart. Crops begin to mature in 75 days.

Canning notes. Mixed frozen orange- and green-fleshed muskmelon balls make a refreshing dessert and represent quite a saving on the supermarket price tag. Muskmelons are harvested in fall and keep well for many weeks in a cool, dry, dark place. Pickle melons that haven't ripened by frost time.

Varieties. For warm areas of the country Honey Mist, a green; Golden Beauty Casaba (120 days to maturity), a white; and Honey Dew (110 days), a green are delicious melons. They take a long growing season and are hard to mature well in cooler regions. Early Hybrid Cranshaw (90 days), a salmon-pink melon on the large size, can be grown almost everywhere. Among muskmelons (the white-veined, orange-fleshed melons we call cantaloupes), Mainerock Hybrid is one of the earliest and so is best for cool regions. It matures in 75 days. Burpee's Netted Gem is a small muskmelon ready in 85 days. Hearts of Gold (90 days) is another small muskmelon with a specially nice flavor. Hale's Best matures in 85 days. Iroquois is a good choice for areas where wilt in cucumbers, melons, and squashes is a problem. It matures in 90 days. Burpee's Hybrid Cantaloupe (82 days) is considered one of the most flavorful and is offered by many seedsmen. Since the green-fleshed melons are longer to mature, in northern gardens consider growing your own muskmelons and mixing the meat with purchased honeydews grown in warmer regions.

Tips. Plant seeds indoors in individual peat pots 4 weeks before planting date, which should be about 6 weeks after the average date of the last frost—well into mid-spring. Cover the young plants with hot caps or plastic tents to encourage rapid development. You get better melons faster if you can underline the planting bed with about 4 inches of rotted manure or compost. Plant melons as cucumbers in hills, 4 plants to a hill, and train the runners outward. Melons will climb with a little help and can mature fruit in this vertical position as long as the developing fruit can be rested on small shelves or in net bags to keep the weight from pulling down the vine. Mulch well around plants to keep humidity in and weeds out. Soil for melons should include a light spring liming; they don't respond to acid soils. Keep melons watered—never from overhead—as the fruits begin to plump out. Harvest when the stem parts from the fruit with a slight pull; as long as it resists, the melon is not quite ripe.

Companion plants. Melon vines can be planted at the foot of tall vegetables, such as corn.

Caution: Don't plant melons in rows in which cucurbits (cucumbers) grew, are growing, or will grow.

OKRA

Sow seed in late spring ½ inch deep, gradually thin to 15 to 24 inches apart, in rows 20 inches apart. Harvest begins in about 56 days.

Canning Notes. I can okra in soups and sometimes with other vegetables. Since it is grown mainly in the south and is available there much of the year, fresh from the garden, it isn't one of the best bets for canning.

Varieties. Clemson Spineless (56 days to maturity), 4 to 5 feet tall, is one of the best of the okras and is advertised in most catalogs. Dwarf Long Green Pod (52 days) is a smaller plant, 2 to 2½ feet tall, and is a variety offered for the north as well, though it takes longer to mature than the others. There are two types of okra—tall growers, to train on a wall, and small growers, 2 to 4 feet high. For a long-season harvest, make a second planting 6 weeks to 2 months after the first.

Tips. Eight to ten plants will be more than enough for most families. Plant in loose, well-fertilized soil and sow in furrows ½ inch deep; cover with ½ inch of soil, tamp, and water often until the seedlings appear. When the plants are 3 inches high, thin so dwarf varieties stand 15 inches apart, tall varieties 24 inches apart. Gather pods when 2½ to 3 inches long. If stems don't cut easily with a knife, okra may be too tough to be worth working with. Don't let okra pods go to seed or plants will stop producing. You can plant a second crop until 2 months before the date of the first frost in warmer areas.

Companion plants. Precede okra by any of the early-spring vegetables—peas, beets, carrots.

ONIONS

Plant sets (or sow seed) in early spring 1 inch deep, 8 inches apart, in rows 12 inches apart. Crops begin to mature in late summer.

Canning notes. The small white onions used to make creamed onions are well worth canning, and so are onion chips and green onions. Dried large onions braided and hung in a cool, dark, dry place will keep well all winter.

Varieties. Yellow Globe is one of the best keeping onions, and another is Ebenezer, a flattened onion with yellowish skin. For summer use fresh. At the same time give a small patch in the garden to Everygreen Long White Bunching onions, which produce scallions in about 60 days and will winter over in milder areas to give more scallions in spring. White Portugal onions are dug for tiny pickling onions while still small. When they reach 2 inches around, they are dug for canning. When canning or pickling is the reason for growing onions, set out as seed.

Tips. In the south, fall planting of onion seeds produces spring crops. You can grow your own onion sets from seeds started indoors 6 weeks before the date of the last frost. Plant sets or sow seeds outdoors about 2 weeks before the average date of the last frost. Fertilizer is the key to big onions. Add 1 pound of 4-8-4, or an equivalent product, and extra humus to every 20 feet of onion row. Plant sets with tips pointed up. If you plant onion seedlings—some companies ship these in very early spring—set them in furrows 2 inches deep, cover with 2½ inches of soil, and tamp. Mulch the row well after planting and water thoroughly. Onions can be thinned (use the thinnings as green onions for freezing or use fresh) until they stand 8 inches apart in the rows; or else set out onion sets and seedlings 8 inches apart in the rows. When flowers appear at the tips of the onion stalks, bend the stalks in half and plan to harvest about 10 days later. Pull the onions up by the roots if the soil is loose; if hard packed, dig with a spading fork, making sure you are well under the onion before you lift. Strew the onions on garden soil in the sun to dry out for a few days, then rub off the soil, braid the stems into bunches 18 inches long, and store in a cool, dry place for use through winter. Perennial bunching onions—green onions—can be left in the garden through winter and picked as needed.

Companion plants. Like garlic, onions are believed to be able to deter pests by their pungent odor, so plant onions near tall, vulnerable plants such as roses or members of the cabbage family.

PARSNIPS

Sow seed in early spring ½ inch deep, gradually thin to 3 to 4 inches apart, in 12 inches rows apart. Harvest roots in fall or allow to winter over in the row.

Canning notes. This is a vegetable that freezes itself—the ground can be your deep freeze—so it's well worth giving space to.

Varieties. All American (95 days to maturity) is a good choice for the casual gardener with stony soil. Hollow Crown is excellent for flavor but requires deep, stone-free soil. It takes about 105 days to mature. Harris Model is another popular variety across the country.

Tips. Like carrots, parsnips require deeply dug soil and grow the best-shaped roots when the soil is free of stones or lumps of any kind. They need a well-drained but rich soil and lots of humus. If your carrot bed must be especially prepared to create these conditions, it makes sense to prepare the parsnip bed next to it and to work the two beds together. The roots develop at a depth of 12 to 18 inches, so the soil must be prepared to this depth. Include lots of organic matter. Parsnip seeds, like carrot seeds, are slow to germinate. Water the row well after planting and cover it with white plastic. Remove the plastic after germination. Thin the seedlings to stand 3 to 4 inches apart in the rows. Parsnips truly taste better after freezing in the ground. The freezing process converts starch in the roots to sugar. Parsnips can be left in the rows through winter and dug whenever the ground thaws enough, or may remain to become the first spring crop.

Companion plants. Plant quick-to-sprout radish seeds when you sow parsnips, to mark the row.

PEAS

Sow seeds in earliest spring 1 to 2 inches deep, gradually thin to 3 inches apart, in rows 20 to 30 inches apart. Crops begin to mature in 58 days for early varieties, 80 days for late varieties.

Canning notes. Peas are one of the best canning and freezing vegetables, either alone or mixed with other vegetables. And since they are one of the first crops in and out of the ground, they allow the gardener to plan two crops in one row. They'll go up, if you want to save space by growing a vertical garden, or they can be planted in low-growing bush varieties with somewhat lower yields. Climbers are best for canning needs since they give the highest yield in the smallest space. Sugar peas, or edible-podded peas, for Chinese cooking are fun to try when you have extra space.

Varieties. The sweetest peas grow from wrinkled seed and these come in both early and main-crop varieties. They are choice for canning and freezing. Burpeeana Early (63 days to maturity) is a vine that grows only 18 to 24 inches tall and is an excellent choice for the small garden. Burpee's Blue Bantam (64 days) grows on vines 15 to 18 inches tall and is an excellent choice for freezing. Green Arrow (70 days) grows on bushes 24 to 28 inches tall and is resistant to downy mildew and Fusarium wilt. The earliest of all the peas, a smooth-seeded, not-quite-so-sweet type, is Alaska (55 days). It can be sown 2 weeks before any of the other varieties and produces a heavy yield. Oregon Sugar pea (68 days) is one of the edible-pod or sugar peas used in Chinese cooking. It grows on vines 28 inches tall. Sweet-pod Brand (68 days), a Burpee seed, is considered one of the best of the sugar peas. Vines grow to 4 feet high. Pick these peas before they start to swell in the pods for best flavor. Dwarf Gray Sugar (65 days) is an old standby among sugar peas. It needs no staking since the vines are 2 to 2½ feet tall. Cowpeas, planted after the soil has warmed, are good choices for warm areas where beans may not grow. They can be eaten fresh at the green shell stage, or allowed to ripen and are dried for storage.

Tips. Peas grow in cold weather and are almost the first crop to go into the ground. If you prepare the soil in the fall you can plant even before frost is out of the ground, especially early varieties such as Alaska. Sow one of these early varieties at 10-day intervals in the month before the last frost is expected, then sow succession plantings of the sweeter wrinkle-seed varieties. A last sowing of peas for fall harvest can be made 30 days before the first frost. The low growers are easiest since they need no staking. To stake tall growers, affix chicken wire to a nearby wall or string it between poles in the open garden. Plant peas on either side of chicken wire supports in the open garden. You can also grow peas on leafless branches stuck into the soil or over brush piled over the soil. However, they are easiest to pick when growing on tall, straight staking. Pea seeds are subject to fertilizer damage but do best in a rich soil. Dig a furrow 4 inches deep and mix a low-nitrogen fertilizer and lots of humus and sand with the bottom soil. Cover the improved soil with a layer of plain soil and plant the peas on this layer. Cover with an inch of soil and a thick hay mulch. The hay will let the soil warm the seeds better than could cool winter earth. Water after planting. As the plant tendrils develop, lead them to the stake or chicken wire; once under way they'll do their own climbing. A side dressing of a low-nitrogen fertilizer when peas have reached a height of 6 to 8 inches will improve the crop to canning proportions. Mulch to keep weeds from robbing the row of nutrients. Harvest the peas just before the pods reach full size—smaller peas are better. Pick from the bottom of the plant; the peas mature there first. Don't let mature pods stay on the plant as they'll slow production. When the plants have stopped producing, remove the vines to make way for other crops.

Companion plants. Any of the late-spring vegetables can follow peas in the rows.

PEPPERS

Sow seed ¼ inch deep in flats indoors, and set plants out in mid-spring. Keep 18 inches between plants, 20 to 24 inches between rows.

Canning notes. Growing your own hot peppers makes sense if you want to can peppers or mixed pickles and peppers, or make relishes. In mild areas you can grow the sweet pimientos to pack in oil. The sweet bell peppers can be frozen raw or cooked for canning in sauces for spaghetti and other Mediterranean dishes. Peppers bear fruit over a period of many weeks once they begin to produce, so plan to can these in small lots. A dozen pepper plants should give enough to use fresh and to can or freeze for winter use.

Varieties. Some of the best varieties of hot peppers are Red Chili, which grows to 18 inches tall and bears 2-inch long fruits. Fresno Chili is similar but has 3-inch fruits. Long Red Cayenne reaches to 30 inches and has fruits 4 to 5 inches long. Hungarian Wax bears long yellow peppers 6 to 8 inches long, and Large Cherry has round fruits ½ inch across. These mature in 65 to 70 days. Burpee's Early Pimiento (65 days) and Pimiento Select (75 days) are good choices if you want to put up pimiento strips. Their fruits are bright red when mature. The green, bell-type peppers also turn red when ripe but haven't the characteristic pimiento flavor. California Wonder (75 days) has nice thick flesh and is a good pepper for freezing. For cooler regions New Ace Hybrid (68 days) is a better choice because it begins to bear sooner.

Tips. In most areas there's only one crop of peppers. Set out in mid-spring as plants. In warm areas plants can be set out for a second crop 90 days before the average date of the first frost. Start seeds indoors 8 to 10 weeks before planting time and protect them after transplanting with hot caps or plastic tenting. In the warmth of a personal greenhouse they grow to maturity more quickly. If you don't have room in the garden row, plant peppers, hot or sweet, among ornamentals or in containers. The plants are pretty, especially when the fruit begins to redden. If you don't have time to start your own, garden centers generally offer started seedlings of varieties best suited to your area. Fertilize the soil for peppers lightly with a low-nitrogen fertilizer. Pick peppers as they become fully ripe; they are better then. Don't let ripe peppers sit on the plants or you will slow or stop production. Protect plants against early frosts in the north with plastic tents and the peppers will go on bearing into Indian summer in a good year.

Companion plants. Sow early radish or lettuce to occupy the rows you are readying for a mid-spring planting of peppers. In some warm areas spinach has time to mature before the peppers are set out.

POTATOES

Set out in early spring. Sow potato pieces 4 to 6 inches deep, 18 inches apart, in rows 2 to 3 feet apart. Crops begin to mature in 80 to 100 days.

Canning notes. To my mind, potatoes are not successful either canned or frozen, though occasionally I freeze a stew with potatoes in it. The stew will be much better if it is combined with potatoes cooked just before serving. However, potatoes are good winter keepers and are worth row space on that count, especially if you want to grow gourmet varieties.

Varieties. Any of the exotic potatoes sold in specialty shops can be planted after they have sprouted eyes. The potatoes you buy at the supermarket can be cut up for planting. Cut the potato into pieces with two eyes to each piece and as much potato flesh as possible. Early varieties of common potatoes offered by farm supply houses and some seedsmen include Pontiac, Red La Soda, and Red Pontiac. Kennebec and Sebago are late varieties. Seedsmen sell potatoes protected against the various diseases this relative of tomatoes and eggplant is subject to.

Tips. Plant early potatoes in early spring at about the date of the last frost. Plant varieties for fall crops about 4 months before the date of the first frost. Potatoes are most successful in soil that is naturally sandy and rich in humus. If you can, plant them in a row where peas were the previous crop. Don't plant potatoes in soil recently limed or to which fresh manure has been added. Plant potato pieces eyes up 18 inches apart in trenches 4 to 6 inches deep. Cover with 2 or 3 inches of soil or with 5 or 6 inches of straw instead of soil. The potatoes grow on underground stems formed by the plants. Above these stems the plant grows a whole leafy plant with small white flowers. When these die down, it is time to dig or pick (if under straw) the potatoes. When the plants are 5 inches high, hill the earth up around the plants. If growing potatoes for fall harvesting, dig the potatoes either when the vines die down or when frost kills them. Dig for potatoes carefully to avoid spearing them with your fork and work each hill well. Allow the potatoes to dry on the garden row for a day or two, then pack them into bushel baskets. They keep best when stored at about 50 degrees Fahrenheit in a dark place that has a little humidity.

Companion plants. Tomatoes and eggplants aren't good companion crops. Radishes and garden cress can be sown over potato tubers in early spring. So can lettuce.

PUMPKINS

Sow seed in mid-spring 1 inch deep, gradually thin to 5 feet apart, in rows 5 feet apart. Crop begins to mature in early fall, 100 to 120 days after planting.

Canning notes. Plant a half packet of pumpkin seeds to supply jack-o'-lanterns for Halloween, and for meat to purée, freeze, or can for pies, soups, and for use as a vegetable dish. You can store pumpkins for several months in a dry, cool place.

Varieties. Big Tom, ready in 120 days, produces 8-pound pumpkins good for all purposes. Small Sugar or Small Sugar Pie, ready in 100 days, is a superb pie pumpkin that reaches about 7 inches in diameter. Jack-o'-lantern (100 days) is specially for Halloween use but is not as fine for cooking. Funny Face Hybrid (110 days) is a semi-bush type, good for small gardens, and it makes good pies and keeps well too.

Tips. Set pumpkins to run through the row of corn, Brussels sprouts, or other tall garden citizens. The big leaves will act as a mulch to keep weeds away and the soil cool and moist. Or grow a few plants in containers and let the vines run. Mulch the area around. Pumpkins can grow down a wall or up a trellis, as long as you provide supports for each fruit as it begins to mature. You can start pumpkin seeds indoors in individual peat pots 3 to 4 weeks before planting time, but this isn't necessary as even in cool northern gardens they'll ripen before the first killing frosts. There is only one crop annually. After each plant has set 3 to 4 fruits, pinch out the tips growing beyond; the remaining pumpkins will grow bigger and ripen sooner. After pumpkins have turned orange all over, they are ripe. However, they will finish ripening in the shelter of a shed or porch overhang if they must be picked before. Don't expose them to frosts; they become damaged and then won't keep. To keep pumpkins between a September harvest time and Halloween's October 31 date, pile them in a cool garage corner.

Companion plants. Sow pumpkins at the feet of any of the tall vegetables—corn, tomatoes, cabbages.

RADISHES

Sow seed, broadcast, in earliest spring or early fall over prepared beds. Crops are ready in 20 to 60 days, depending on varieties.

Canning notes. Radishes aren't for canning, but do use them to fill rows of slow-growing seeds, such as carrots, and to fill up empty garden rows in early spring or early fall.

Varieties. Among the quick growers ((22 days or less) are varieties such as French Breakfast, Scarlet Globe, and Red Boy. For a continuous crop you can plant simultaneously with early types others, such as Champion or Crimson Giant, which mature in about 28 days. A second crop of radishes to plant in late summer for fall and winter use includes varieties such as White Chinese and Long Black Spanish. These take about 60 days to mature. As soon as the ground can be worked, sow a package of an early variety and a package of a later type, and you'll have radishes for over a month. In the cool of late summer, plant the fall and winter types, and store the roots in damp sand in a cool spot sheltered from frosts; you'll have radishes through early winter.

Tips. Prepare beds for planting, rake well and scatter seed broadcast, then tamp firmly into place. No mulch is needed as the seeds will be up and the crop harvested before weed season gets under way. Watering with a fine mist after sowing will encourage quick germination. Harvest radishes when the shoulders poke through the soil. Harvest radishes as they are ready. If they stay in the ground, they grow big and become woody.

Companion plants. Early radishes can precede any of the late- or mid-spring vegetables. Or plant them with any of the tall early-spring vegetables including carrots and parsnips.

RHUBARB (PERENNIAL)

Set out roots in early spring 10 inches deep, 3 feet apart, in rows 3 feet apart. Crops are perennial and mature in mid-spring, annually.

Canning notes. Stewed rhubarb, canned, is a delight and fresh rhubarb, frozen, makes superb pies. Rhubarb jam is another treat. Two plants per family member will give plenty to use fresh and for putting up.

Varieties. MacDonald rhubarb gives sauces and pies in a lovely, greenish-pink. Valentine is wonderfully sweet in pies or stewed and is a nice deep-red color. Victoria is a green, slightly more sour, type. Take your pick. Valentine is considered by many the best of all rhubarbs.

Tips. Rhubarb is a handsome perennial with big green leaves and pretty red or reddish stalks. It can go into a bed of ornamentals or be grown in a small ornamental clump in a container on the patio, as long as there is enough soil around the roots to keep them from freezing and thawing too often in winter. In summer the plants send up tall spikes of off-white florets that are very pretty, though they really should be removed to preserve the plant strength for growing edible stalks. Since it is a perennial, prepare the soil well to a depth of 12 to 16 inches, incorporating plenty of fertilizer and humus. Each spring, scatter 1 pound of a high-nitrogen fertilizer such as 10-6-4 around each plant. Mulch in fall for winter protection. Every 7 or 8 years, divide your rhubarb plants. To divide, dig the plants in the fall and divide the roots into sections each having three buds and a healthy section of the old root. Replant at once and don't plan to harvest until the second season after planting. As a rule, a light harvest can be taken the third year and a full harvest the year after. Harvest stems by gripping near the base and twisting sharply to one side. Don't pick away more than a third of any plant in one season. Remove leaves, as they are considered poisonous.

Companion plants. Early radish can be grown around rhubarb before leaves begin to bush out in spring.

RUTABAGA

Sow seed in mid-spring ½ inch deep, gradually thin to 8 inches apart, in rows 18 inches apart. Crops begin to mature in 85 to 90 days.

Canning notes. Rutabaga—yellow turnips—are such good winter keepers there's little point in canning unless you consider canning or freezing as half the cooking, a device that speeds winter meal preparation. Keep washed, wax-dipped roots in a cool, dark, moist place —they'll last all winter.

Varieties. Purple-Top Yellow (90 days) is a variety that keeps well.

Tips. There's just one crop in most areas, planted in mid-spring, or any time up to four months before the average date of the first frost. Roots are best when about 3 to 4 inches around, but they needn't be dug until the heat is past and the moist cool air of fall is around. Dig them carefully to avoid damaging the roots with the spading fork, and let sit a day or two in the row; then bury the roots in a damp sand in a cool, dark place with good air circulation, or else dip the roots in melted paraffin and store in a cool cellar.

Companion plants. Early crops of lettuce, radishes, or carrots can precede the sowing of rutabaga.

SALSIFY

Sow seed in mid-spring ¼ inch deep, gradually thin to 3 to 4 inches apart, in rows 12 inches apart. Crops begin to mature in about 120 days.

Canning notes. Salsify is often called "oyster plant" and makes a nice change in the winter vegetable menu. Though it can be frozen, it is an excellent winter keeper that can be dug and stored in moist sand or wintered over in the row. The roots are long, thin, and whitish, about 8 by 1½ inches and tapered like carrots. One packet will produce as much as the average family will want and should occupy about a 25-foot row.

Varieties. Many catalogs offer Sandwich Island Mammoth (120 days). Scorzonera is called "black salsify," a dark-skinned relative of salsify.

Tips. Seed can be sown before the last frost in spring. A second crop can be planted 4 or 5 months before the date of the first frost. Like carrots, salsify does best in loose, rock-free soils, deeply dug. Follow planting tips under Rutabaga. Store the roots—not waxed —in damp sand, or leave in its row for next spring's digging.

Companion plants: See Rutabaga.

SPINACH

Sow seed in early spring ¼ inch deep, gradually thin to 4 inches apart, in rows 12 inches apart. Crops mature in 40 to 50 days.

Canning notes. Because true spinach gives just one cutting, the yield is lower per foot of row space than other boiling greens, such as New Zealand spinach. Consider planting one row of early-spring spinach to eat fresh. For canning, plant New Zealand spinach, Malabar, or Tampala, big plants you can pick repeatedly, and they give all-summer spinach crops. Or, plant kale and/or Swiss chard, as they yield through summer. Plan to put up spinach in small lots, picking twice as much as needed for dinners (or else picking all that is ready) and freezing the extras while preparing dinner.

Varieties. Bloomsdale Long-Standing (48 days) is a good all-purpose spinach for spring planting. Winter Bloomsdale (45 days) is a good one to plant for a fall crop. Virginia Savoy and Hybrid 7 are resistant to downy mildew and are indicated for fall planting where this problem exists.

Tips. Spinach does best in a soil above pH 5.6. If yours is below, add a dusting of lime several weeks before planting the spinach row. Add to the row half a bushel of rotted or dried manure, or a high-nitrogen fertilizer such as 10-6-4. When plants are 5 inches tall, an additional feeding of nitrate of soda, scratched into the soil on either side at the prescribed rate, improves the crop. Plan to sow one crop as soon as the ground can be worked; by the time heat arrives it will be out of the ground. If the plants show signs of bolting (main stems shooting skyward), harvest the whole crop right then; once bolted, spinach quality is very poor. Sow a second crop about 60 days before the average date of the first frost. In warm areas of the country, spinach can be left in the row for winter use if protected with a good blanket of straw. You can harvest some side leaves from young spinach plants or let the whole plant mature and cut it from the root as you do heading lettuce. The only caution is: Wash it in seven or eight changes of water before using, as sandy spinach is awful.

Companion plants. Sow any of the mid- or late-spring crops in rows vacated by early-spring spinach.

SPINACH—NEW ZEALAND, MALABAR, AND TAMPALA

Sow seed in mid-spring ¼ inch deep, gradually thin to 6 inches apart, in rows 18 inches apart. Crops begin to mature in 70 days.

Canning notes. New Zealand spinach and the type of boiling greens called Malabar spinach and Tampala are easy to grow in areas where real spinach is a tricky crop or will bolt in summer. And New Zealand spinach is really good and has the further advantage of being a long-season crop. You can freeze it in small lots. Tips can be picked at will all summer until frost. Other spinach substitutes are Swiss chard and kale.

Varieties. New Zealand, Tampala, and Malabar spinach are offered under those names in the spinach sections of major catalogs. They mature in 70 days.

Tips. Plan on one crop planted in mid-spring. New Zealand spinach seed is slow to germinate, so soak it overnight in warm water before sowing. Keep weeds out of the garden until the spinach is up and running. It will climb, so if you are short of space plant it against a mesh fence or a support of your devising. Plant 6 to 8 seeds every foot in furrows ¼ inch deep, cover with ¼ inch of fine soil, and tamp. Mulch around the sowing. Thin seedlings to stand 4 to 6 inches apart when seedlings are 3 inches high and pull mulch up around the seedlings. When the plants are half grown, scratch a handful of nitrate of soda in around each to provide nutrients for this long-standing crop. Harvest after plants are flourishing, break off 3-inch tips as needed. Don't take too much from any individual plant at one time.

Companion plants. These spinaches can be preceded by any of the early spring seeds—radishes, lettuce, peas.

SUMMER SQUASH

Sow seed in mid-spring 1 inch deep, gradually thin to 6 inches apart, in rows 2 to 3 feet apart. Crops begin to mature 45 to 50 days after planting.

Canning notes. Frozen squash isn't the best vegetable in the world, but it can be good if the squash is very small and firm when picked and if it isn't overblanched before freezing. I don't think it is good enough to warrant planting a whole row for freezing, but do plant it for eating fresh in summer and freeze the extras. Once the bushes start to produce, they'll ripen fruits until frosts.

Varieties. Both the summer squashes called zucchini (long and green) and the shorter plumper yellow types begin to produce in midsummer. Early Golden Crookneck (53 days to maturity) is one of the best yellow squashes for freezing. Hybrid Zucchini Squash (50 days) is the green squash recommended for freezing. There are many other fascinating squashes to grow for use fresh—the pretty White Bush Patty Pan, for instance—but I haven't found them particularly good for putting up.

Tips. There are vining squashes and bush-type squashes. I've found the bush type easier to grow and prolific producers. Sandy soil, well supplied with humus, gives good crops; 5-10-10 seems to be the best fertilizer. Mulch along the rows after the seedlings are up to help keep the moisture supply even. Harvest the fruits as they reach about 6 inches in length; when the skins are so thick you can't pierce them with your fingernails, the fruits will be full of seeds and rather tasteless. Keep squashes picked to keep the bushes producing.

Companion plants. Radishes, lettuces, early peas, or turnips can precede the planting of squash.

Caution Note: Don't plant squashes where cucumbers or melons were the previous crop.

WINTER SQUASH

Plant in mid-spring. Sow 6 seeds to a hill, thin seedlings to 4 per hill. Space hills 6 feet apart. Crops begin to mature in 90 to 110 days, depending on variety.

Cannng notes. Hubbard squash, purée and frozen, makes divine pies and an excellent vegetable. The other winter squashes I find better served fresh. The fall and winter squashes store and keep well.

Varieties. Waltham Butternut (85 days to maturity); True Hubbard (115 days), a big squash; Blue Hubbard (120 days), which is even larger; and Buttercup (105 days), a turban-shaped squash are good choices for winter keeping. Bush Acorn Table King and Burpee's Bush Table Queen mature in only 75 to 80 days and are also good winter keepers.

Tips. There's only one crop of winter and fall squash, to be sown as seed in mid-spring. When the squashes are 4 to 5 inches tall, thin 4 to a hill. When the vines begin to really run, scratch a handful of fertilizer into the soil around each plant. Pick fall and winter squashes only after they have matured, that's when the flavor is best. If Butternut squash still has little streaks of green on it, it usually hasn't as full a flavor as when after all green has gone. Leave fruits a few days in the row to harden before storing, at temperatures of 45 to 55 degrees Fahrenheit. Squashes are damaged by freezing, so protect them with plastic tenting if real frosts threaten before they have quite matured.

Companion plants and caution. See Summer Squash.

STRAWBERRIES (PERENNIAL)

Set out in early spring, 1½ inches deep, 18 inches apart, in rows 4 feet apart. Crops begin second season for standard types, first season for everbearer types.

Strawberry plant at left is too far below ground level; the one in center is too far above ground level; the one at right is correctly planted. Tamp soil around planted roots carefully to dispel air pockets.

Canning notes. Strawberries are one of those luxury foods that freeze beautifully or make gorgeous jam; they are well worth giving as much space to as you can. Since 35 plants will yield between ½ and 1 quart of berries, in order to have as many berries as you can eat fresh, freeze, and can, try to find room for 35 plants per family member. Though they are somewhat expensive to put in, the plants send out runners on which baby plants grow so you can perpetuate the strawberry patch at no further expense.

Varieties. A variety of strawberry seed now offered as Alexandria grows to maturity the first season. Any number of standard one-crop varieties are offered by catalogs. They are offered in very early, early, mid-season, late, and everbearer varieties. The everbearers usually give one rather heavy crop over a period of weeks and a scattering of berries the rest of the season. By planting one very early (such as Blakemore or Earlidawn), one early (such as Premier, or Fairfax), one mid-season (such as Sparkle or Redchief), one late mid-season (such as Guardian), one late such as ((Mariate), and one of the everbearers (such as Superperfection or Ozark Beauty), you can have a season-long crop of berries.

If you have no room for big strawberries, consider growing the little alpine or wild strawberries as edging plants for your ornamental borders and container gardens or at the feet of tubbed trees. Among the nicest is Baron Solemacher, a rather tender alpine strawberry, to sow as seed; it will bear fruit the first season. In areas where the winter cold is severe, plan to replant it annually.

Tips. Strawberries do best in sandy, slightly acid, fertile soil. Dig a shovelful of acid humus such as peat moss into the soil for each plant and add a handful of 5-10-5 or 4-8-4 into the ground for each 20 feet of row. Or set the bed over a 2-inch deep layer of well-rotted manure or compost along with a supply of fertilizer. When setting out berry plants, avoid having the sun reach the roots. Set the plants into furrows 1½ inchs deep and 4 inches wide. The crowns must be set at the exact level at which they grew before. To get this just right, hold the plant by its center stem and spread the roots out over a small hump in the trench floor. Cover with 1¼ inches of soil and firm the soil around the roots. If frost threatens the first season, protect the plants with bushel baskets or hot caps or plastic tenting. During the first season, keep all berries of the standard types from setting fruit by removing the blossoms as they appear. Keep the flowers picked on the everbearer types through the early part of the summer and let them set some fruit toward the end of the season after they are well established. The second season, let all the flowers set fruit.

If you let them, strawberry plants will send out runners that will root baby plants and form matted rows. Make new berry rows by digging rooted plantlets, severing them from their runners, and setting out in early spring in new rows. Though some commercial growers and organic farmers allow matted rows to go on growing, the common practice with strawberries is to keep runners cut and to dig up the original bed every 4 years to replace it with production from new beds. Two years before the beds are to be changed, root as many runners as you will need to fill the new beds. Transplant the rooted plants the following spring. The year after, discard the old plants and harvest from the new.

Strawberries require winter protection in areas where there are frosts. Once the temperature has reached the low 20s, cover the bed with 6 inches of mulch; when the ground freezes hard, add another foot of mulch. Remove most of the mulch in early spring so the sun can warm the bed. The second reason the beds are in, feed the plants in early spring with 5-10-5 at the specified rate. Broadcast fertilizer carefully when the leaves are dry, avoiding the leaves. Use a feather duster to remove any fertilizer that does get on the leaves. When berries are shiny, dark red, and plump, they are ready for harvest. Pick them promptly, as they become overripe and useless within a day or two. Since they are acidic, harvest into wooden or plastic containers.

Companion plants. Plant strawberries at the feet of tubbed trees. You can grow lettuce as the edges of runner-trimmed berry beds.

SWEET POTATOES

Set out in late spring. Plant pieces 5 inches deep, 18 inches apart, in rows 2 to 3 feet apart. Crop matures in 120 to 150 days.

Canning notes. Sweet potatoes canned make good pies; pureed sweet potatoes, frozen, are pretty good too. The tubers don't keep as well as the white Irish potatoes, but can be stored in the winter for several months. However, sweet potatoes require a great deal of heat and lots of time to mature their crops, so this isn't a good idea for northern gardens.

Varieties. Varieties advertized in catalogs serving warm regions include Rose Centennial and Centennial. Porto Rico is a popular variety, and so is Georgia Red. If you want to try a few in a container garden in a very hot patio corner of a northern garden, cut up sprouted eyes of sweet potatoes purchased at the local food shop, sprout them in a warm room by setting the tapered ends of the potatoes in glasses of water (you can hold them there by fixing toothpicks in them). Keep the water level even

Tips. Plant sweet potatoes in sandy soil that is rich. Use low-nitrogen fertilizers only, such as 5-10-5. Dig a trench 5 to 6 inches deep and mix into the soil at the bottom of the trench 2 pounds of fertilizer for every 50 feet of row. Over this lay humusy but unfertilized soil to a depth of 2 inches, set the tubers on this soil, and cover with ridges of unfertilized soil about 9 inches high. Dig the crops after frost has killed the tender tips of the potato vines.

Companion plants. Any of the early- or mid-spring vegetables can precede sweet potatoes.

TOMATOES

Set out plants in mid-spring and space 2 to 3 feet all around. Crops begin to mature in 52 to 80 days.

Canning notes. Tomatoes are the number-one garden plant in popularity and one of the most rewarding of all canning materials. They make purée, paste, soup, sauce, and jam. Wonderful relishes are made from the green fruits at the end of the growing season. To have plenty for canning and eating fresh you might plant up to 5 plants per family member.

Varieties. There are lots of quick-to-mature small tomato varieties to grow for eating fresh: Patio Hybrid and Small Fry Hybrid are two

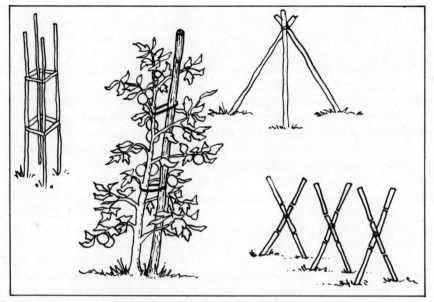

Four ways to stake tomatoes

of these small types that will grow anywhere—in containers as well as in the open garden. They produce fruit within a few weeks of planting seedlings. For canning and preserving, Heinz 1350 (75 days to maturity) is considered one of the best. Roma VF (76 days) is a plum-shaped tomato considered exceptionally good for paste and for cooking and canning whole. San Marzano (80 days) is grown for canning whole, purée, and paste. Burpee's Big Boy Hybrid (78 days); Monte Carlo Hybrid (VFN) (75 days); Beefmasket Hybrid (75 days), a meaty beefsteak type; Spring Giant Hybrid (65 days), an early one good for cool areas; and New Yorker (64 days), another early one are other excellent tomatoes for putting up. Red Cherry (72 days) is a small tomato for pickling and preserving; Yellow Pear (70 days) and Yellow Plum, small yellow tomatoes, are grown for pickling and preserving.

Tips. There is only time for one tomato crop in most areas, but it is a continuous crop once it begins to mature. Plant small varieties that are quick to mature for immediate use fresh, and slower tomatoes ready at the end of the season for putting up.

Start seedlings indoors 4 to 6 weeks before planting time, which is in mid-spring. Cover the planted seedlings with brown paper bags or plastic tenting to keep them warm through their first days in the garden. I have set tomatoes out earlier than this with all sorts of elaborate protection, but they sulked until the weather warmed. Indoors, seedlings germinate at 70 to 80 degrees Fahrenheit (the hybrids like it hottest), but the seedlings grow best at temperatures ranging between 60 and 70 degrees. You can start the seedlings in flats, but I suggest you transplant them to individual peat pots when they have four or six leaves so that the plants you set out will be bushy and will grow vigorously. If you want tomatoes as soon as possible, provide them with a soil really rich in humus and in fertilizers. Low-nitrogen fertilizers seem to produce fewer leaves and more tomatoes. My choice is 4-8-4 or well-rotted manure. Tomato soil, a commercial product, is great for containers. When the tomato plants have doubled planting size, scratch a small handful of 4-8-4 into the soil around each plant and mulch well to preserve moisture in the soil and keep out weeds. Staked tomatoes produce more abundantly so stake those meant for canning. Use a single pole, as long as it is set 6 inches into the ground and is sturdy, about 1¾ by 2 inches. Almost anything vertical, however, will make a support for a tomato plant, from a trellis to a sturdy drainpipe. Size and quantity of tomatoes is improved if you keep all suckers growing between major branch stems snipped out. Harvest tomatoes when dead ripe, especially for canning. When early, light frosts threaten, cover the tomatoes with sheets of plastic or old cotton sheets, and you should still have bearing plants in Indian summer. When hard frosts threaten, pull up the plants and hang them upside down from rafters in the basement, or else strip the plants of all green and half-ripe tomatoes. Those that are whitening usually will ripen to red. The really green one make good piccalilli and other preserves. You can store ripening tomatoes for fresh use in newspapers in an airy, cool, dark room, and they will keep for several weeks.

Companion plants. Precede tomatoes with any of the early-spring crops—such as lettuce, peas, radishes. Grow herbs, cucumbers, or pumpkins at the feet of tall-staked tomatoes.

TURNIPS

Sow seed in early spring ½ inch deep, gradually thin to 6 inches apart, in rows 18 inches apart.

Canning notes. I have frozen mashed young turnips and found them good, but this isn't a crop I count on freezing. For turnips meant to store in a cool place, grow rutabaga (yellow turnips) instead.

Varieties. There can be two turnip crops, one in early spring and one sown in late summer for fall harvesting. Early Milan (45 days) and Tokyo Cross (35 days) are two good varieties for early-spring crops. They are small and have a really delicate flavor. Foliage, or Shogoin, Turnips take 70 days to mature roots, but meanwhile, in about 30 days, their foliage becomes an edible boiling green, so they give two crops in one. Just Right Hybrid (60 days) is another turnip whose greens are delicious as a boiling green. The early turnips can go in 30 days before the last average frost date. The late types are best planted 12 to 6 weeks before the average date of the first frost.

Tips. Turnips are handled the same as rutabaga. When picking turnip greens, harvest only tender young leaves, and never strip a plant of more than one-fourth to one-third of its foliage.

Companion plants. Sow turnip seeds at the edges of early peas. When the peas come out, the turnips will have the rows to themselves.

7

Canning
Vegetables and Fruits

If you have canned before, you can skip the next several pages. If you've never canned, the information that follows is important—first of all, to help you understand that it really is a simple process and secondly, to alert you to the areas where things can go wrong.

There are three basic ways to can. All three begin the same way, with the cleaning and cutting up or other preparation of the food to be processed. The real differences in canning methods are in the processes by which the foods are guarded against spoilage.

The processes are: (1) the pressure-canner method, which processes the foods at 240 degree Fahrenheit in a pressure canner (or a pressure cooker, as you'll see below); (2) the boiling-water bath, which processes the foods in water boiling at 212 degrees in a large, lidded kettle; (3) the open-kettle method, which consists of cooking the ingredients in a kettle (usually, while you stir, hence the open or uncovered kettle). Open-kettle processed foods include well-cooked jellies and such, and these can be sealed with paraffin and stored without further processing. Further processing is desirable for some open-kettle recipes, as explained later.

Each of the recipes in the next two chapters for canning garden foods is processed by one of these three methods. General instructions for each method and for the handling and sealing of canning jars are given below.

CAUTIONS FOR PRESSURE CANNING

General Information

A pressure canner is just a big pressure cooker. It processes foods at 240 degrees Fahrenheit. This high degree of heat is necessary to guarantee the destruction of the types of organisms that can cause spoilage in foods low in acid content. Foods, like soils, have varying degrees of acidity. Acidity is a natural preservative; when it is present in large amounts in foods, the foods can be processed at lower temperatures. When it is not, the foods *must* be processed at 240 degrees, and the pressure canner reaches and holds this temperature, whereas boiling water does not.

Suggestions that you can "cold-seal" canned foods (no processing after sealing) are not considered wise by the USDA. Nor is "oven processing." Foods in jars that have been correctly processed, handled, and stored will not spoil. Though new methods may eventually evolve, for now pressure canning is the only method considered safe for low-acid foods.

Don't be afraid to can your garden produce. Follow canning instructions carefully, and your canned foods will be safe. If you fail to follow instructions carefully, symptoms of spoilage will warn you. Bubbly gases, liquids that have spurted from the containers, moldy or soft or slimy foods, liquids that become cloudy, once-clear liquids that develop sediment, jars that leak, tops that bulge, and strange odors are indications to be wary. If you have any doubts about your canned goods, heat the contents for 10 to 15 minutes at boiling point before using. If the food then gives off an odor, discard it.

Improperly processed foods are not always lethal. Foods that darken in the top of the jar; fruits that darken after they've been removed from the jar; pink, blue, or purple streaks in apples, pears, and peaches; green vegetables that darken or lose their color or turn brown; yellow crystals in canned green vegetables; white crystals in canned greens; fruits that float in the jar—these are all the result of imperfections in the canning process and are probably all right. Too much heat, less than fresh ingredients, or salt-containing fillers can cause these defects without spoiling the foods. Both the harmless imperfections and the outright spoilage are usually the result of one or more of three bits of carelessness in canning: carelessness in packing, in timing of processing, or in testing jar seal.

Follow Processing Instructions Exactly

Of the various bacteria and organisms that can cause spoilage, botulism—*Clostridium botulinum* is its scientific name—is the most frightening. It has no odor and doesn't change the look of the foods. A bacterium that is harmless when there is oxygen present, botulinus thrives in the absence of oxygen, as for instance in sealed canned foods. It does not do well in high-acid foods but will flourish in low-acid foods. Low-acid foods must be processed by pressure canner for the length of time given in order to remove all danger of the possibility of botulism. The recipes below tell which process to use for each food canned. Follow the instructions exactly, in particular as they relate to timing, for pressure canning low-acid foods, and make sure your pressure canner is in perfect working order, as described below.

Follow Sealing Instructions Exactly

Foods on the screw caps or jar rims can cause spoilage and imperfect sealing of your canned goods and result in any one or more of the symptoms, both hazardous and nonhazardous, described above. Follow sealing and testing instructions exactly, and make sure your jars are in perfect condition.

Use the Ingredients Called For; Don't Substitute

Syrups that are too light or salt that contains a filler meant to keep it from caking can cause some of the harmless symptoms described, and though these aren't necessarily hazardous, they may make the foods look odd, which will make you nervous. So, in the beginning anyway, use the ingredients recommended.

Salt labeled "pure" or "canning" or "kosher" has no sediment dropout to cloud liquids and cause concern. Use this salt; then any cloudiness in jars you will know comes from other causes—possibly starch in the vegetable, possibly improper processing. If in doubt, heat the food 10 to 15 minutes at boiling point and discard if there is any odor.

Iodine in salt will discolor canned goods, though it won't harm them. Use salt without iodine to avoid this cause of discoloration.

Once you know your way around in canning and have developed confidence in your canned products, you can consider changing recipes to suit personal tastes. However, even then don't alter processing times called for and don't deviate from correct sealing and processing procedures.

Store Canned Goods Properly; Label and Date Your Jars

Canned goods can last indefinitely if they are stored in a dry, dark (light alters color) place, between 35 and 60 or 70 degrees. Canned goods that go down to 32 degrees will freeze. After they thaw, the seal may be broken and the food will then spoil.

Canned foods taste best when used within twenty-four months (two years). Label your jars and date your labels: Use older goods first. Note on your labels any special touch, flavoring agent, or variety of the vegetable or fruit grown. Those you find especially good can then be grown again for canning. Note the recipe used and its source when labeling, then you can repeat big successes.

EQUIPMENT HANDY FOR CANNING AND PRESERVING

A pressure canner, a boiling-water bath, or a big kettle for open-kettle canning are major pieces of equipment, and each is described below along with jars to use. Whichever canning method you use, you will need or find handy the following:

A jar lifter, sold at hardware stores and dime stores
A large, wide-mouth funnel, preferably made out of glass or plastic for high-acid foods
A food mill that will cut down slicing and cutting chores
Large glass measuring cups (two come in handy)
Sharp knives
A rack (cake rack will do) for holding jars while they cool (or use a couple of clean towels)
A footed colander for straining juices to make jellies (or use doubled cheesecloth)
A jelly thermometer
A mesh colander for the hot-pack process: It holds foods in boiling water in a process that precooks before canning and processing
A ladle for dipping and pouring the liquids used to fill food jars

Equipment of glass, enamelware, or plastic that resists heat is

Tools that make canning and freezing easier

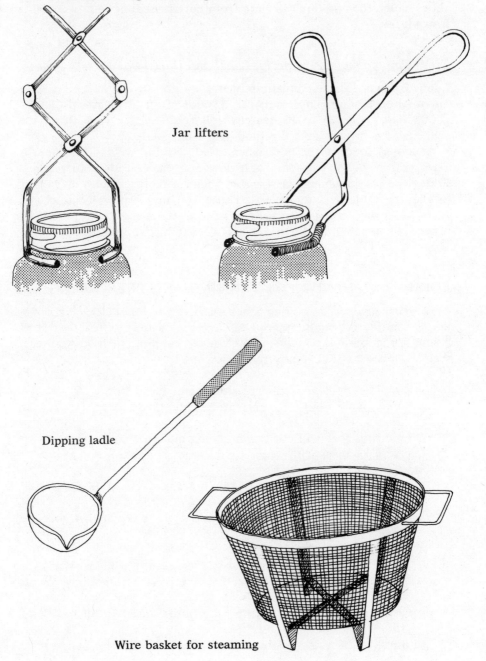

Jar lifters

Dipping ladle

Wire basket for steaming

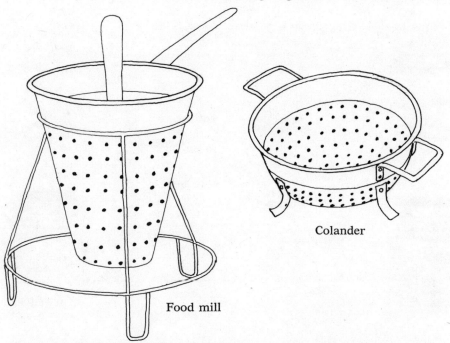

Colander

Food mill

the best investment because it can be used when working with high-acid foods, which may be discolored by contact with brass, copper, iron, or other metals. Most of the equipment used for canning you will find handy for freezing as well.

Canning Jars

The term "can" refers to a tin can, and it is possible to use tin cans for canning. However, it's a complicated process with special requirements in equipment, so most canning is done in glass jars, which also are called "canning jars."

You can use "found" jars for some kinds of preserving, but for foods to be processed either in the pressure canner or the boiling-water bath, use regular canning jars. These come in two basic shapes: straight-sided and shouldered or slope-sided.

Straight-sided jars are best for freezing and for jellies, since the straight sides make it easy to turn out the contents. They range in size in my area from ½ to 1½ pints.

Mason jars are those with sloped shoulders and a pinched-in neck. They come in both wide-mouth, which are easier for filling, and narrow-mouth types. They range from 1-pint to 2-quart (½-gallon)

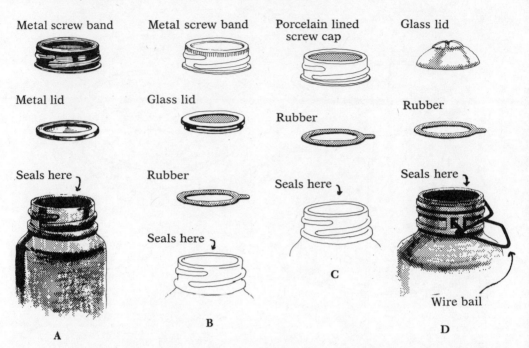

Metal screw band

Metal screw band

Porcelain lined screw cap

Glass lid

Metal lid

Glass lid

Rubber

Rubber

Seals here

Rubber

Seals here

Rubber

Seals here

Seals here

C

Wire bail

A

B

D

Flat metal lid is rested on the rim of the jar, with the sealing compound down. The metal band screws over, holding the flat metal lid firmly to the jar rim. Put the screw lid down on top of the flat metal lid, and screw the band on firmly. This is not a self-sealing type.

Seal sealing canner is put together in the sequence illustrated. Place the wet rubber ring on the glass lid. The lid goes on top of the rubber, then the screw band is fitted over both and screwed down tightly. Then, turn the band back to loosen it a little. After the processing, and as soon as you remove the jar from the canner, screw the band down tightly to complete the seal.

Place the wet rubber ring on the shoulder of the jar and screw the band down over it. Then, turn the screw band back to loosen it a little. When you take the jar from the processing kettle, screw the cap down tightly to complete the sealing process.

Place the wet rubber ring on the jar and set the glass lid in place over it. Then, lift the lower wire bail up over the top of the glass lid and slide it into the groove there. Then, push the larger bail wire down against the side of the jar. The jar is sealed. Don't touch the bails after the processing.

sizes. Use the larger sizes for big batches of picnic pickles and for the snack foods your family enjoys often. Put up other foods in jars large enough to provide enough for one family meal. I use as a gauge ½ cup of vegetables or fruit for each family member.

Both types of jars have various types of caps and sealing systems, illustrated on the facing page. Follow instructions with the illustrations exactly when handling the jars.

You will also find on the market small quilted jars for gift packaging of preserves. These come in small and in ½-pint sizes. Mason domes make them suitable for foods to be processed. There are also quilted jelly glasses. They are to be sealed with paraffin, and the caps are simply protective coverings for the paraffin. Don't put them through heating processes.

Found jars (empty peanut butter jars or jelly glasses, for instance) may not stand up to the high heats of processing, so do not use these for foods to be processed. You can use them for the recipes in which processing is not required.

SEALING

General Instructions

Canned goods are vacuum-sealed by the processing. When a jar is closed at normal temperature, the air pressure within and without the jar is the same. As the jar is heated, everything in it expands (therefore we leave headroom, as you will see below), the air inside the jar is forced out, and the air pressure inside becomes less than that outside. As the jar cools, everything in it shrinks, a partial vacuum is formed, and atmospheric pressure of almost fifteen pounds per square inch, at sea level, holds the lid down and keeps the jar sealed. The sealing compound on Mason dome lids and the rubber of the rings used with zinc caps keep the air from returning into the sealed jar. Naturally, the seal must be perfect if the foods inside are to be preserved.

To guarantee a good seal, make sure lids and jar rims are absolutely clean of foods. Make sure you leave headroom so foods can expand without pressuring the jar lid, and make sure you treat each type of jar lid in the way suggested in the illustration.

Be absolutely certain that jar rims have no hairline cracks. Run your finger over the rim of each jar before using. Follow the instructions for testing your jar seal after cooling the jars, with each

Three ways to test the seal after processing in a pressure canner or a boiling-water-bath canner: You can hear a metallic snap as the lid becomes sealed while the jar is cooling; listen for it. Tap the lid with a spoon. A clear ringing sound means the jar is correctly sealed; when food is touching the lid, the sound will be dull. Feel the seal—press the center of the lid. If it is down and won't move, the jar is sealed. Tilt the jar to one side; if no food seeps out, the seal usually is perfect. If the jar is not sealed, reprocess the food. When the seal is assured, remove the screw band, wash it, and store for use the next time.

jar each time you can. Once the seal is secure, you can remove the screw cap, wash it thoroughly, and store it.

The Effect of Altitude

Altitude affects the number of pounds of pressure at which you pressure can. In boiling-water-bath processing, it affects the length of time you process the foods in the bath. The pressure poundages and boiling-water-bath processing-time periods for the recipes in this book are for specific altitudes. If you live at higher altitudes, refer to the Altitude Charts to adjust either the pressure poundage or the time of processing, depending on which method is called for.

PRESSURE CANNING FOR LOW-ACID FOODS

General Instructions

If you have a small pressure cooker, consider doing your first pressure canning in it. It must be of a type that offers a selection of 5-, 10-, or 15-pound pressure settings. A 4-quart pressure cooker will process 4 1-pint jars. For ½-pint and 1-pint jars (all a small pressure cooker can handle), add 20 minutes to the pressure-canner time indicated in the recipes to compensate for the quick climb the small pressure cooker takes at the start of the process and for its quick cooling at the end. Don't wet to lower the temperature after the processing, as you do when cooking daily meals with a pressure cooker.

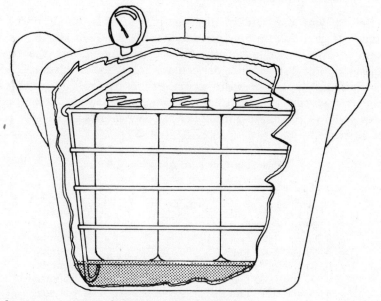

Typical pressure canner shown in cross section

A pressure canner (a larger version of a pressure cooker) is a must if you are going to process in large jars. Pressure canners come in sizes ranging from the small 6-quart type, which holds 7 quarts, to the large, which is called 22-quart by most makers. This size holds 20 pint jars, arranged one on top of the other, or 7 quart jars.

The major difference between the various makes is in the type of pressure gauge used. Some manufacturers offer a "weight-gauge control," and other offers a "dial-gauge control." Each type offers 5-, 10-, and 15-pound pressure readings intended for canning.

Accuracy of the pressure readings is all-important in home canning. The USDA recommends that dial-type pressure gauges be checked every year before the canning season. The County Extension home economist, usually associated with the Extension Service (see Appendix), may be able to refer you to a local source for checking a dial gauge or may be able to give you the address of the manufacturer of your equipment so that you can return it for checking. The type of gauge called "weight-gauge control" does not need annual checking. If you buy a pressure canner second hand, make sure that whatever type of gauge control it has is checked for accuracy before you do any canning whatsoever.

Each time before canning, clean the petcock and the safety valve of your canner, then wash and dry the canner well.

Before you use any of the recipes in this book, check your altitude. If you live at an altitude over 2,000 feet above sea level, correct with a pencil according to the Altitude Chart the pressure poundage called for in each pressure-canning recipe given. The chart gives readings possible with a dial-gauge control. If your canner doesn't allow such fine adjustments as half pounds, round off the figures given to the highest number. In other words make 11½ pounds read 12 pounds.

PRESSURE-CANNING ALTITUDE CHART

ALTITUDE ABOVE SEA LEVEL	PROCESS RECIPES AT:
2,000 to 3,000 feet	11½ pounds
3,000 to 4,000 feet	12 pounds
4,000 to 5,000 feet	12½ pounds
5,000 to 6,000 feet	13 pounds
6,000 to 7,000 feet	13½ pounds
7,000 to 8,000 feet	14 pounds
8,000 to 9,000 feet	14½ pounds
9,000 to 10,000 feet	15 pounds

STEP-BY-STEP PRESSURE CANNING

Gather the Materials

Harvest the foods to be canned. Estimate the number of jars needed by fitting the raw foods into the jars you plan to use. A handful of beans fitted into a pint jar will tell you about how many beans 4-, 6-, or 8-pint jars can handle; a few baby beets fitted into a wide-mouth jar will give you a notion of how many jars you'll need to handle the current harvest. Halve a couple of peaches, and you'll see how many jars you need for the peaches gathered. Store the freshly gathered ingredients in the refrigerator while you get ready to can. Wash the jars and their lids thoroughly in hot soapy water (or in the dishwasher) and keep them hot. Then there will be no danger of the jars cracking when boiling-hot canning liquid is poured into them. Don't run rubber rings or compound-covered Mason jar caps through the dishwasher. Hand-wash them in hot water and set them in a pan with hot water over them to keep them hot.

Preparation

Wash your vegetables or fruits thoroughly in cold water, in as many changes of water as is needed for the water to drain absolutely clear without a grain of sand or dirt in it. Lift the foods from the water rather than draining the water off. Then you can see if the bottom of the sink really is sand-free or not.

Follow the recipe chosen to prepare the vegetables for canning. Wash, peel, scrape, slice, dice, or whatever. Sort them according to thickness and size, since these factors affect processing and appearance. Big beans and little beans aren't as attractive in the same jar as beans of similar lengths. Make this deluxe product look like a deluxe product. Prepare only as many vegetables or fruits as your processer can handle at one time. Then, while the processing is in progress, you can prepare a second batch.

Cold Pack or Hot Pack

Hot or cold packing is the step before you put the foods into the jars for processing. Cold packing means placing raw foods into the jars. Hot packing means precooking the foods to some degree before processing.

The advantages of cold packing are that you eliminate precooking the foods. The disadvantages are that raw-packed foods sometimes float to the top of the jar and spoil its looks, and they take more processing time.

The advantages of hot packing are that foods are unlikely to float, processing takes less time, and the jars are better filled because of the air and moisture released during the precooking process. The recipes give processing times for hot-pack processing and tell how long each food must be precooked for hot-pack processing.

To ready for hot packing, place the prepared foods into water that is boiling hard. Don't cover the kettle. Let the water return to a boil and time the cooking period from the moment it begins to boil again. Lift the food from the water but don't discard the water. Usually it is used to fill the jars after the food has been packed into them.

Packing and Sealing the Jars

To pack the jars, pour the food pieces through a wide-mouthed funnel if they are small enough. This keeps jar threads clean. Pack starchy vegetables, such as corn, to within 1½ inches of the jar rim and add boiling water to within 1 inch of the rim. Pack nonstarchy products, such as snap beans, to within 1 inch of the jar rim and fill with boiling liquid, leaving ½ inch of headroom between the liquid and the rim top. Air bubbles will form along the sides of the jar after the boiling liquid is added. Remove these by running a rubber spatula around the inside of the jar. Wipe the jar threads and top clean, cap, and seal.

Packing the Canner

A few minutes before you are ready to pack the jars, place the pressure canner over medium heat, set the rack in the bottom of the canner, and add 1 inch of boiling water to small canners, 2 inches to large canners. Or follow the specific instructions that come with your canner. After each jar has been filled and capped, set it on the rack in the canner to keep hot. Space the jars so that steam circulates freely around each. Adjust the canner cover and fasten, following the manufacturer's instructions carefully.

Processing

The minute the lid is closed, steam will begin to escape from the open petcock. Allow it to escape for 7 or 8 minutes while pressure builds up. Then close the petcock. Start counting the processing time when the amount of pressure required for your altitude is showing on the pressure gauge. Watch the pressure for a few moments, and adjust the heat under the canner if necessary to keep the pressure steady. Process exactly as required by the recipe.

Cooling

Lift the canner from the heat and set on another, unlighted, burner the moment the processing time is up. Wait 2 minutes (or the time given in the manufacturer's instructions), then open the petcock. If no steam escapes, remove the cover.

Use a thick oven mitt or a jar lifter to remove the jars. Set them cap side up on a rack to cool or on several folded towels. Avoid placing the jars on a cold surface. The cooling area should be away from drafts or sudden cold. Cool 12 hours.

Testing the Seal

After the jars have cooled, test the seal as instructed on page 114. If a jar fails to seal, repack it and reprocess, or refrigerate and use the food as soon as possible.

Storing

Store your jars in a cool, dark, dry place with a temperature between 35 and 60 to 70 degrees.

BOILING-WATER-BATH CANNING FOR HIGH-ACID FOODS

General Instructions

Boiling-water-bath canning, or water-bath canning, is a process very similar to pressure canning. The main difference is in the equipment used. Instead of a pressure canner, the jars are processed in a very large, very deep kettle that has a lid. You can use any giant kettle you have (if it has a lid) as long as it accommodates a rack that will hold the jars above the floor of the kettle (away from the direct heat of the burner) and as long as it is deep enough to allow the water to reach 2 to 4 inches over the tops of the jars to be processed. You can use a pressure canner as a boiling-water-bath canner as long as it is deep enough. By leaving the petcock open, steam will escape and the pressure will not build up.

Processing times for the recipes in this book are for altitudes at or below 1,000 feet above sea level. If your altitude is higher, check the Boiling-Water-Bath Altitude Chart before you treat any of the recipes to boiling-water-bath processing.

BOILING-WATER-BATH ALTITUDE CHART

IF ALTITUDE IS OVER:	ADD TO PROCESSING TIMES 20 MINUTES OR LESS	ADD TO PROCESSING TIMES OVER 20 MINUTES
1,000 feet	1 minute	2 minutes
2,000 feet	2 minutes	4 minutes
3,000 feet	3 minutes	6 minutes
4,000 feet	4 minutes	8 minutes
5,000 feet	5 minutes	10 minutes
6,000 feet	6 minutes	12 minutes
7,000 feet	7 minutes	14 minutes
8,000 feet	8 minutes	16 minutes
9,000 feet	9 minutes	18 minutes
10,000 feet	10 minutes	20 minutes

Preparing Fruits

Many of the recipes using water-bath canning are for fruits, which are usually packed in syrup. Some fruits, particularly cherries, freeze well, so, before you can your fruits, consider that as an alternative.

Apples, peaches, pears, and some other fruits change color when cut or peeled. Drop these as you ready them into an ascorbic-acid solution of 2 tablespoons each of salt and vinegar to each gallon of cold water. Or make an ascorbic-acid solution using mixtures sold by drugstores and hardware stores for this purpose. Fruits sometimes change color after canning. If this will trouble you, to each quart of fruit packed add ¼ teaspoon of pure ascorbic acid before adding the syrup to the jar. If you are using a mixture of ascorbic and citric acid, follow the manufacturer's instructions.

I use light, medium, or heavy syrup for canning fruits. Prepare the syrup according to the following table. Measure the sugar into a saucepan, add the water, and stir over low heat until the sugar dissolves; then keep the syrup hot but not cooking until you are ready to pour it into the fruit-packed jars.

Syrups for Fruit Canning

Light:	2	cups sugar* + 4 cups water = 5	cups syrup
Medium:	3	cups sugar + 4 cups water = 5½	cups syrup
Heavy:	4¾	cups sugar + 4 cups water = 6½	cups syrup

I prepare 1 to 1½ cups of syrup for each quart or 2 pints of fruit to be canned. Syrup keeps, so if you have lots left over, refrigerate it and use another day.

Procedure

Use the same procedure in water-bath canning as for pressure canning, with these differences:

Before you begin to pack the jars, set the rack in the bottom of the water-bath canner, and half-fill the canner with boiling water. Have ready a large kettle filled with water that is very hot but not boiling. As each jar is capped, place it on the rack in the canner. When the canner is loaded, pour the very hot water down along the

---

* You can use corn syrup or honey as a sweetener for fruit syrups and in the making of some preserves. As a rule of thumb, use half the amount of sugar called for and half honey or corn syrup. Brown sugar can be used instead of white at the same rate, but it will make a less-sweet syrup.

sides of the canner. Don't pour it over the jars. Add enough water to cover the tops of the jars by 2 to 4 inches, depending on the depth of your canner. Place the lid on the canner. Bring the water to a boil over high heat. When the water begins to boil, start timing the processing. Very often, pints are processed in 25 minutes, quarts in 30 minutes. This varies according to altitude (see the Altitude Chart). After the water has begun to boil, watch it for a few moments to make sure it is staying at a steady, gentle boil. Adjust the heat if necessary. When the processing time is up, remove the jars at once with a jar lifter or a heavy oven mitt, and proceed as for pressure canning. Store boiling-water-bath-processed foods the same as pressure-processed foods.

OPEN-KETTLE CANNING FOR PRESERVES

General Instructions

Jams, marmalades, and other preserves, such as pickles and relishes, are usually high in natural preservatives, such as sugar and acid, and are generally fully cooked (in an open kettle so you can stir as the contents simmer) before they are sealed into jars. Because of their natural preservatives and/or the long cooking period, they generally do not require processing to ensure the inhibition of spoilage bacteria. However, some do require processing, generally with a boiling-water bath. For others, processing is optional.

Plan to process in a boiling-water bath if your storage room is above 50 degrees Fahrenheit. If preserves or pickles are stored at warmer temperatures (as in centrally heated modern apartments) or if you live in a humid, warm climate, it is a good idea to give your preserves extra protection from mold and other organisms by processing them for the times recommended in the recipes before storing.

Jelly is an exception: Do not process jelly in a boiling-water bath. Do sterilize jars for jelly by boiling for 2 minutes.

Preserves to be processed must be packed into canning jars. Jellies and preserves not to be processed can be sealed with paraffin and don't have to be in rim-perfect canning jars, since they won't have to stand up to high heats. Some authorities suggest you sterilize jars not to be processed. I put them through the dishwasher or wash them in very hot soapy water, as described for cleaning of canning jars on the preceding pages. If you are going to pack boiling jams into them, place the jars in a kettle of hot water so they can warm some minutes before they are packed. That will guarantee them against cracking when the boiling jam is added.

When you process open-kettle preserves in a boiling-water bath, fill the jars to within ½ inch of their tops to allow for expansion. Preserves to be processed are generally in the boiling-water bath about 10 to 15 minutes.

The Boiling-Water-Bath Altitude Chart tells how many minutes to add, depending on altitude, to processing times for open-kettle-canned goods that are to be processed in a boiling-water bath.

About Making Jellies and Jams

Vegetables and fruits turned into jams and relishes and fruits made into jellies must be wholesome and in good condition, just like those for canning and freezing. For jelly making, you'll need an additional piece of equipment; a jelly bag, which allows you to strain the juice that will be made into jelly. However, several pieces of clean cheesecloth set into a colander, preferably enameled or plastic, will do as well.

The Sheeting Test

Sweets meant to jell, such as jellies and jams, are cooked with sugar to the point at which the pectin in the fruits and the sugars combine to produce a gel. On a jelly thermometer—another handy gadget— the point is 220 to 222 degrees Fahrenheit. You can also tell when the gel point is reached because the liquid simmering in the kettle will "sheet" on a spoon rim or the tines of a fork as the gel stage is reached. See the accompanying illustration for jelly at the "sheeting" stage. Depending on weather—humidity affects sheeting—use both the thermometer and the sheeting test. I check the thermometer, then try a sheeting test just to make sure my jellies and jams are ready to set.

Paraffin for Sealing Jellies

Paraffin for sealing jellies is sold at hardware stores and in most supermarkets. Melt it in the top of a double boiler over hot water. Paraffin catches fire very easily if melted over the burner in a regular saucepan. Keep it hot as you work by leaving it over the water that melted it, and reheat as needed. Pour a ¼-inch layer of paraffin into the jar. Poured paraffin should be pricked with a fork to eliminate

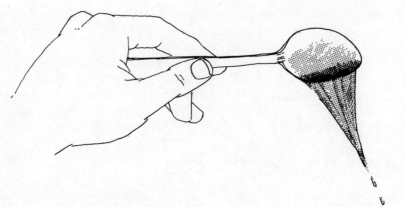

Boiling jellies and jams pour from a spoon or the tines of a fork in "sheets," rather than in a thin stream, once they have reached the gel point. Toward the end of the cooking, test for "sheeting" often, and the moment the "sheeting" stage is reached, remove the kettle from the heat.

bubbles. After it has set, you may need to add a little more paraffin as it tends to set with a depression in the center; the center is sometimes so thin that the jelly can break through.

Note: You can can fruits without sugar or sugar syrup. Sugar makes canned fruits more to our taste, but it can be omitted from canning recipes for fruits, or you can substitute your preferred artificial sweetener at the rate prescribed by the manufacturer for regular use. You cannot omit sugar from jellies or jams since the sugar is one of the ingredients responsible for a gel condition.

8

Recipes for Canning Vegetables

PICKLED ARTICHOKE HEARTS

Boiling-Water Bath

Preparation: For every 15 small artichokes, you will need 4 cups of white vinegar; 8 cups of water; 1 cup white-wine vinegar; 1 peeled, crushed clove of garlic; and 1 tablespoon of salt. Cut the stems from the artichokes and remove all the tough outer leaves. In a large kettle bring the white vinegar and 4 cups of water to a boil; turn the artichokes into the kettle, cover, and simmer until a leaf comes away easily when tugged. Drain the artichokes and cut them in half from top to bottom. Scoop out the hairy choke in the center of each artichoke half and discard it. In a saucepan combine the last 4 cups of water, the wine vinegar, garlic, and salt and bring to a boil.

Packing: Pack the artichokes halves into hot pint canning jars, leaving ½ inch headroom, and pour the vinegar mixture over them, leaving ¼ inch headroom. Seal.

Processing: Process 15 minutes for altitudes up to 1,000 feet above sea level.

124

ASPARAGUS

Pressure Canned

Preparation: Measure the number of jars needed and thoroughly wash the asparagus. Peel away the woody skin up to the tip and cut away the tough end, making all spears the size of the jars to be used. Make them short enough to allow 1½ inches headroom in the jar.

Hot packing: Bring a kettleful of water to a rapid boil and lay the asparagus on a rack or in a colander set in the boiling water. When the water returns to a boil, boil 3 minutes. Lay the canning jars on their sides. Lift out the rack or colander. Slide the asparagus into the jars. Add ½ teaspoon of salt to each pint jar, 1 teaspoon for each quart jar. Bring the cooking water back to a boil and fill each jar with it, leaving 1 inch headroom. Seal.

Processing: Process quarts 30 minutes, pints 25 minutes, at 10 pounds pressure for altitudes up to 2,000 feet above sea level.

DILLED KENTUCKY WONDER BEANS

Boiling-Water Bath

Preparation: For each 4 pounds of green beans (enough to fill 8 pint jars), you will need 4 cups of boiling water; 2 cups of white vinegar; 4 tablespoons of salt; 4 teaspoons dill weed; ½ teaspoon cayenne pepper; 4 peeled cloves of garlic, crushed; and 6 cups of cold water. Wash the beans, remove the stem ends, but leave the pointed ends. Cut them lengthwise to fit pint jars, allowing ½ inch headroom. Set the beans in a medium kettle and pour the boiling water over them. Return to boiling and simmer 3 minutes. Drain the beans.

Packing: Pack the beans lengthwise into pint canning jars. Combine the remaining ingredients in a small saucepan and bring to a boil. Pour the boiling pickling liquid into the jars, leaving ¼ inch headroom. Seal.

Processing: Process 10 minutes for altitudes up to 1,000 feet above sea level.

LIMA BEANS

Pressure Canned

Preparation: Wash and shell the beans. Hard-to-open pods yield if you plunge them for 1 minute into boiling water, cool, then yank down hard on the tip of the string. Measure the number of jars needed.

Hot packing: Place the beans in a colander and bring a kettleful of water to a rapid boil. Set the colander of beans in the water. Bring the water back to a boil and boil rapidly for 3 minutes. Lift out the beans and pack into hot jars leaving 1½ inches headroom. Add ½ teaspoon of salt to each pint, 1 teaspoon to each quart jar. Cover with the boiling water, leaving 1 inch headroom. Seal.

Processing: Process quarts 50 minutes, pints 40 minutes, at 10 pounds pressure for altitudes up to 2,000 feet above sea level. If beans are extra large, process an additional 10 minutes for both pints and quarts.

GREEN OR WAX SNAP BEANS

Pressure Canned

Preparation: Wash and sort according to size and cut away tip ends. Measure the number of jars needed. If sizes are very uneven, cut all the beans into 2-inch lengths.

Hot packing: Bring a kettleful of water to a rapid boil, place the beans in a colander, and place the colander in the water. When the water returns to rapid boil, time for 3 minutes, then remove the beans. Place in hot jars, leaving 1 inch headroom. Add ½ teaspoon of salt for each pint jar, 1 teaspoon for each quart jar. Cover with boiling bean water, leaving ½ inch headroom. Seal.

Processing: Process quarts 25 minutes, pints 20 minutes, at 10 pounds pressure for altitudes up to 2,000 feet above sea level.

BEET-AND-ORANGE CONSERVE

Boiling-Water Bath

Preparation: For every 18 medium beets, you will need 2 large oranges, 2 medium lemons, 4 cups light corn syrup, 4 cups sugar, 2 cups slivered blanched almonds (optional), and 2 tablespoons ground ginger. Remove the beet foliage, leaving 2 inches, wash the beets, and cook in boiling water about 15 minutes or until the skins slip off easily. Remove skins and tap root. Grate the beets. Slice the unpeeled oranges and lemons into the thinnest possible pieces. Seed them. In a large kettle combine the beets, the orange and lemon slices, corn syrup, and sugar. Over medium heat, bring the mixture to a boil, stirring. Reduce the heat and simmer 40 minutes, stirring occasionally. Add the almonds and the ginger and simmer 5 more minutes.

Packing: Turn into hot ½-pint jars, leaving ¼ inch headroom. Seal.

Processing: Process 5 minutes for altitudes up to 1,000 feet above sea level.

BEETS

Pressure Canned

Preparation: Remove leaves, leaving 2 inches of leaf stem on the beets. Wash thoroughly and grade according to size.

Hot packing: Bring a kettleful of water to a rapid boil. Place beets, in graded sizes (that is, one size at a time), in a colander and immerse in the water. Boil until the skins slip off easily, which will be about 20 minutes for small beets. Remove the beets from the boiling water and plunge into cold water. Skin them and remove the tops. Slice, dice, or leave them whole and pack into hot jars, leaving 1½ inches headroom. Add 1 teaspoon salt to quart jars, ½ teaspoon to pint jars. Add the boiling beet water to the jars, leaving 1 inch headroom. Seal.

Processing: Process 35 minutes for quarts, 30 minutes for pints. Add 10 minutes more if beets are packed whole, whether in quarts or pints. Pressure reading should be 10 pounds for altitudes up to 2,000 feet above sea level.

SAUERKRAUT

Boiling-Water Bath

Preparation: For each pound of cabbage, you will need 1 teaspoon of salt. Remove any outside or damaged leaves from the cabbage, core it, and quarter it. Shred the cabbage. In a large earthenware crock or a glass bowl layer the cabbage with salt, packing each layer firmly. Leave headroom of several inches at the top of the crock —sauerkraut ferments. Fill a large plastic trash bag with water, making sure there is no leakage, and set it on top of the kraut. It should have enough water in it to fill the crock completely and to act as a rather heavy weight. (Its purpose is to keep cabbage in the crock below the level of the brine that forms as the salt draws the moisture from the cabbage.) Set the cabbage for fermentation, which takes 5 to 6 weeks, in a place where the temperature is between 68 and 72 degrees. Fermentation is evident by the formation of bubbles which work their way to the surface of the crock. When fermentation ceases, it is time to process the kraut.

Packing: Heat the undrained kraut to simmering, somewhere between 185 and 210 degrees Fahrenheit on a jelly thermometer. Do not let it boil. Pack it at once into hot pint or quart jars, leaving 1 inch headroom, and cover with hot, not boiling, brine from the cooking kettle, leaving ½ inch headroom. If there's not enough juice, add hot brine (2 tablespoons of salt for 1 quart of water). Seal.

Processing: Process quarts 20 minutes, pints 15 minutes, for altitudes up to 1,000 feet above sea level.

Cooking: Cook sauerkraut 15 to 30 minutes before serving. I rinse the brine from mine before I cook it.

CABBAGE-AND-BEET-RELISH

Boiling-Water Bath

Preparation: For each 2 cups of fine-chopped cabbage, you will need 2 cups of grated cooked beets, ¼ cup of prepared horseradish or horseradish sauce, ½ cup of sugar, and 1½ cups of cider vinegar. Core the cabbage and soak in a brine made of 1 gallon of water and 3 tablespoons of salt for 1 hour. Rinse thoroughly and grate the cabbage. Measure it and rinse it again. Let drain while you prepare the beets. Wash the beets, removing all but 2 inches of foliage, boil the beets until the skins slip off easily, then skin them. Grate the beets and measure.

Packing: Combine all the ingredients except the vinegar in a glass bowl, then pack into hot ½-pint jars. Heat the vinegar to boiling and pour it at once over the mixture in the jars, leaving ½ inch headroom.

Processing: Process for 15 minutes for altitudes up to 1,000 feet above sea level.

CARROTS

Pressure Canned

Preparation: Select baby carrots, remove the tops and tips, wash, but don't peel. Grade the carrots according to size and plan to process similar sizes in batch lots. Measure the number of jars needed.

Hot Packing: Bring a large kettleful of water to a rapid boil, place the carrots, one size at a time, in a colander and plunge into the boiling water. When the water returns to a boil, boil 3 minutes for average sizes, 5 minutes for larger sizes. Remove the carrots and pack into jars. Fill with boiling carrot water, leaving 1 inch headroom. Add ½ teaspoon of salt to pint jars, 1 teaspoon to quart jars. Cover with boiling water, leaving ½ inch headroom. Seal.

Processing: Process quarts 30 minutes, pints 25 minutes, at 10 pounds pressure for altitudes up to 2,000 feet above sea level.

CARROT JAM

Boiling-Water Bath

Preparation: For each 8 cups of grated raw carrots (I prefer late carrots for this), you will need 6 cups of sugar, the juice and grated rind of 4 lemons, 1 teaspoon of ground cloves, 1 teaspoon of ground allspice, and 1 teaspoon of ground cinnamon. Wash, grate, and measure the carrots into a big kettle. Grate the rind from the lemons, then juice them, strain the juice, and then measure it into the kettle. Measure and add all the other ingredients. Turn the heat to medium-low and stir until the sugar has dissolved. Keep the mixture at a very low simmer and stir occasionally until it thickens enough to mound a little on a spoon.

Packing: Turn into hot ½-pint canning jars and seal.

Processing: Process 10 minutes for altitudes up to 1,000 feet above sea level.

CARROT-AND-ORANGE MARMALADE

Boiling-Water Bath

Preparation: For every 6 cups of grated raw carrots you will need 3 oranges, 6 lemons, 8 cups of water, about 8 cups of sugar, and a pinch of salt. Wash, grate, and measure the carrots. Grate the rinds from 1½ oranges and 3 of the lemons, then juice all the oranges and lemons and set aside. Turn the grated fruit rinds into a big kettle, add half the water, and cook rapidly for 30 minutes. Add the grated carrot and the rest of the water and boil 20 minutes more. Add the fruit juices. Measure the mixture. For each cup of the mixture add to the kettle ⅔ cup of sugar. Bring to simmer and cook for an hour, stirring occasionally, or until the mixture mounds on a spoon. Add the salt just before it finishes cooking.

Packing: Turn hot into ½-pint jars, leaving ½ inch headroom, and seal.

Processing: Process 10 minutes for altitudes up to 1,000 feet above sea level.

CAULIFLOWER

Pressure Canned

Preparation: Cut florets into 2-inch pieces and discard the main stalk. Measure the number of jars you will need. Soak the florets in a solution of 1 quart of water mixed with 1 teaspoon of salt for 1 hour. Rinse in clear water.

Hot packing: Bring a kettleful of water to a rapid boil, place the florets in a colander, place the colander in the water, bring back to a rapid boil, and boil 3 minutes. Lift the florets from the water and pack into hot jars, leaving 1 inch headroom. Cover with cooking water, leaving ½ inch headroom. Seal.

Processing: Process quarts 35 minutes, pints 30 minutes, at 10 pounds pressure for altitudes up to 2,000 feet above sea level.

CELERY IN TOMATO JUICE

Pressure Canned

Preparation: Wash and remove the leaves from celery and cut into 1-inch pieces. Prepare enough to fill whatever number of jars you plan to can. Measure out enough tomato juice (see recipe for Seasoned Tomato Juice, page 139) to fill the jars. Place the celery in a large kettle over medium heat, along with 2 teaspoons of salt and 1 garlic clove, peeled and minced, for each 12 cups of celery. Add the tomato juice, cover, bring to a simmer, and simmer for 5 minutes.

Hot packing: Pack the celery into jars, leaving 1 inch headroom, and cover with boiling tomato juice, leaving ½ inch headroom. Seal.

Processing: Process quarts 35 minutes, pints 30 minutes, at 10 pounds pressure for altitudes up to 2,000 feet above sea level.

CREAMED CORN

Pressure Canned

Preparation: Cream corn when you are working with ears that have less than perfect kernels. Have everything ready to can before you begin, and process the corn as soon as you have picked it. Husk the corn, remove the silks under cold running water, and dry the ears. With a sharp knife, cut the kernels from the cobs halfway to the cobs. Use the same knife to press out the meat from the kernel halves remaining on the corn.

Hot packing: Have a few quarts of water at boiling point. Place the kernels in an empty kettle and just cover with boiling water. Bring back to a boil and boil 3 more minutes. Pack into pint jars, leaving 1½ inches headroom. Add ½ teaspoon of salt per jar. Fill the jars to within 1 inch of the tops with boiling corn liquid. Add extra boiling water if needed to fill the jars.

Processing: Process pint jars 85 minutes at 10 pounds pressure for altitudes up to 2,000 feet above sea level.

CORN KERNELS

Pressure Canned

Preparation: Have everything ready to can before you pick the corn. Pick fully ripe ears. Can at once. Husk the ears, wash away the silk under cold running tap water, dry the ears, and, with a sharp knife pressed against the kernels, slice the kernels from the husks. Don't scrape the cob. Measure the number of jars needed.

Hot packing: Have ready a few quarts of boiling water. Spread the kernels over the bottom of a heavy kettle and barely cover with boiling water. Bring the water back to a boil and, as soon as it is boiling, drain the kernels, reserving the liquid. Pack the kernels into the jars, leaving 1½ inches headroom at the top. Add 1 teaspoon of salt for each quart jar, ½ teaspoon for each pint jar. Fill the jars with the corn liquid, leaving 1 inch headroom. If there isn't enough, add a little more boiling water. Seal.

Processing: Process quarts 1 hour and 25 minutes, pints 55 minutes, at 10 pounds pressure for altitudes up to 2,000 feet above sea level.

CORN-AND-TOMATO RELISH

Boiling-Water Bath

Preparation: You will need ½ cup granulated sugar; 2 table-spoons salt; 1 tablespoon turmeric; 8 cups corn kernels; 2 cups chopped ripe tomatoes; 2 cups peeled and chopped onion; 2 cups peeled and chopped cucumber; 2 cups stemmed and seeded sweet green pepper; 1 cup chopped celery; 2 dried red hot peppers, seeded and crushed; 1 cup cider vinegar; 2 teaspoons mustard seed; ¼ cup cold water; and 2 tablespoons cornstarch. Combine the sugar, salt, and turmeric in a large kettle and add the vegetables, vinegar, and mustard seed. Bring to the boiling point, reduce the heat, and sim-mer 30 to 40 minutes. stirring occasionally. Combine the cold water and the cornstarch and stir into the hot mélange. Stir at a simmer until slightly thickened, about 5 minutes.

Packing: Pour into hot pint jars, leaving ½ inch headroom. Seal.

Processing: Process 15 minutes for altitudes up to 1,000 feet above sea level.

CUCUMBER DILL PICKLES

Boiling-Water Bath

Preparation: For every 20 cucumbers (4 to 6 inches long) you will need 1½ tablespoons of mixed pickling spices, ¾ cup of salt, 1 cup of cider vinegar, and 4 quarts of hot water. You also need fresh dill, though pickles can be made with dried dill weed or seed. Begin by placing a layer of dill and one-fourth of the spices in an earthen-ware crock or a large glass bowl that is narrow. Cover the dill with a layer of washed, stemmed cucumbers, unpeeled. Continue to make layers of cucumbers, dill, and spices until all the cucumbers are used up, and end with a layer of dill and spices. My crock does this many cucumbers in four layers, but it could be done in three or two layers. Heat the vinegar and the water gently in a small sauce-pan and dissolve the salt in it. Allow the brine to cool and pour it over the cucumbers. Cover the cucumbers with clean cloth or cheese-cloth, set a large plate on the cloth, and weight the plate with a bottle filled with water. (Its purpose is to keep the cucumbers under the brine.) Cure the cucumbers 2 to 4 weeks at 68 to 72 degrees Fahrenheit. If the brine level falls below the cucumbers, make addi-tional brine and pour it over the cucumbers. Skim the scum from the crock daily. The cucumbers are cured when they are uniform in color, without whitish spots.

Packing: Prepare fresh hot brine, using 1 cup of vinegar, 4 quarts of water, and ¾ cup of salt, and boil for 5 minutes. Pack the cucumbers into hot canning jars, leaving ½ inch headroom, and fill the jars with hot brine, leaving ¼ inch headroom. Seal.

Processing: Process quarts and pints 10 minutes for altitudes up to 1,000 feet above sea level.

Note: For kosher dill pickles, pack with 1 peeled clove of garlic, 1 bay leaf, 1 piece of hot red pepper, and 1 teaspoon of mustard seed per jar. Add these to the jars after they are packed and before you pour in the pickling liquid.

YELLOW CUCUMBER PICKLES

Boiling-Water Bath

Preparation: This is a recipe to use with lemon, or yellow, cucumbers. For every 12 yellow cucumbers, large size, you need 4 quarts of water, 1½ cups of salt, 1 gallon of cider vinegar, 8 cups of sugar, ¼ cup of mustard seed, and ¾ cup of whole mixed pickling spices tied into a cheesecloth bag. Wash, peel, and seed the cucumbers and cut into strips ¾ by 2½ inches long. Set in a large bowl or big earthenware crock. Mix the water and the salt, pour it over the pickles, and let stand 12 hours. Drain the pickles. Combine the vinegar, sugar, and mustard seed and place 5 cups of this mixture with the bag of pickling spices in a kettle with a broad bottom. (I use an enameled chicken casserole that is very large.) Bring the vinegar mixture to a boil and cover the bottom of the kettle with one layer of cucumber strips. Return the vinegar to a boil and lift out the cucumber slices at once.

Packing: As each load of cucumbers is removed from the vinegar, pack it into a hot canning jar and pour boiling vinegar mixture over it, leaving ¼ inch headroom. Seal the jars and set in the boiling-water-bath canner. Keep the spices in the vinegar; don't place in the jars. Add more vinegar to the kettle and repeat the process until all the slices have been through the vinegar. If you run out of vinegar solution, make more.

Processing: Process the jars 15 minutes for altitudes up to 1,000 feet above sea level.

MUSTARD PICKLES

Boiling-Water Bath

Preparation: Make this with 1½- to 2½-inch pickling cucumbers. For each 3 dozen cucumbers, you will need 1 cup of salt, 4 cups of water, 6 medium green tomatoes, 1 small head of cauliflower, 3 sweet green peppers and 3 sweet red peppers (or 6 sweet green peppers), 2 cups of peeled tiny pickling onions (or use onion slices), ½ cup of sugar, ½ cup of flour, 1 tablespoon turmeric, ½ cup of water, ½ cup of prepared mustard, and 5 cups of white vinegar. Make a brine of the salt and water. Wash the cucumbers. Wash and stem the tomatoes and cut them into wedges resembling the size of the cucumbers. Cut the cauliflower into 1½-inch florets, discarding the core, and soak the florets in cold water. Stem, seed, and wash the peppers and cut them into 1-inch strips that are thin. Place all the vegetables except the onions in a crock, pour the brine over them, and let stand overnight in a place as close to 68 degrees as you can find. In the morning drain and thoroughly rinse the vegetables in cold water. In a small bowl combine the sugar, flour, and turmeric and stir in the water a little at a time, making a smooth paste. Stir in the mustard and as much vinegar as will go into the bowl. Turn into a kettle, finish adding any leftover vinegar, and simmer over low heat until the mixture thickens to the consistency of a light cream sauce. Turn the drained vegetables into the mustard sauce and bring to a simmer. Simmer 15 minutes.

Packing: Pack into hot pint jars, leaving ¼ inch headroom.

Processing: Process pints or quarts 10 minutes for altitudes up to 1,000 feet above sea level.

BREAD-AND-BUTTER PICKLES

Boiling-Water Bath

Preparation: For 24 to 30 small pickling cucumbers, you will need 6 medium onions, peeled and thinly sliced; ¾ cup of salt; 2 cups of water; 1 quart white vinegar; 4 cups of sugar; 3 tablespoons of celery seed; and 3 tablespoons of mustard seed. Wash the cucumbers well, remove the stem ends, and cut the cucumbers into slices ¼ inch thick. Don't peel. Measure out 6 quarts (24 cups). Arrange the cucumber and onion slices in layers in a large earthenware or glass crock, and sprinkle each layer with salt. Cover and let stand for 3 hours, draining juice every half hour or so. Combine the water, vinegar, sugar, and celery and mustard seeds in a medium kettle and stir until the sugar dissolves. Bring to a boil and boil 3 minutes. Turn the cucumber slices into the pickling liquid, bring back to a boil, but do not boil.

Packing: Turn the cucumbers and onion slices at once into hot canning jars, and distribute the celery and mustard seeds evenly among the jars. Pour the hot brine over the jars, leaving ¼ inch headroom. If there's not enough brine, make a little more. Seal the jars.

Processing: Process quarts and pints 15 minutes for altitudes up to 1,000 feet above sea level.

SWEET GHERKIN PICKLES

Boiling-Water Bath

Preparation: Use only tiny gherkins for this. For each 2 quarts (3 pounds) of gherkins, you will need 2½ cups water, ½ cup of salt, 2 quarts cider vinegar, 4 cups sugar, 2 tablespoons whole allspice, 1 tablespoon celery seed, ½ cup mustard seed, and 1 3-inch stick of cinnamon and 2 tablespoons of whole cloves tied into a cheesecloth bag. Wash the gherkins and leave the stem ends on. Place them in a large crock. Mix the water and the salt in a kettle and bring to the boiling point. Pour it over the gherkins; there should be enough to completely cover them. Let them stand 24 hours. Drain and rinse the gherkins. Bring the vinegar to boiling, pour it over the gherkins and let stand 24 hours more. Then drain the vinegar into a kettle. Add the sugar and the spices and boil the mixture quickly for 5 minutes.

Packing: Pack the gherkins into hot ½-pint jars, leaving ½ inch headroom. Pour the boiling vinegar over them, leaving ¼ inch headroom. Seal.

Processing: Process the gherkins for 5 minutes for altitudes up to 1,000 feet above sea level.

HORSERADISH SAUCE

(For Refrigerator Storage)

Preparation: For each cup of peeled, grated, fresh horseradish, you will need ½ cup of white vinegar and ¼ teaspoon of salt. Combine all the ingredients in a blender, pack into dry jars, and seal tightly. Refrigerate.

MIXED VEGETABLES

Pressure Canned

Preparation: You can combine any two vegetables you like for canning, as long as each is processed for the correct length of time. Prepare each vegetable as directed under the instructions given individually (peas and carrots, for instance). Then combine them in hot jars, and cover with boiling cooking liquid, leaving 1 inch headroom if one of the vegetables is starchy.

Processing: Process quarts and pints for that period of time required by the longest-processing vegetable of the pair. Process at the pressure called for by the vegetable requiring the highest pressure.

OKRA, TOMATOES, AND ONIONS

Pressure Canned

Preparation: Wash the okra, drop into boiling water for 1 minute, remove, and break off the stem ends, then drain and dry. Wash and stem the tomatoes, then scald and peel. Then cut the okra and the tomatoes into pieces of similar size. Measure the jars needed and add half an onion, peeled and cut into pieces the same size as the tomatoes and okra, for each jar to be filled.

Hot packing: Place the tomato, okra, and onion pieces in a large heavy kettle over low heat with 1 teaspoon of salt and ¼ bay leaf for each quart. Add ¼ cup of water to the bottom of the kettle, turn heat to medium-high, and simmer the vegetables for a full 3 minutes after the liquid in the kettle begins to boil. Pack into hot quart jars, leaving 1 inch headroom, and cover with cooking liquid. Add enough boiling water to fill the jars to within ½ inch of the tops. Seal.

Processing: Process quarts 40 minutes, at 10 pounds pressure for for altitudes up to 2,000 feet above sea level.

WHOLE ONIONS

Pressure Canned

Preparation: Dig small onions and peel under cold water (to keep you from crying). Measure the number of jars needed.

Hot packing: Bring a kettleful of water to a rapid boil. Place the onions in a colander and set into the kettle. When the water returns to a boil, boil for 5 more minutes. Remove the onions and pack into hot jars, leaving 1 inch headroom. Fill the jars with cooking liquid, leaving ½ inch headroom. Seal.

Processing: Process quart and pint jars 40 minutes, at 10 pounds pressure for altitudes up to 2,000 feet above sea level.

PEAS WITH GREEN ONIONS

Pressure Canned

Preparation: Shell the peas and grade them according to size—big or small. Canned big peas are good in salads; I love canned tiny peas with seafood. Measure the jars needed. Peel green onions (or tiny white onions) 1½ inches around, allowing one for each quart jar, half an onion for each pint.

Hot packing: Place the small peas and the onions that go with them in a colander, bring a kettleful of water to a boil, and boil 3 minutes. Big peas are boiled 5 minutes. Pack the peas, each size in its own container, along with its onion companion. Seal.

Processing: Process quarts 40 minutes, pints 35 minutes, at 10 pounds pressure for altitudes up to 2,000 feet above sea level.

PIMIENTOES AND SWEET PEPPERS

Pressure Canned

Preparation: Wash the peppers, place in boiling water for 12 minutes, cool, skin, and remove stem ends and seeds.

Packing: Flatten the pimientoes in layers in pint jars, filling the jars to within ½ inch of the top. Don't add water or anything else; these are dry packed.

Processing: Process pint jars for 10 minutes, at 10 pounds pressure for altitudes up to 2,000 feet above sea level.

SUCCOTASH

Pressure Canned

Preparation: Have everything ready to can with, and shell 10 or 12 cups of lima beans (or other fresh shell beans) as described under Lima Beans. Pick the corn, husk it, remove the silks under cold water, and place in a kettleful of boiling water. Bring the water back to a boil and boil 5 minutes. Remove the corn and reserve the water. With a sharp knife, cut the kernels from the corn husks. Don't scrape the cobs. Measure the corn and add, for each cup of corn, ⅔ cup lima beans. Cover the beans with the water the corn boiled in, bring to a boil, and boil 3 minutes. Remove the beans.

Hot packing: Combine the corn and the beans and pack into hot jars, leaving 1½ inches headroom. Bring the cooking water back to a boil and fill the jars, leaving 1 inch headroom. Add 1 teaspoon of salt for each quart jar, ½ teaspoon for each pint jar. Seal.

Processing: Process quarts 1 hour and 25 minutes, pints 1 hour, at 10 pounds pressure for altitudes up to 2,000 feet above sea level.

SWEET POTATOES

Pressure Canned in Syrup

Preparation: Wash the potatoes and boil for 20 minutes. Then remove the skins, which should slip off easily, and cut the potatoes into medium pieces. (Finish cooking extras that don't fill a jar and serve for dinner.) Prepare a medium syrup while the potatoes are cooking (see Syrups for Fruit Canning Table, page 120).

Hot packing: Pack the potato pieces into hot jars and fill with boiling syrup, leaving 1 inch headroom. Seal.

Processing: Process quarts 90 minutes, pints 55 minutes, at 10 pounds pressure for altitudes up to 2,000 feet above sea level.

TOMATO CHUTNEY

Boiling-Water Bath

Preparation: You will need 30 large ripe tomatoes, 6 large apples, 6 large pears, 6 large peaches, 4 large onions, 2 cups cider vinegar, 4 cups granulated sugar, 2 tablespoons unrefined salt, and 1 packet mixed pickling spices tied into a cheesecloth bag. Wash, scald, skin, stem, and core the tomatoes, apples, and pears. Peel and seed the peaches. Peel the onions. Chop all these together coarsely. Place all the remaining ingredients in a large kettle. Set over high heat and bring to a rapid boil. Add the vegetables and fruits, bring back to a boil, and boil until thick, about 20 minutes. Remove the pickling spices.

Packing: Pour into hot jars, leaving ½ inch headroom. Seal.

Processing: Process 5 minutes for altitudes up to 1,000 feet above sea level.

TOMATO CONSERVE

Boiling-Water Bath

Preparation: You will need 18 cups ripe tomatoes, stemmed, cored, and chopped; 3 teaspoons ground ginger; 6 cups sugar; and 3 lemons, sliced paper-thin. In a medium kettle place the tomatoes over low heat, stirring occasionally, and simmer 45 minutes. Add the ginger, sugar, and lemon. Simmer until the tomato juice is thick enough to mound on a spoon.

Packing: Pour into hot pint jars, leaving ½ inch headroom.

Processing: Process 10 minutes for altitudes up to 1,000 feet above sea level.

SEASONED TOMATO JUICE

Boiling-Water Bath

Preparation: Use overly ripe, but not spoiling, tomatoes to make juice, or the parts of any less than perfect tomatoes, but make sure the pieces used are absolutely sound. Obviously enough, juicy tomatoes make better juice than meaty ones like the beefsteak or the plum tomatoes. Wash and core the tomatoes and cut into small pieces. Simmer over medium heat, stirring, until the juices render, about 5 minutes. Press through a food mill or a sieve; discard pulp.

Hot packing: Measure and return the sieved juice to the kettle and add, for each quart of juice, ½ bay leaf, ½ teaspoon of oregano or basil, and salt to taste. Bring to just below a boil and pour into hot jars, leaving ¼ inch headroom.

Processing: Process quarts 15 minutes, pints 10 minutes, for altitudes up to 1,000 feet above sea level.

Note: To make canned tomato juice that is unseasoned, omit herbs and salt.

SPICY TOMATO PASTE

Boiling-Water Bath

Preparation: Use meaty red tomatoes for this. It takes about 8 quarts of chopped tomatoes to make 8 ½-pints of paste. You won't use it (usually) in more than ½-pint lots. Wash the tomatoes, stem and core them, cut them into thin chunks, and place them in a large heavy kettle with 1½ cups of washed, seeded sweet green peppers; 2 bay leaves; 2 cloves of garlic, peeled and minced; and 2 teaspoons of dried or 2 large sprigs of fresh basil (optional). Add 1 teaspoon of salt and a pinch of ground cloves. Over medium heat, simmer, stirring, until the tomatoes are soft, about 5 minutes. Press through a sieve or a food mill and discard pulp. Turn the paste into the kettle and simmer uncovered until it mounds on a spoon, stirring occasionally. This will take about 2½ hours.

Hot packing: Turn into hot ½-pint jars, leaving ¼ inch headroom, and seal.

Processing: Process ½-pints 45 minutes for altitudes up to 1,000 feet above sea level.

TOMATO PUREE

Boiling-Water Bath

Preparation: Use juicy tomatoes for this, or combine meaty and juicy types. It takes about 4 quarts of chopped tomatoes to make about 8 half-pints of purée. Prepare the tomatoes as described for Spicy Tomato Paste, and turn into a large kettle. For each 4 quarts of chopped tomatoes, add 3 cups of peeled chopped onions; 1 large garlic clove, peeled and minced; 1½ cups seeded, cored, chopped green peppers; 1 tablespoon of salt; 1 stalk of celery, minced; ½ teaspoon of dried (or 1 teaspoon minced fresh) oregano; and a pinch of dried thyme. Simmer until tender, then press through a sieve. Return the purée to low heat and simmer 1½ hours, stirring often.

Hot packing: Turn into hot ½-pint canning jars, leaving ¼ inch headroom.

Processing: Process ½-pints 45 minutes for altitudes up to 1,000 feet above sea level.

TOMATO SAUCE FOR PASTA

Boiling-Water Bath

Preparation: I make this to serve on spaghetti. You will need 8 pounds tomatoes, 1 teaspoon celery seed, 1 teaspoon powdered mustard, ¼ teaspoon thyme, ½ teaspoon oregano, 2 cups chopped fresh mushrooms, 2 tablespoons white vinegar, 2 teaspoons salt, and

1 bay leaf. Wash the tomatoes and stem, core, and quarter them. In a large kettle, bring the tomatoes to simmering. Add the celery seed, mustard, thyme, and oregano and boil 10 minutes, stirring often. Put through a sieve, a food mill, or the blender, a few cups at a time. Return to the kettle. Add the chopped mushrooms, vinegar, salt, and bay leaf. Bring to a boil and simmer 45 minutes. uncovered. Stir occasionally. The sauce is ready when it has thickened to the consistency of light catsup. Remove the bay leaf.

Packing: Pour into hot pint jars and seal.

Processing: Process 30 minutes for altitudes up to 1,000 feet above sea level.

GREEN TOMATO PRESERVES

Boiling-Water Bath

Preparation: You will need 11 cups stemmed, cored, and chopped green tomatoes; 8 cups granulated sugar, and 2 lemons, sliced paper-thin. In a medium kettle place the chopped tomatoes, cover with boiling water, and simmer 5 minutes. Drain. Add the sugar to the tomatoes and let stand at room temperature for 4 hours. Drain the syrup into a small kettle and, stirring constantly, boil the syrup rapidly over high heat, until it spins a thread when dropped from a spoon, about 15 minutes. Return the tomatoes to the syrup, add the lemon slices, and boil until the syrup is thick and clear, about 10 minutes.

Packing: Pour into hot pint jars, leaving ½ inch headroom.

Processing: Process 10 minutes for altitudes up to 1,000 feet above sea level.

KOSHER GREEN TOMATO PICKLES

Boiling-Water Bath

Preparation: You will need 24 cups small whole green tomatoes, 6 whole stalks celery, 1½ whole sweet green peppers, 6 cloves garlic, 2 quarts water, 1 quart cider vinegar, 1 cup salt, and 6 large sprigs fresh dill or 2 tablespoons dill seed. Wash, dry, stem, and core the tomatoes and pack into 6 hot quart jars. Press the tomatoes down so each jar is well filled. Leave ½ inch headroom at the top. Into each quart jar press 1 whole stalk of washed and dried celery, ¼ washed and dried seeded green pepper, and 1 garlic clove, peeled.

Place the water, vinegar, and salt in a medium kettle. Bring to a boil. Add the dill and simmer 5 minutes.

Packing: Pour the hot brine over the pickles in each jar, leaving ½ inch headroom at the top. Add 1 dill sprig, if you are using fresh dill, to the top of each jar. Seal.

Processing: Cap and process 15 minutes for altitudes up to 1,000 feet above sea level.

Store the processed jars for 4 to 6 weeks before using.

WHOLE TOMATOES

Boiling-Water Bath

Preparation: Have tomato juice handy for filling the jars. Measure the number of jars, allowing several extra tomatoes for each jar. Wash the tomatoes, remove any green or spoiled areas, stem them, and scald half a minute in boiling water. Skin the tomatoes.

Hot packing: Bring the tomato juice to boiling, and simmer the tomatoes, several at a time, for 1 minute, or only long enough so they flatten when pressed. Pack the tomatoes into hot canning jars, leaving 1 inch headroom. To each pint jar add ½ teaspoon of salt; for each quart, add 1 teaspoon. When the tomatoes are all in, fill the jars with tomato juice just below a boil, leaving ½ inch headroom. Seal.

Processing: Process quarts of red tomatoes for 45 minutes, pints 35 minutes, for altitudes up to 1,000 feet above sea level. Process pink, yellow, and other low-acid tomatoes 55 minutes per quart, 45 minutes per pint, for altitudes up to 1,000 feet above sea level.

PICCALILLI

Boiling-Water Bath

Preparation: You will need 4 cups chopped green tomatoes; 4 cups shredded cabbage; 2 sweet green or red peppers, seeded and shredded; 2 large onions, peeled and minced; ¼ cup unrefined salt; 1½ cups cider vinegar; 1½ cups water; 2 cups firmly packed light-brown sugar; 1 teaspoon dry mustard; 1 teaspoon ground turmeric; and 1 teaspoon whole celery seed. Wash, dry, stem, core, and chop the tomatoes. Mix with the cabbage, red and green peppers, and onions. Sprinkle with the salt and let stand overnight at room temperature. In the morning pour off the liquid and squeeze the vegetables to remove any remaining liquid. Place the vinegar, water, sugar, and spices (knotted into a cheesecloth bag) in a medium kettle and bring to a boil. Simmer 5 minutes, then stir the vegetables into the boiling syrup.

Packing: Bring back to a full rolling boil, turn into hot pint jars, leaving ½ inch headroom at the top. Seal.

Processing: Process 5 minutes for altitudes up to 1,000 feet above sea level.

CHILI SAUCE

Boiling-Water Bath

Preparation: You will need 16 cups of chopped ripe tomatoes; 1 medium onion, peeled; 1½ cups granulated sugar; ¾ teaspoon Tabasco sauce; ½ teaspoon curry powder; 2 cups vinegar; 5 teaspoons unrefined salt; 2 teaspoons ground ginger; 1 teaspoon ground cinnamon; and 1 teaspoon powdered mustard. Wash, scald, skin, stem, and core the tomatoes and chop coarsely with the onion. Place in a large kettle and add all the remaining ingredients. Over medium heat, bring the mélange to a boil and simmer 2 hours, stirring frequently.

Packing: Pour into hot pint jars and seal.

Processing: Process 5 minutes for altitudes up to 1,000 feet above sea level.

CATSUP

Boiling-Water Bath

Preparation: You will need 12½ pounds ripe tomatoes; 2 medium onions, peeled; water; ¼ teaspoon cayenne pepper; 2 cups cider vinegar; 1½ tablespoons broken stick cinnamon; 1 tablespoon whole cloves; 3 cloves garlic, peeled and minced; 1 tablespoon paprika; 1 cup granulated sugar; and 2½ teaspoons salt. Wash, stem, core, and slice the tomatoes and simmer until soft in a medium kettle over medium heat. Slice the onions into a kettle. Add enough water to cover and boil until tender, 5 or 10 minutes. Press the cooked onions and tomatoes through a sieve and mix well together. Stir in the cayenne pepper, return the ingredients to the large kettle, and boil rapidly until the mélange has reduced to half its original volume, about 30 minutes. Place the vinegar in an enamel or glass pan. Place the spices (except the paprika) and the garlic cloves in the vinegar and simmer 30 minutes. Bring to a rapid boil, cover, and remove from the heat. Allow this to stand at room temperature, covered.

When the tomato mixture has cooked down, stir in the vinegar mixture; there should be about 1¼ cups. Add the paprika, sugar, and salt and boil rapidly until thick, about 10 minutes.

Packing: Pour into hot pint jars, leaving ½ inch headroom. Seal.

Processing: Process 5 minutes for altitudes up to 1,000 feet above sea level.

PICKLED ZUCCHINI SLICES

Boiling-Water Bath

Preparation: For this you will need about 10 or 12 6-inch-long very fresh zucchini squashes, along with 1 cup of salt, 1 cup of sugar, 3 cups white vinegar, 6 tablespoons dry mustard, 2 tablespoons ground ginger, 2 tablespoons curry powder, and 12 peppercorns. Wash the zucchini and cut into ½-inch rounds, unpeeled. In a large glass bowl layer the zucchini slices with the cup of salt. Let stand 24 hours. Drain and rinse the zucchini in cold water, then set in a large kettle. In a small saucepan, combine the sugar, vinegar, and spices and boil for 5 minutes. Pour the boiling mixture over the zucchini, bring the liquid back to the boiling point, and cook rapidly for 5 minutes. The zucchini slices should be translucent but not soft.

Packing: Lift the zucchini slices into hot pint canning jars and leave ½ inch headroom. Pour in the boiling pickling liquid, leaving ¼ inch headroom. Seal.

Processing: Process 5 minutes for altitudes up to 1,000 feet above sea level.

9

Recipes for Canning Fruits

APPLE-BLUEBERRY JAM

Boiling-Water Bath

Preparation: For each 4 cups of blueberries you will need 4 medium tart apples, ½ cup of water, 6 cups of sugar, and 2 teaspoons of strained lemon juice. Wash and drain the blueberries, and combine with the sugar, water, and lemon juice in a large kettle. Wash, stem, core and peel the apples, and chop them. As you measure each cupful, turn it into the kettle, and mix with the kettle contents. Turn the heat to medium-low and, stirring constantly, heat until the sugar has dissolved. Raise the heat and cook rapidly, stirring, about 20 minutes or until the jam is thick.

Packing: Pour into clean ½-pint canning jars and seal.

Processing: Process 10 minutes for altitudes up to 1,000 feet above sea level.

APPLE BUTTER

Boiling-Water Bath

Preparation: You will need 4 pounds of acidy apples, such as MacIntosh, plus 2 cups of apple cider, 3 to 4 cups of sugar, ½ teaspoon ground cloves, ½ tablespoon ground cinnamon, and ½ teaspoon ground allspice. Stem the apples and cut them into the kettle. Cover at once with the cider and bring to simmer, stirring. Cook until the apples are soft, then rub them through a sieve. Measure the mixture and add exactly half as much sugar as you have cups of apples. Return to the kettle with the sugar and the spices, and simmer until the mixture is dark and thick. It may take as long as 2 hours. Stir often. This is something to do while you are reading a book.

Packing: Turn into hot pint jars, leaving ½ inch headroom. Seal.

Processing: Process 10 minutes for altitudes up to 1,000 feet above sea level.

CLOVELLY APPLE CHUTNEY

Boiling-Water Bath

Preparation: You will need 6 large, acidy apples; 4 cloves of garlic, peeled and minced fine; 1 tablespoon of salt; 2 tablespoons of mustard seed; a few grains of cayenne; 2½ cups of dark brown sugar, firmly packed; a 15-ounce package of seedless raisins; 5 slices of sugared ginger, cut fine; and 3 cups of cider vinegar. Place all the ingredients except the apples in a large kettle. Then pare and core the apples and cut them into small pieces into the kettle. As you add pieces, keep coating them with the mixture in the kettle. Over medium heat, simmer the chutney until it becomes thick, stirring often. It will probably take an hour, or perhaps two.

Packing: Pour into hot ½-pint jars, leaving ½ inch headroom, and seal.

Processing: Process 10 minutes for altitudes up to 1,000 feet above sea level.

APPLE JELLY

Open-Kettle Canned

Preparation: You need acidy apples for this, such as MacIntosh. Wash apples and remove stems and blossom ends. Cut them into a medium kettle over medium-low heat, stirring occasionally as you work. When finished, add enough water to cover the apple pieces and cook 15 minutes, stirring. Mash the fruit through a dampened jelly bag or wet cheesecloth, and let drip overnight into a bowl. Measure the juice and turn it into a large kettle. Add 1 cup of sugar for each cup of juice measured. Boil over high heat, stirring, until the jelly thermometer reads 220 degrees and a few drops run from fork tines in a sheet. Remove from the heat and skim off the froth.

Packing: Turn at once into hot jelly jars, leaving ½ inch headroom. Allow to cool. Then, very slowly, pour melted paraffin onto the jelly until ¼ inch thick. Add a second coat after first cools.

APPLE-HERB JELLY

Open-Kettle Canned

Follow the recipe for Apple Jelly, but add for each cup of measured juice 1 sprig of your favorite herb, 1 tablespoon of white vinegar, and only ¾ cups of sugar. Remove the herbs after the sheeting stage has been reached.

APPLE-MINT JELLY

Open-Kettle Canned

Follow the recipe for Apple Jelly, but for every 2 cups of juice add 4 sprigs of fresh peppermint, minced, or another strongly flavored mint to the strained juice. After the sheeting stage has been reached, quickly stir in enough green food coloring to suit your taste and proceed with the recipe.

APPLE JUICE

Boiling-Water Bath

Preparation: About 15 to 20 large apples (10 pounds) makes 4 pints of juice. All you add to the juice is water and sugar to taste. Wash and core the apples, cut them into rounds, and put them through a food chopper. Place in a large kettle and add 1 cup of water for every 15 to 20 apples. Over medium heat, stir until the mixture begins to simmer. Strain overnight through 2 thicknesses of cheesecloth. Squeeze the bag in the morning to extract the remaining juice. Turn back into the kettle and add sugar to taste. Heat just enough to melt the sugar.

Packing: Turn into hot canning jars, leaving ½ inch headroom.

Processing: Process 10 minutes for pints or quarts for altitudes up to 1,000 feet above sea level.

APPLE RINGS

Boiling-Water Bath

Preparation: Wash, core, and peel the apples and drop into an ascorbic-acid solution. Slice into rings ½ inch thick, returning each slice to the solution as you cut. Measure the number of jars needed. Prepare a light syrup (see page 120), about 1½ cups for each quart jar. Add to the syrup 5 or 6 drops of red food coloring to make a dark, rich red. Add ½ teaspoon of cinnamon powder for each cup of syrup. Drain and rinse the apple slices, dry them, and drop into the boiling syrup. Bring the syrup back to a boil and simmer 5 minutes.

Hot packing: Remove the rings and pack into hot jars, leaving 1 inch headroom. Fill the jars within ½ inch of their tops with the boiling syrup. Seal.

Processing: Process quarts 25 minutes, pints 20 minutes, for altitudes up to 1,000 feet above sea level.

APPLESAUCE

Boiling-Water Bath

Preparation: Allow about 5 large firm apples for each pint of applesauce. Wash, core, peel, and quarter the apples and drop into an ascorbic-acid solution as you work to keep them from discoloring.

Hot packing: When all are ready, drain and rinse the apple slices and turn into a large kettle with 1 cup of water for each 5 apples. Turn the heat to medium-high and simmer until soft. Mash them fine, and add ¼ to ½ cup of sugar (if you like things sweet), a tiny pinch of salt, and 1 (or 2) teaspoon of cinnamon for each 5 apples. The salt makes the sauce sweeter. Bring the applesauce back to a boil. Pack at once into hot pint jars and seal.

Processing: Process pints 25 minutes for altitudes up to 1,000 feet above sea level.

APRICOTS

Boiling-Water Bath

Preparation: Measure the number of jars needed for your apricots, then wash the fruit and scald them in boiling water half a minute to facilitate skinning. Skin the apricots, remove the stems, and slice at one end so you can remove the pits. As you skin each piece, drop it into the ascorbic-acid solution to keep the color from changing. Make enough medium syrup (see page 120) to fill the jars.

Hot packing: Remove the apricots from the acid solution, rinse well, drain, and dry. Drop several at a time into boiling syrup. Boil each batch 3 to 5 minutes (depending on size), remove from the syrup, and pack into hot jars, leaving 1 inch headroom. When all the apricots are done, fill the jars with boiling syrup, leaving ½ inch headroom.

Processing: Process quarts 30 minutes, pints 25 minutes, for altitudes up to 1,000 feet above sea level.

APRICOT JAM

Boiling-Water Bath

Preparation: For each 8 cups of peeled, crushed apricots, you will need ¼ cup of strained lemon juice, 6 cups of sugar. Stem and wash the apricots. Pour the lemon juice into a bowl. Peel the apricots, crush them in a blender or by hand, and toss each cupful as it is ready into the lemon juice. When all the apricots are ready, combine with the sugar in a large kettle over medium-low heat. Heat, stirring, until the sugar dissolves, then turn the heat to high and cook rapidly until the jam thickens enough to mound on a spoon. Keep stirring as it cooks.

Packing: Pour into hot pint jars leaving ½ inch headroom and seal.

Processing: Process 10 minutes for altitudes up to 1,000 feet above sea level.

BERRIES

Boiling-Water Bath

(These are so much better preserved frozen.) Preserve berries frozen if they are perfect; otherwise use them for jams or jellies. If you can't do either, then you can put them up hot pack in a light or medium syrup.)

Preparation: If you've grown ground-high berries with straw or plastic under them, they are probably clean and won't need washing. High bush berries like raspberries shouldn't need washing unless they grow near a dusty area or where sprays have been used. I prefer to can them unwashed. Pick the berries over, removing any spoiled specimens, and rinse quickly in icy water. Drain well.

Hot packing: Place them in a large kettle with ½ cup of sugar for sour berries, ¼ cup for very ripe, sweet berries, and let stand for 2 hours. Place over medium heat and cook, stirring constantly, until the sugar dissolves and the berries are boiling hot, about 2 minutes. Pour immediately into hot jars, leaving ½ inch headroom. Fill the jars with hot berry liquid. If there isn't enough to fill the jars, make and add boiling hot medium or light syrup (see page 120). Leave ½ inch headroom in the jar tops. Seal.

Processing: Process quarts 15 minutes, pints 10 minutes, for altitudes up to 1,000 feet above sea level.

BERRY JAMS

Boiling-Water Bath

Preparation: You will need about ⅔ cup of sugar for each cup of cooked berries. Combine ripe and underripe berries. Discard any spoiled fruit and wash the berries. Over medium heat in a large kettle, heat the berries until the juices run, then turn the heat to high and boil, stirring, until the volume in the kettle is reduced by about half. Measure the fruit and add ⅔ cup of sugar for each cup of fruit. Stir over low heat until the sugar has dissolved, then turn the heat to medium-high and boil until the jelly thermometer reads 220 degrees and the jelly makes a good sheeting test. Remove from the heat and skim away the froth.

Packing and processing: Turn into hot ½-pint canning jars, leaving ¼ inch headroom, and process 10 minutes for altitudes up to 1,000 feet above sea level.

Note: For blackberry jam add 1 cup of sugar for each cup of fruit measured after the first cooking.

SWEET OR SOUR CHERRIES

Boiling-Water Bath

Preparation: Canned cherries are packed in syrup. I like a light syrup for sour cherries and a medium or heavy syrup with sweet cherries. (See page 120.) Wash, drain, and stem the cherries and pit them with one of those little gadgets sold at hardware stores.

Or, prick each cherry with a needle to keep it from bursting during the processing. Measure the number of jars needed.

Hot packing: Make the canning syrup and bring to a boil. Drop cherries into the syrup, bring it back to a boil, and leave 1 minute for small cherries, 2 minutes for larger ones. Turn them in the boiling liquid with a spoon as they cook to make sure all are scalded. Remove the cherries and pack into hot jars, leaving 1 inch headroom. Add boiling syrup, leaving ½ inch headroom. Seal.

Processing: Process quarts 15 minutes, pints 10 minutes, for altitudes up to 1,000 feet above sea level.

CRABAPPLE JELLY

Open-Kettle Canned

Follow the recipe for Apple Jelly. Work only with 4 cups of fruit at a time.

CRANBERRY SAUCE

Boiling-Water Bath

Preparation: Most of us don't grow cranberries, but they make good preserves, so here's how: To make 2 pints of sauce, work with 1 quart of fresh cranberries. Pick over the berries, discarding any imperfect or spoiled fruit.

Hot packing: Turn them into a kettle with 1 cup of water. Simmer on medium heat until the berries begin to pop from their skins, about 5 minutes. Press the kettle contents through a sieve. Return the mixture to the kettle and stir in 2 cups of sugar. Simmer until the sugar has dissolved, about 3 minutes. Pack into hot pint or ½-pint jars, leaving ½ inch headroom. Seal.

Processing: Process pints and ½-pints 10 minutes for altitudes up to 1,000 feet above sea level.

FRUIT BUTTERS

Boiling-Water Bath

(Fruit butters can be made from whole fruit, but they can also be made from the pulp that is usually discarded after juice has been extracted for the making of jelly.)

Preparation: To make fruit butters from jelly pulps, place the pulp in a small kettle and add just a little water, enough to cover the pulp. Turn the heat to medium-high and bring the mixture to simmering. Simmer 5 minutes. Press the mixture through a sieve. Now measure the amount of pulp you have (along with its juice) and add ⅔ cup of sugar for every cup of pulp. Return this to the kettle and simmer slowly, stirring often, until the mixture has thickened. It can take an hour or more.

Packing: Turn into hot pint jars, leaving ½ inch headroom, and seal.

Processing: Process 10 minutes for altitudes up to 1,000 feet above sea level.

GRAPE JELLY

Open-Kettle Canned

Preparation: For every 2 pounds of ripe grapes you will need 6 cups of water, and 3 cups of sugar. Remove the stems and any spoiled or green fruit. Wash well. Turn into a medium kettle, add 2 cups of the water, and simmer until the fruit is soft. Strain overnight through a damp jelly bag or wet cheesecloth set in a colander. Return the pulp to the kettle, add 4 cups of water, and simmer half an hour. Strain this juice, discard the pulp, and combine the two juices in a kettle. Stir in the sugar, boil rapidly until the jelly thermometer reads 220 degrees and a sheeting test is successful. Remove from the heat and skim the froth.

Packing: Turn into hot jelly jars, leaving ½ inch headroom. Allow to cool, then slowly pour melted paraffin into the jars, until ¼ inch thick. Add a second coat after the first cools.

GRAPE-JUICE CONCENTRATE

Boiling-Water Bath

Preparation: Try this with Concord grapes after you have made all the grape jelly you want and still have lots to put up. For each 6 pounds of Concord grapes (about 14 cups) you will need 2 cups of water and 1½ cups of sugar. Wash the grapes, stem them, and measure out 14 cups. Combine the grapes and the water in a large kettle and, over low heat, bring to a boil. Simmer covered until tender, about 30 minutes. Strain the juice through a double layer of cheesecloth, then refrigerate for 24 hours. Strain again, omitting the sediment at the bottom of the container. In a large kettle combine the grape juice and the sugar and stir over medium heat until the boiling point is reached.

Packing: Pour into hot pint jars, leaving ¼ inch headroom. Seal.

Processing: Process 10 minutes for altitudes up to 1,000 feet above sea level.

Use: Pour the juice over cracked ice and dilute with cold water to suit your individual taste. Add a spritz of lemon juice or a sliver of thin lemon rind to make things a little different.

MUSKMELON CANTALOUPE PICKLE

Boiling-Water Bath

Follow the recipe for Pickled Watermelon Rind, using muskmelon or cantaloupe rind.

PEACH CHUTNEY

Boiling-Water Bath

Preparation: To make this you will need 5 cups of pitted, sliced, not-too-ripe peaches; ¼ cup of chopped, seeded sweet pepper; ¾ cup seedless raisins; 2 cups of sugar; ½ cup of cut-up sugared ginger; 1½ cups of cider vinegar; and ¼ teaspoon of salt. Tie into a small cheesecloth bag ¼ teaspoon whole cloves, ¼ teaspoon whole allspice, and ⅔ inch of a cinnamon stick. Combine all the ingredients in a large kettle and, bring to a boil over medium heat. Boil, stirring often, until the mixture is dark and thick, about 1½ hours.

Packing: Turn into hot ½-pint jars, leaving ½ inch headroom, and seal.

Processing: Process 10 minutes for altitudes up to 1,000 feet above sea level.

HALVED PEACHES

Boiling-Water Bath

Preparation: Measure the number of jars needed for your peaches; then scald the fruit in a lot of boiling water to make skinning them easy. Scald about 30 seconds, or 1 minute if they are underripe. Cool, skin, and halve the fruit. Discard the stones. As you work, drop each piece into ascorbic-acid solution to keep the flesh from discoloring.

Hot packing: Make a medium syrup (see page 120). While it is readying, drain and thoroughly rinse the peach halves. Drop the halves a few at a time into the boiling syrup and simmer for 3 minutes after the syrup boils up again. As each batch is finished, pack it into hot canning jars, leaving 1 inch headroom. When all the peaches are done, pour boiling syrup into the jars, leaving ½ inch headroom. Seal.

Processing: Process quarts 25 minutes, pints 20 minutes, for altitudes up to 1,000 feet above sea level.

PEACHES IN A PICKLE

Boiling-Water Bath

Preparation: For every 30 peaches you will need 90 whole cloves; 6 cups of sugar; 4 cups cider vinegar; 4 cups water; and, tied into a cheesecloth bag, 8 3-inch cinnamon sticks, 24 whole cloves, and 2 teaspoons whole allspice. Scald the peaches in boiling water 30 seconds (or 1 minute for underripe peaches), cool, and skin. Press 3 cloves into each peach. Combine the rest of the ingredients in a large kettle. Over medium heat, stirring, bring to simmer. Add the peaches, and simmer until they are barely tender—15 minutes for smaller peaches, 20 minutes for larger ones.

Packing: Pack the peaches into hot quart jars, pressing them gently into the containers. Leave ½ inch headroom. Boil the syrup about 10 minutes or until it has become a little thicker. Remove the bag of spices and pour the boiling syrup into the jars, leaving ¼ inch headroom. Seal.

Processing: Process quarts 15 minutes, pints (you can't get many peaches into a pint jar) 10 minutes, for altitudes up to 1,000 feet above sea level.

PEACH JAM WITH SPICES

Boiling-Water Bath

Preparation: You will need about 3 or 4 cups of cut-up peaches (4 pounds), 2 cups of water, 2 or 3 cups of sugar, 1 teaspoon ground cinnamon, and ½ teaspoon ground allspice. Pit the peaches and wash them. Cut them into small pieces into a kettle to which you have added the water. Simmer over low heat until soft, then rub through a sieve and measure. Add the sugar and return to the kettle. Then, add the spices. Cook slowly, stirring occasionally, until the mixture is thick enough to mound on a spoon.

Packing: Turn into hot ½-pint jars, leaving ½ inch headroom. Seal.

Processing: Process 10 minutes for altitudes up to 1,000 feet above sea level.

PEACH-AND-MUSKMELON MARMALADE

Boiling-Water Bath

Preparation: You will need 3 oranges, halved and seeded; 2 lemons, halved and seeded; 4 cups of peeled, diced muskmelon (or cantaloupe); 4 cups peeled, diced peaches; and 5 or 6 cups of sugar. You can add Maraschino cherry halves, just enough to add color, if you like. Finely chop the oranges and lemons without peeling them. In a large kettle bring the muskmelon and peaches to a low boil and simmer for 2 minutes, then mix in the orange and lemon and stir in the sugar. Over moderate heat, simmer until the mixture thickens, stirring occasionally. When the mixture responds to the sheeting test, it is done.

Packing: Pour into hot ½-pint jars and add a cherry half or two to each jar. Seal.

Processing: Process 10 minutes for altitudes up to 1,000 feet above sea level.

PEACH-PINEAPPLE JAM

Boiling-Water Bath

Preparation: For each 5 cups of quartered ripe peaches you will need 2 cups of drained, cubed pineapple; 6 cups of sugar; 1½ cups of chopped walnut meats; and 1 4-ounce jar of Maraschino cherries, halved, along with the juice. Wash, stem the peaches, and prepare an ascorbic-acid solution. Scald the peaches 30 seconds to 1 minute (for underripe peaches) to make skinning them easy. As each is skinned, drop it into the ascorbic-acid solution. Prepare the rest of the ingredients. Remove the peaches from the ascorbic acid, rinse well, cut and measure them, and place with the pineapple and the sugar over medium-low heat in a big canning kettle. Simmer, stirring, until thick and clear. Add the nuts, cherries, and cherry juice, and simmer 1 minute more.

Packing: Let the mixture stand until cool, then pour into clean, dry ½-pint glasses for canning. Seal.

Processing: Process ½ pints 10 minutes for altitudes up to 1,000 feet above sea level.

PEARS

Boiling-Water Bath

Preparation: Pears for canning should be ripe but not soft. Pick them ripe but before they begin to feel soft to the touch. Wash the pears and measure the number of jars needed. Prepare an ascorbic-acid solution and, as you peel, halve, and core the pears, drop them into the solution.

Hot packing: Prepare a light syrup (see page 120). Drain and rinse the pears well and drop several halves at a time into the boiling syrup. Cook each batch 5 minutes, then remove and pack into hot jars, leaving 1 inch headroom. When all the pears are done, fill the jars with boiling syrup, leaving ½ inch headroom. Seal.

Processing: Process quarts 25 minutes, pints 20 minutes, for altitudes up to 1,000 feet above sea level.

PEARS IN CINNAMON SYRUP

Boiling-Water Bath

Follow the recipe for Pears, but make a medium syrup and add 2 sticks of cinnamon and 8 drops of red food coloring for each quart of syrup. Remove the cinnamon before packing the pears.

PEARS IN MINT SYRUP

Boiling-Water Bath

Follow the recipe for Pears. Make a medium syrup, color it with green instead of red food coloring (8 drops to each quart), and cook the pears 10 minutes in the syrup before packing.

PEARS IN A PICKLE

Boiling-Water Bath

Follow the recipe for Peaches in a Pickle, but use fully ripe pears instead of peaches. As you finish peeling each pear, drop it into an ascorbic-acid solution to keep it from discoloring. Rinse the pears well before proceeding with the recipe.

PLUMS

Boiling-Water Bath

Preparation: Wash the plums, and measure the number of jars needed. Prick each plum with a sterilized needle before continuing. This will keep them from bursting during processing.

Hot packing: Prepare a medium syrup (see page 120). Simmer the plums, several at a time, in the syrup for 2 minutes; then remove and pack into hot jars, leaving 1 inch headroom. When all are cooked, fill the jars with boiling syrup, leaving ½ inch headroom. Seal.

Processing: Process quarts 25 minutes, pints 20 minutes, for altitudes up to 1,000 feet above sea level.

QUINCE JELLY

Open-Kettle Canned

Though few of us grow quinces, the jelly is so good, you might consider planting some. Follow the recipe for Apple Jelly, but work only with 4 cups of fruit at a time.

RHUBARB SAUCE

Boiling-Water Bath

Preparation: Red or green rhubarb stalks are equally suited to this recipe. If your stalks are greenish, add a little red food coloring to heighten the color. Remove the foliage and wash the stalks. Cut into 1½-inch pieces and add sugar at the rate of ½ cup for each quart of rhubarb, if you like rhubarb sour; 1 cup if you like rhubarb sweet. Toss well and let stand for 4 hours at room temperature.

Hot packing: Turn the rhubarb into a heavy kettle and set over low heat. Heat until the juices begin to flow, stirring constantly. Then add ½ teaspoon vanilla for each 4 cups of rhubarb, cook ½ minute more, and pack into hot jars, leaving ½ inch headroom. Seal.

Processing: Process quarts and pints 10 minutes for altitudes up to 1,000 feet above sea level.

RHUBARB-STRAWBERRY CONSERVE

Boiling-Water Bath

Preparation: For each 2½ pounds of rhubarb (about 4 cups of 1-inch pieces) you will need 7 cups of sugar and 4 cups of strawberries. Wash the rhubarb and remove the foliage. Cut it into 1-inch pieces and measure it into a big kettle. Measure the sugar and add to the kettle. Measure the strawberries, and wash them quickly in icy water; then turn them into the kettle. Over low to medium-low heat, bring the kettle to a boil, stirring all the while, until the sugar melts. Turn the heat to medium-high and boil rapidly until thick enough to mound on a spoon.

Packing: Turn into ½-pint jars and seal.

Processing: Process 10 minutes for altitudes up to 1,000 feet above sea level.

STRAWBERRY JAM

Boiling-Water Bath

Preparation: For each 8 cups of strawberries, you will need 7 cups of sugar and 3 tablespoons of strained lemon juice. Wash, drain, and hull the berries, discarding any spoiled fruit. Combine sugar and berries in a large heavy kettle and, over low heat, bring to a boil, stirring. When the sugar has dissolved, add the lemon juice, turn the heat to medium-high, and boil until thick, about 40 minutes. Stir often. When thick, remove from the heat and skim the froth, though you needn't be as meticulous about jam as about jelly.

Packing and processing: Turn into pint jars and process 10 minutes for altitudes up to 1,000 feet above sea level.

STRAWBERRY JELLY

Open-Kettle Canned

Preparation: For each 12 cups of berries, you will need 7½ cups of sugar and 1 bottle of liquid pectin. Wash, hull, and sort the berries, discarding spoiled fruit. Crush the berries and strain the juice through a jelly bag or a doubled, dampened square of cheesecloth set into a colander. Strain overnight. Measure the juice into a kettle and stir in the sugar. Turn the heat to medium-low and stir until the sugar is dissolved. Turn heat to medium-high and bring quickly to a full, rolling boil. Add the pectin and bring again to a full, rolling boil. Boil hard for 1 minute. Remove from the heat and skim the foam well.

Packing: Pour into sterilized, hot jelly jars in ½-pint sizes. Allow to cool, then pour melted paraffin over the jelly ¼ inch thick. After the paraffin has cooled, add another thin coat and store.

PICKLED WATERMELON RIND

Boiling-Water Bath

Preparation: The rind of 2 small, early watermelons will make about 8 ½-pints of pickled rind (about 4 pounds). For each 8 cups of prepared rind you will need ½ cup of salt; 5 pints of water; 2 trays of ice cubes; 2 cups of white vinegar; and 35 whole cloves and 4 1-inch sticks of cinnamon, tied into a cheesecloth bag. You will also need a lemon, seeded and sliced very thinly. Remove all the pink meat from the melon and pare away the outer rind. Cut the inner rind into 1-inch cubes and set in a large bowl. Combine the salt and 4 pints of the water, stirring until the salt dissolves. Add a trayful of ice cubes to the brine and pour over the rind. Let stand 6 hours. Drain the rind and rinse well. Set in a kettle with 1 cup of water, bring to simmer, and cook until just tender. Don't cook it mushy. Drain the rind. Combine the remaining ingredients in a small saucepan, with the exception of the lemon. Boil for 5 minutes, then pour over the rind, add the sliced lemon, and let stand overnight. In the morning bring the kettle to a boil and simmer until the rind is translucent, about 10 minutes.

Packing: Pack the rind into hot ½-pint or pint canning jars, leaving ½ inch headroom. Bring the syrup to a boil and fill the jar, leaving ¼ inch headroom. Seal.

Processing: Process ½ pints and pints 5 minutes for altitudes to 1,000 feet above sea level.

10

Recipes for Freezing Vegetables

You can freeze almost everything that grows in your garden, including the herbs. However, there's a way that's best and easiest to put up each item you grow.

The absolutely easiest way with some foods is to leave them in the ground and dig them as needed, as long as the ground hasn't frozen, and then to take up the last of the crop the following spring. See the list of vegetables that can winter over in their rows, given in Chapter 2.

Some other vegetables can be left in the garden until a severe frost is expected and then dug and stored. In most areas, these require light covering with straw or hay, or plastic tenting loosely applied. Or, they can be harvested in midfall and stored in a cool root cellar or an indoor cellar at between 45 and 55 degrees Fahrenheit. Store these vegetables layered with damp sand, and sprinkle water on the sand monthly to maintain humidity. See the list of vegetables to store in a cool place, also given in Chapter 2.

The list of vegetables I have found freeze well follows. Many of these can be stored or put up in other ways.

Vegetables That Freeze Very Well

Artichokes	Onions, whole or chopped
Asparagus	Green onions
Lima beans	Peas
Snap beans	Sweet peppers
Broccoli	Pumpkin
Brussels sprouts	Rhubarb
Cauliflower	Spinach
Chard	Winter squash
Corn	Sweet potatoes
Herbs	Tomatoes
Kale	Zucchini
Okra	

This list reflects my personal prejudices. I have found that foods that depend on texture for some of their appeal—carrots, for instance—lose it in freezing and are better put up in other ways. While pumpkin (which is on the list) and carrots (which aren't) have somewhat similar textures, I use pumpkin mashed or puréed to make pies, so the fact that freezing spoils the texture doesn't matter. Carrots I prefer whole to mashed, so I can them instead.

Whether I can or freeze a garden product depends not only on my preferences but on space. When I have a huge freezer, I can freeze most of the things I want. When I have a small freezer, I can instead of freeze anything that lends itself to canning. It's easier to find storage space for canned goods than for frozen goods.

EQUIPMENT

If you don't have a big freezer, experiment with freezing garden produce in the freezer space over your refrigerator before you go out and buy a big freezer to contain a summer's worth of growing. If freezing is just one of several ways you preserve food, then the rule of thumb is that you will need three cubic feet of space per family member for freezing. If you are going to do a lot of freezing, six cubic feet per family member is a better size. You can buy home freezers with up to thirty cubic feet of storage space. A refrigerator-freezer with separate doors is a good choice if you need no more than ten to sixteen cubic feet of space all told and if floor space is at a premium. Separate, upright freezers range in size from six to

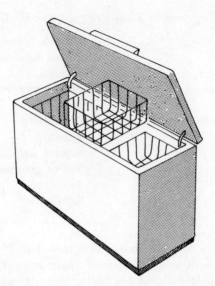

Chest freezers pack in food very efficiently but make it a little harder to get at than upright types.

Upright freezer is easier to draw food from and takes less floor space—but many claim the "cold falls out" when the door opens, lowering the temperature inside.

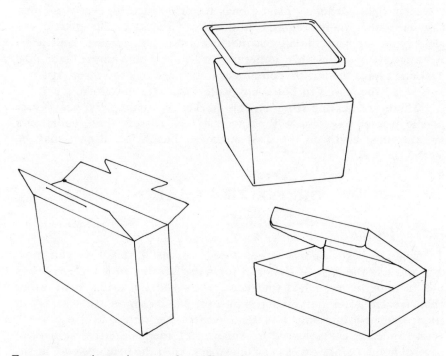

Freezer containers in waxed cardboard come in many practical shapes.

twenty-two cubic feet. Chest-type freezers for the home go up to twenty-five-plus cubic feet. These are average sizes—there are larger units on the market for commercial and other purposes.

There are pros and cons for each type. Upright freezers make food easier to get at, but the cold "falls out" when you open the door. The key factor in choosing a freezer is certifying that it will maintain a temperature of minus 10 degrees Fahrenheit so that when unfrozen food is placed in the freezer, the temperature won't go above 0 degrees, a maximum for good freezer storage.

If you can, get a freezer with an alarm system that warns when the energy supply or the cooling system goes wrong. Otherwise, you can have a whole freezer of food spoiling and not know it.

The freezer is the only item of major expense needed for freezing food. The next biggest investment is in freezer containers. In the wrong containers frozen foods deteriorate as the dry, cold air draws moisture from them. Available today are folding cartons with replaceable liners, waxed fiberboard containers, plastic and glass containers, aluminum bake-and-freeze containers, and plastic bags of freezer weight. Ordinary plastic bags won't do instead, except as interior wrapping. Many freezer containers are reusable. The plastic and glass types are reusable almost indefinitely, as long as you don't warp (plastic in the dishwasher sometimes warps) or chip the rims or lids. You don't have to sterilize containers to be used or reused for freezing. Just wash them well in hot soapy water, air dry, and store.

There are heating irons on the market for sealing the heavy-duty plastic freezer bags. Since the bags can't be reused, these containers are the most costly in the final analysis, though initial cost may be less.

THE FREEZING PROCESS

Harvesting for Freezing

To have the best possible frozen foods, harvest just before you process, and use the best of the crop for freezing. Big, tough green beans will taste better Frenched (halved) and cooked and eaten fresh rather than frozen. After harvesting, pick over your crop, setting aside for immediate use anything less than perfect and any odd sizes. Don't freeze or can vegetables with bruises; cut them out. If you harvest several hours before processing, clean and keep the produce cool in the crisper. If foods are allowed to stand for several hours between harvesting and processing, changes will take place—sugars will become starches—and the end product won't be as good as it might have been.

Blanching

Your kitchen already contains everything you need for blanching vegetables and fruits for freezing—a big kettle in which to boil the blanching water and a wire colander in which to set the food to be blanched. A wire basket heats up more quickly than a metal colander. If you use a colander, add 3 or 4 seconds to the blanching time to allow for the heat lost to the warming of the colander. In addition to these, you need a sink, ice cubes, and the containers for freezing —and that's all.

If you are planning to freeze a lot of vegetables at any one time, you'll need a lot of ice to cool the blanched foods. So, the night before, make as much ice as you can in the freezer. Use bread loaf tins as freezing trays—they make big cakes of ice that melt less quickly than small cubes.

You can use the blanching water eight times before changing it. This is not true when strongly flavored foods or highly colored foods are blanched. Herbs, for instance, will flavor whatever comes after them in the blanching water, so the water must be changed each time you change the herb. The water beets have blanched in will color whatever comes after them, so change the water before doing, for instance, wax beans.

The cooling water can be used as long as it contains ice and stays clear.

Packaging Frozen Foods

Green beans that have yellowed and have a dry, fibrous look are typical of vegetables wrapped in containers that failed to keep the air out. Large crystals in foods are symptomatic of slow freezing. Package well and freeze quickly.

Try to fill containers full so there are no air spaces. Wrapped foods, such as meats, are without air spaces, but bagged foods are not. To get all the air out of bagged foods, gather the open end of the bag into one hand, put your mouth over the end, as over the end of a balloon, and suck in, drawing all the air out until the package sides gather around the food. Seal the bag with a tie twist.

When the container is a box, carton, or glass jar that won't be filled by the food inside, line the container with a plastic storage bag. Glass containers must have ¼ to ½ inch of headroom above the contents—so here the rule doesn't apply. Why store things in cartons if you are first going to package them in plastic bags? Because square cartons stack better in the freezer and make filling the freezer easier and more efficient. The extra protection of the carton helps keep foods in better condition, too.

In addition to freezer storage containers sold commercially, you can use some improvised containers. Milk cartons and other household waxed containers will crack at 0 degrees, and aren't reliably airtight for that reason. Coffee cans with plastic lids make good freezer containers, but the insides tend to rust when wet, so line the cans first with freezer film or bags. Coffee cans and big freezer film bags are great for storing small bundles of frozen goods, such as herbs, quarter- or half-cup lots of chopped onions, sweet pepper rings, and similar foods. Glass jars are fine for the freezer, as long as they are straight-sided; curved glass jars can't be emptied of frozen foods until the foods have thawed completely, and they thaw more slowly in the container than out of it.

When you are freezing a completely cooked food like soup or meat and tomato sauce for spaghetti, and you will want to thaw in a hurry, freeze it in a plastic bag set inside the pot you will heat it in later. Once frozen, remove the bag from the pot, overwrap in freezer-weight plastic or paper, and store in the freezer. When it is time to eat the soup or sauce, remove it from the freezer, put it in hot water long enough to melt the frozen food free of the plastic then set the food in the pot you froze it in originally and turn on the heat. In a matter of minutes you can have a potful of bubbling soup or sauce.

Label Your Frozen Goods

It is useful to label the foods you freeze, giving the contents, the date frozen, and the number of portions enclosed. There are pens especially for labeling frozen goods. The freezing date tells how soon the food must be used to avoid deterioration. Freeze portions in lots large enough to serve your family. A pint package of vegetables (two cups) will serve three or four people—three if they are hearty eaters, four if they aren't.

Keeping Frozen Foods

The Ball Corporation, makers of canning equipment, suggests the following times for keeping frozen foods: Citrus fruits, three to four months; noncitrus fruits, twelve months; herbs, raw, eight months; herbs, blanched, twelve months; jams, twelve months; onions, raw, three to six months; prepared casseroles, sauces, soups, stews, six months; pies, baked, one month; pies, unbaked, three months; vegetables, cooked, one month; vegetables (except onions), blanched, twelve months.

Loading the Freezer

The trick in loading the freezer is to keep the temperature from rising above 0 degrees Fahrenheit. If you put a ton in at once, the temperature will almost surely rise. About two to three pounds of food per cubic foot of freezer space is about as much as any freezer can freeze in twenty-four hours. Foods that take longer to freeze may not be as good as those frozen more quickly. Place each new packet to be frozen either in a flash-freeze compartment, which some freezers have, or in contact with the freezing coils. Leave space between each package. When the next new load goes into the freezer, place the first packages elsewhere in the unit and set the newly processed packages on the freezing coils.

Saving Freezer Contents If the Power Source Fails

Emergency measures for the freezer that loses its power source are: If you expect a power shortage, turn the freezer to its coldest point and keep the door of the freezer closed until the power goes on again. A loaded freezer at 0 degrees will usually stay cool enough to keep foods frozen for two days as long as the door isn't opened. Half loaded, the freezer will warm more quickly. If a power failure is prolonged and there is a lot of food in the freezer, put dry ice into it. About fifty pounds of dry ice will keep the temperature of food in a well-loaded twenty-cubic-foot unit below freezing for three or four days. If the freezer is only half loaded, the same amount of ice will keep it cool only two or three days. Don't touch dry ice with your hands, and make sure the room is well ventilated while you work.

Thawing Frozen Foods

Never thaw more than you can use at one time. Frozen foods spoil more quickly than fresh foods. Stews, sauces, and soups can be thawed overnight by placing them in the refrigerator. Or, freeze each in a plastic bag inside its cooking pot, and, once frozen solid, liberate the pot. When thawing, turn it from the plastic bag back into the cooking pot (it will be the same shape) for heating in a hurry. Or, thaw it in cold water in its freezer container. Unwrapped and set near the stove, berries and vegetables thaw in just an hour or so.

Thawed foods can be refrozen if they are only half thawed and if there are still ice particles in the package. Half-thawed foods may lose quality. If they are half thawed several times, they eventually won't be worth eating. Precooked foods may be refrozen if it is certain the temperature did not go above 32 degrees.

STEP-BY-STEP INSTRUCTIONS FOR FREEZING VEGETABLES

1. Select a 5- or 6-quart kettle that has a lid and, over high heat, bring 4 quarts of water to a rapid boil. This will blanch 4 cups of prepared vegetables.

2. While the water is coming to a boil, strip away the foliage, if any, and wash the vegetables; then cut away any damaged or spoiled portions. Prepare by slicing, chopping, or quartering.

3. Clean the sink and fill it full of cold water. Add a trayful of ice cubes, or a cake of ice, to the water.

4. Place 4 cups of prepared vegetables in a wire basket, or a metal colander, and plunge the basket or colander into the boiling water. Cover the kettle at once and immediately start counting out the blanching time required by each recipe.

5. The instant the blanching time is up, remove the basket or colander from the kettle and plunge it into the ice water. Cool it there exactly the length of time the vegetables were blanched. Remove at once, drain quickly, then spread the vegetables on a clean towel or paper towel to dry.

6. Fill your freezer packages as full as possible, close, seal, label, and place at once in the coolest part of the freezer—the freezing coils usually on the floor—or in the fast-freeze compartment. Leave some space between packages. In a few hours or the next day, remove the newly frozen goods from the fast-freezing area. Place newly frozen goods under previously frozen goods, so you will use up the older packages first.

RECIPES FOR FREEZING VEGETABLES

ARTICHOKES

Preparation: Pick young artichokes and remove the stem and stiff, prickly outer leaves down to the tender inner leaves and the heart. Wash well, slice the artichokes through the center lengthwise, and cut out the hairy choke.

Blanching: Blanch in boiling water 3 minutes for the smaller artichokes, and 4 minutes for larger sizes. Cool, drain well, pack, label, and freeze.

Cooking: Place frozen pint package in ½ cup of boiling water, cover, return to a boil, and simmer until a fork pierces the heart easily. Sprinkle with salt, toss with butter, and sprinkle with a little lemon juice before serving.

ASPARAGUS

Preparation: Pick spears of similar thickness for freezing. If the garden offers a mixed bag of sizes, sort the sizes into small, medium, and large. Wash spears thoroughly to remove all sand from inside scaly leaves and cut away the tough end, making all spears the length of the freezer package. If you have leftover green ends that are tender, can these. They make a nice salad vegetable, cold.

Blanching: Blanch 4 minutes for thickest asparagus, 3 minutes for medium, and 2 minutes for thin spears. If you find yourself blanching one containerful and the spears are of mixed sizes, put the largest in first for 4 minutes, 1 minute later add the mediums, and 1 minute after that add the thin ones. Cool, drain, dry, pack, label, and freeze.

Cooking: See instructions for Artichokes.

LIMA BEANS

Preparation: Rinse and shell the beans. Hard-to-open pods are easier to strip if you plunge them into boiling water for 30 seconds, then pull down hard on the end string. Sort the shelled beans according to size.

Blanching: Blanch larger beans 4 minutes, medium 3 minutes, and small 2 minutes. If blanching a mixed collection, see instructions for Asparagus. Cool, drain, pack loosely into container, label, and freeze.

Cooking: Turn the frozen beans into 1 cup of rapidly boiling water, cover, bring to a boil, simmer 4 to 5 minutes or until tender. Drain, shake dry over the heat, salt to taste, toss with butter, and serve.

SNAP GREEN OR WAX BEANS

Preparation: Pick slim, very young beans of uniform length, wash well, snip off ends, and sort according to thickness. If you are including thick, older beans, slice them in half lengthwise down the center, not down the seam. This is called "Frenching" the beans.

Blanching: Blanch whole young beans 3 minutes, thin young beans and Frenched beans 1 minute, and whole beans cut into 1- to 1½-inch pieces 2 minutes. Cool, drain, dry, pack, label, and freeze.

Cooking: Turn frozen beans into ½ cup of rapidly boiling water, bring the water back to a boil, cover, and simmer 2 to 4 minutes for Frenched beans, 4 to 5 minutes for whole beans. Salt to taste, top with butter, and serve.

BROCCOLI

Preparation: Pick young heads with tightly curled buds. Remove the thick outer skin of the stalks and slice the heads into spears with stems about 1 inch thick. Lengths should be uniform. Young leaves may be left on. Soak the broccoli in a solution of brine—1 teaspoon of salt to each quart of water—for 1 hour. Rinse in two changes of water.

Blanching: Blanch 3 minutes for thicker heads and 2 minutes for thinner heads. Cool, drain, dry, pack, label, and freeze.

Cooking: Turn frozen package into ½ cup of boiling water, cover, return to a boil, and simmer 4 to 5 minutes until stems are tender. Drain, salt lightly, toss with butter, and serve.

BRUSSELS SPROUTS

Preparation: Pick small dark-green sprouts with closely packed leaves for freezing. Remove the stems and soak the sprouts in a solution of brine—1 teaspoon of salt to each quart of water—for 1 hour. Rinse in two changes of cold water. Sort sizes.

Blanching: Blanch large sprouts 5 minutes, medium sprouts 4 minutes, and small sprouts 3 minutes. Cool, drain, dry, pack, label, and freeze.

Cooking: Turn frozen sprouts into ½ cup of rapidly boiling water, cover, bring back to a boil, and simmer 5 minutes or until sprout stem ends pierce easily with a fork. Drain, salt lightly, toss with butter, and serve.

CAULIFLOWER

Preparation: Select pure-white, tightly curled heads for freezing. Break the heads into florets 1 to 2 inches across, and discard the central stems. Soak florets in a brine solution—1 teaspoon of salt to each quart of water—for 1 hour. Rinse in three or four changes of water.

Blanching: Blanch 1 minute. Cool, drain, dry, pack, label, and freeze.

Cooking: Turn frozen cauliflower into ½ cup of rapidly boiling water, cover, bring water back to a boil, and simmer until stems pierce easily with a fork. Drain, salt lightly, toss with butter, and serve.

CHARD

Preparation: Pick young, shiny, bright-green, tightly curled leaves. Tear off 1- to 1½-inch pieces of the leafy greens. (The central stems, cooked like asparagus, salted and buttered, are very good.)

Wash the greens well in three changes of water or until there is no sand left in the sink. Pack the green bits tightly into the colander.

Blanching: Blanch exactly 1 minute. Cool, drain, pressing out the water, until none is left. Pack, label, and freeze.

Cooking: Turn the frozen chard into ½ cup of boiling water, bring back to a boil, simmer 3 minutes or until chard is thawed and bubbling hot. Drain, salt, butter, and serve.

WHOLE EARS OF CORN

Preparation: Pick ripe, but tender, young ears of corn. While the blanching water is heating, husk the ears and pass under cold water to remove silk. Do not freeze any ears with blemishes; use fresh.

Blanching: Blanch large ears 7 minutes, medium 5 minutes, and small 4 minutes. Cool, drain, dry, pack, label, and freeze.

Cooking: Turn the frozen ears into a large kettle full of boiling salted water, bring the water back to a boil, and boil rapidly, covered, for 5 minutes or until the kernels are tender and the cobs are heated through.

WHOLE KERNELS OF CORN

Preparation: Husk just-picked corn and remove the silk under running cold water.

Blanching: Blanch ears 10 minutes for large ears, just long enough to cook the kernels. Cool, drain, dry the corn, and with a sharp knife held close to the cob slice off the kernels whole. Pack into freezer containers, label, and freeze.

Cooking: Turn frozen kernels into ½ cup of simmering milk (or water) and simmer for 2 or 3 minutes or until milk has evaporated. Salt lightly, add pepper, butter, and serve.

HERBS

See Chapter 12, Herbs for Cooking, Canning, Freezing, and Drying.

KALE

See Chard.

LETTUCE AND SALAD GREENS

Lettuce leaves frozen with tiny green peas are a nice touch. Handle the lettuce like chard and combine with blanched peas, then freeze.

MIXED VEGETABLES

Preparation and blanching: Prepare and blanch each of the vegetables in the combination as described for that vegetable, then combine and freeze.

Cooking: To cook, follow the instructions for the vegetable in the combination which requires the longest cooking period. Onions and tomatoes, tomatoes and zucchini, and tomatoes and okra are among my favorite mixed vegetables. See also the Succotash recipe.

OKRA

Preparation: Pick very young, tender fresh pods, wash well, and sort into uniform sizes.

Blanching: Blanch large pods 2 minutes, medium 2 minutes, and very small 1 minute. Cool, drain, dry, pack, label, and freeze.

Cooking: Frozen okra isn't my favorite vegetable to serve alone, though my family loves breaded, butter-fried young okra slices. I usually use the frozen pods for gumbo recipes.

CHOPPED ONIONS

Preparation: Pick large, mature onions, skin them, slice off the root ends, and chop coarsely. You can chop in the blender at slow speed, in small lots, or in a food chopper. Place the onions in a plastic freezer bag, draw out the air, and seal with a twist tie. Or divide into ¼- or ½-cup lots and seal in small bags enclosed within a large bag. Or cut into ¼-inch slices and pull the slices apart to make rings and freeze these.

Use: Use like fresh onions. The texture will be softer, less crisp but that's almost the only difference.

GREEN ONIONS

Preparation: Pick onion thinnings or bunching onions, clean them, slice off the root ends and the toughest portions of the stalks, and peel the onions one layer down. Chop with a knife or food chopper into ¼- or ½-inch sizes. Proceed as for Chopped Onions.

WHOLE ONIONS

Preparation: Harvest small onions 1 to 3 inches around, peel, wash, and grade according to size.

Blanching: Blanch the largest sizes 6 minutes, medium 5 minutes, and small 3 minutes. Drain, dry, pack, label, and freeze.

Cooking: Turn frozen onions into a cupful of boiling water and bring the water back to a boil. Simmer 7 to 10 minutes or until the onions are tender. Serve with salt and butter or in a cream sauce.

PEAS

Preparation: Pick tender young peas, wash the pods, and shell the peas. Sort according to size.

Blanching: Blanch larger sizes 2 minutes and smaller peas 1 minute. Cool, drain, dry, pack, label, and freeze. I pack some in family-sized containers and some in large plastic freezer bags, tied with a wire twist. From these bags I take as needed to make vegetable mélanges.

Cooking: Turn frozen peas into ½ cup of boiling water with 1 small, peeled garlic clove. Bring water back to a boil, simmer 3 to 4 minutes or until a few peas begin to slip their skins. Drain, discard the garlic, salt lightly, butter, and serve.

PEAS WITH ONIONS

Preparation: Prepare tiny new peas as described in Peas. Prepare tiny new onions, as described in Whole Onions. Allow 12 tiny onions for each 2 cups of peas.

Blanching: Blanch the onions for 2 minutes. Add the peas and blanch 1 more minute. Cool, drain, dry, pack, label, and freeze.

Cooking: Follow instructions for Peas, but make sure the onions are cooked through before serving.

SWEET PEPPERS

Preparation: Select ripe, thick-skinned peppers, cut out the stem ends, and use a spoon to scoop out the seeds and white pulp. Wash the insides thoroughly to remove all seeds. Now you can either freeze them raw or blanch and freeze them. Freeze them whole if you want to use them for stuffing. Or freeze in halves, strips, rings, or 1- to 2-inch pieces if they are to be used in stews or sauces. Seal raw, whole peppers or pepper slices or rings into large freezer bags so you can withdraw the amount needed and reseal the bag. Label and freeze.

Blanching: If you prefer to blanch the peppers so they will be partially precooked, blanch whole peppers 4 minutes, half peppers 3 minutes, and rings, pieces, or strips 2 minutes. Cool, drain, dry, pack, label, and freeze.

Cooking: Whole peppers, frozen raw or blanched, can be stuffed like fresh peppers and cooked just a minute or two less than your recipe requires. Peppers in pieces require 4 to 6 minutes of cooking to be tender.

PUMPKIN

Preparation: Cut the pumpkin in half, scrape out all the seeds and stringy part, and bake in a 325-degree oven for 1 hour or until the pumpkin meat is absolutely tender. Scrape from the shell, put through a sieve or a ricer, or mash to a purée. Drain away as much moisture as possible.

Freezing: Pack into 2-cup lots. Some recipes for pumpkin pie call for 1 cup, but many call for 2. Freeze in freezer-weight plastic bags.

Cooking: To serve as a vegetable, let the pumpkin thaw, then reheat it with a few tablespoons of milk or cream and add salt, pepper, and butter to taste. Tastes rather like squash.

SPINACH

Remove the toughest part of the spinach stalks and wash the greens in seven or eight changes of water, or until not a single grain of sand remains in the bottom of the sink. Then follow instructions under Chard.

NEW ZEALAND, MALABAR, AND TAMPALA SPINACH

Pick fresh, young tips from the plants, wash until no sand is left in the washing water, strip leaves from the stems, and proceed as for Chard.

SUMMER SQUASH

Preparation: Select only very young summer squashes, yellow or green, 5 to 6 inches long. Wash them, remove the stem ends, and slice into rounds ¼-inch thick. Do not peel.

Blanching: Blanch for 3 minutes. Cool, drain, dry thoroughly, pack, label, and freeze.

Cooking: Turn frozen squash slices into ¼ cup or less of boiling water, just enough to cover the bottom of the pot. Over medium heat, cook the squash, stirring constantly, until all the moisture has gone from the pot and the slices are translucent. Salt and pepper to taste, toss with butter, or a little olive oil and garlic, and serve very hot.

WINTER SQUASH

Preparation: Pick Butternut squash (the best for freezing) when ripe. Halve, quarter, peel, seed, and scrape away all the stringy parts. Cut into 1-inch-thick chunks and place in a kettle of boiling water. Cover and cook rapidly until you can pierce the pieces easily with a fork, about 15 to 20 minutes. Drain well. Place the pieces back in the pot and shake them over heat until they are dry. Mash to a purée.

Freezing: Pack into 2-cup lots in freezer bags or containers, seal label, and freeze.

Cooking: Turn frozen squash into ½ cup of boiling water, bring back to a boil, cover, and cook 2 minutes. Drain, return to the heat, and stir while mixing in salt, pepper, and butter to taste. You can use Butternut squash to make pie. Just follow your favorite pumpkin pie recipe.

SUCCOTASH

Preparation and blanching: Prepare and blanch a combination of one-third whole kernels of fresh corn, as described under Corn, and two-thirds baby Lima beans, described under Lima Beans.

Freezing: Pack mixture in 2-cup lots in freezer containers, seal, label, and freeze.

Cooking: Turn the succotash into ⅓ cup of rapidly boiling water, cover, return to a boil, and simmer 4 to 5 minutes. When ready, the Lima beans pierce very easily with a fork. Drain, shake over heat to dry, salt and pepper to taste, add butter, and serve.

WHOLE TOMATOES

Preparation: Tomatoes are acid and will discolor if they come into contact with copper, brass, galvanized, or iron utensils. Use glass or enameled utensils instead. Wash and stem tomatoes, remove any bruises or imperfect parts, and dip into boiling water for 30 seconds. Cool quickly in cold water and skin the tomatoes. Place the tomatoes in a kettle over medium heat and heat until the juices begin to run. Lower the heat and simmer 5 more minutes, or until the tomatoes are soft. Remove the tomatoes from the kettle and dip briefly in ice water.

Freezing: Pack tomatoes and the juices remaining in the kettle into plastic or glass freezer containers, squashing the tomatoes a little to get more into each package. Fill the containers with the tomato juices. Add tomato juice (commercial or your own) to fill the containers, leaving ½ inch headroom. Seal, label, and freeze.

Cooking: Thaw and use frozen tomatoes like whole canned tomatoes.

WHOLE GREEN TOMATOES

Preparation: Wash, core, and remove the stems from green tomatoes, then slice them into rounds about ¼- to ½-inch-thick. Place a square of freezer paper between each tomato round.

Freezing: Pack tomato slices into pint containers, seal, label, and freeze.

Cooking: Thaw the slices, and use as you would zucchini or fry them with eggs. There are many ways to use green tomatoes for canning or pickling, so save some of your green tomatoes—don't freeze them all.

ZUCCHINI

See Summer Squash.

11

Recipes for Freezing Fruits

Fresh fruits, correctly handled for freezing and kept at a temperature of 0 degrees Fahrenheit, will keep well up to one year. Precooked fruits, such as applesauce, will be better if used up within four months.

There are several methods for freezing fruit: dry pack; sugar pack; syrup pack; or blanch and pack. General instructions for the first three follow. Review the preceding chapter for general instructions for blanching and freezing and for information and cautions on packaging and storing frozen foods.

Farther along in this chapter you will find recipes for freezing the common garden fruits.

GENERAL INFORMATION ON FREEZING FRUITS

The fruits I have found freeze best include:

Apple slices for baking
Apricot slices for baking
Berries of all sorts
Sour and sweet cherries
Cranberries (though most of us don't grow them)
Melons, cut into balls
Peach slices
Rhubarb pieces, raw

177

Tomatoes are horticulturally classed as a fruit, but since they are generally used as a vegetable, I included them in Chapter 10. Many of the orchard fruits lose their texture after freezing, so that, unless I am putting up slices for pie making, I prefer to put up peaches, pears, and plums as canned goods.

Packaging of Frozen Fruits

Fruits are juicy, so plan to pack them in plastic or glass containers. When you are packing fruits with syrups, fill the containers, leaving ½ inch headroom in large containers and ¼ inch in smaller containers. Put up in one freezer container only as much fruit as you are likely to use to make one pie or cake, or to use for one family meal. One-quart containers of berries give me plenty to serve as dessert for four people. One pint of applesauce serves the same number. By the way, I sometimes freeze leftovers of fresh applesauce. One quart of fruit—4 cups—is as much as I use in a 9-inch pie. When I make 8-inch pies, I still use a quart.

Discoloration in Fruits

Apples (and peaches and pears, too) change color when exposed to the air after peeling. When you are working with these fruits, drop each slice as it is peeled or cut into a solution of ascorbic acid (which is just vitamin C) or citric acid. You can buy these acids at most drugstores, and the containers carry instructions for their use in fruit preparation. Or, mix one gallon of cold water with 2 tablespoons of salt and 2 tablespoons of white vinegar. Leave fruits in these acid solutions no longer than 20 minutes and rinse well before proceeding with the recipe.

Fruits are acid and will discolor if they come into contact with copper, brass, galvanized, or iron utensils. Use enamelware, stainless steel, or glass for working with fruits.

DRY PACK FRUITS

This method is generally used only for berries. Pick over the fruit and discard imperfect berries. Hull the fruit and peel. Drop into an ascorbic-acid solution (see above for proportions) if the fruit is of a type that discolors. Wash in a sinkful of icy water, drain, and dry.

Pack into freezer containers, leaving ¼ inch headroom. Seal, label, and freeze. To thaw, allow a few hours at room temperature, then use as fresh.

SUGAR PACK

Follow the instructions for dry pack, but pack sprinkled with sugar or a combination of sugar and ascorbic acid, added according to package-label instructions. Place a thin layer of sugar, or sugar and ascorbic acid, over the bottom of the container before adding the fruit, and end with a sprinkling of sugar and acid over the last layer of fruit.

SYRUP PACK

Berries that have little juice or flavor, fruits that change color when cut, and fruits to be served in syrups, like peach slices, are often frozen in syrups of varying sweetness. I prefer to can these, but freezing is easier. You can make a syrup for these fruits with water or with the juice from the fruit. To make a sugar syrup, add the sugar to water that has just reached boiling, then stir until the dissolved. Chill before adding to the freezer container.

In freezing instructions here and in other books you will find calls for syrups of various strengths. The chart below conforms to sugar percentages called for by most recipes:

SUGAR SYRUPS FOR FREEZING

Light
(*20 percent*): 1 cup sugar + 4 cups water = 5   cups syrup
Medium
(*30 percent*): 2 cups sugar + 4 cups water = 5⅓ cups syrup
Medium-Heavy
(*40 percent*): 3 cups sugar + 4 cups water = 5½ cups syrup
Heavy
(*50 percent*): 4¾ cups sugar + 4 cups water = 6½ cups syrup

Corn syrups are made by mixing sugar and water over heat until the sugar is dissolved, then adding in the corn syrup, then chilling.

CORN SYRUPS FOR FREEZING AND CANNING

Light: 1 cup sugar + 2 cups corn syrup + 6 cups water = 8 cups
Medium: 2 cups sugar + 2 cups corn syrup + 5 cups water = 8 cups
Heavy: 2 cups sugar + 2 cups corn syrup + 4 cups water = 8 cups

To make syrup with honey, follow the chart for making corn syrups, but substitute honey for corn syrup. Honey has a distinct flavor of its own and will affect the flavor of the fruit.

When making syrups for packing fruits that discolor after peeling or cutting, such as apples, peaches, and pears, add to the syrup after it has cooled the proportion of ascorbic acid called for on the ascorbic-acid package.

RECIPES FOR FREEZING FRUITS FROM THE GARDEN

APPLE SLICES

Blanched and Packed

Preparation: Bring 4 quarts of water to a rapid boil and prepare an ascorbic-acid solution of 1 gallon of cold water to 2 tablespoons of ascorbic acid. Wash, core, peel, and slice the apples into rounds ¼ inch thick and drop them into the ascorbic-acid solution as soon as each is ready.

Blanching: When all the apples are ready, rinse them thoroughly and place in an enameled colander or cheesecloth bag, and drop into the boiling water. Blanch for 2 minutes. Cool in a sinkful of icy water, drain, and dry.

Freezing: Pack in 4-cup lots in large freezer-weight plastic bags. Seal, label, and freeze.

Use: Thaw and use the same as fresh apples for pies, compotes, or sauces.

APRICOT SLICES

Blanched and Packed

Preparation: Bring 4 quarts of water to a rapid boil. Wash, halve, and pit the fruits. Peel and cut into rounds ¼ inch thick.

Blanching: Place in an enameled colander or cheesecloth bag and blanch in the boiling water for 1 minute. Chill in ice water 30 seconds, drain, and dry.

Freezing: Pack, label, and freeze in 4-cup lots.

Use: Thaw and use the same as fresh apricots for pies, compotes, sauces.

BLACKBERRIES

Dry Pack or Sugar Pack
    Preparation: Sort the berries carefully, removing all smashed or spoiled fruit. Wash in ice water quickly; don't let them soak. Drain and let dry thoroughly.
    Freezing: Pack loosely into freezer containers, seal, label, and freeze. Optional: If the berries are very sour, pack with sugar, using ½ cup of sugar for every 4 cups of berries. Toss the berries with the sugar before packing.
    Use: Thaw and use the same as fresh berries.

BLUEBERRIES

Sugar Pack
    Prepare as for Blackberries, and pack with sugar.

SOUR CHERRIES

Dry Pack
    Preparation: Fill a sink full of water and add two or three trays of ice cubes. Soak the cherries about 1 hour. Then drain, stem, dry, and pit them.
    Freezing: Pack in 4-cup lots into freezer container, seal, label, and freeze.
    Use: Use the same as fresh cherries for pies or sauces.

SWEET CHERRIES

Dry Pack
    Preparation: Wash and stem the cherries. Drain and dry.
    Freezing: On heavy-duty freezer film or foil, lay the cherries over the freezing coil of the freezer or in the fast-freeze compartment. When the fruits are frozen hard, bag them in a freezer-weight plastic bag tied with a twist, label, and store in the freezer.
    Use: Thaw the fruits and use the same as fresh cherries.

CRANBERRIES

Dry Pack
    Follow the instructions for Sweet Cherries, but wash the cranberries well first, and stem them.

MELON BALLS

Dry Pack

Preparation: Use mixed half-and-half orange- and green-fleshed melons for this—cantaloupes, honeydew, or casaba. Melons must be really ripe. Halve and seed the melons, scrape away all pulp and strings, and peel, removing all hard rind. (Make pickled melon rind from the rind if you like.) Use a round teaspoon to scoop balls from the melon flesh. Save the remainder and use in fresh fruit salad.

Freezing: Pack the melon balls in pint-sized freezer containers. Sprinkle with 1 teaspoon strained lemon juice (or Cointreau, an orange liqueur). Seal the bags with a twist, label, and freeze.

Use: Half-thaw and serve.

PEACH SLICES

Syrup Pack

Preparation: Prepare an ascorbic-citric–acid solution of 2 table-spoons of the acid to 1 gallon of cold water. Peel the peaches under cold water to avoid getting the fuzz all over your nose. Then slice the peaches from the pits into the acid solution. Make a 40-percent syrup solution. Drain, rinse, and dry the peach slices.

Freezing: Pack the peach slices into containers, cover with syrup, leaving ½ inch headroom. Seal, label, and freeze.

Use: Thaw and use the same as fresh peaches.

RASPBERRIES

Sugar Pack

Preparation: Hull the berries and remove any bruised or spoiled fruit. Wash quickly in ice water, drain, and dry.

Freezing: Pack layered with ⅔ cup of granulated sugar for each 4 cups of berries. Seal, label, and freeze.

Use: Thaw and use the same as fresh berries.

RASPBERRIES

Syrup Pack

Preparation: Follow preparation instructions for Raspberries, Dry Pack, but make a 30-percent syrup solution.

Freezing: Pack the berries into freezer containers and fill with syrup, leaving ½ inch headroom. Seal, label, and freeze.

Use: Thaw and serve.

RHUBARB PIECES

Sugar Pack

  Preparation: Cut away and discard woody ends of the rhubarb stalks and all leafy parts. Cut away any blemished areas and cut the stalks into 1-inch lengths.

  Freezing: Pack loosely, layered with 1 cup of sugar for each 4 cups of rhubarb pieces. Seal, label, and freeze.

  Use: Thaw and use the same as fresh rhubarb, but omit 1 cup of sugar from recipe instructions if you are using the rhubarb for baking.

STRAWBERRIES

Dry Pack

  Follow the instructions for Raspberries, Dry Pack.

STRAWBERRIES

Syrup Pack

  Follow the instructions for Raspberries, Syrup Pack.

FREEZING PIE DOUGHS

Once you have frozen all these lovely fresh fruits for the making of pies and such, you might as well make and freeze your pie doughs. Make the dough, following your favorite recipe, roll it out, and cut into circles to fit your pie tins. Layer the circles with heavy-duty freezer film or freezer paper. Overwrap them in heavy-duty freezer paper, or place stacks of dough circles into a large freezer-film bag and tie it closed. Freeze the dough circles.

  When it is time to make a pie, take two circles for a double crust pie, or one circle for a single crust pie, from the bag, thaw, place in your pie tin, and proceed with the recipe.

  You can freeze the rolled-out dough circles in aluminum or tin pie plates sealed into plastic bags. But to make enough ahead of time to feel you have a real supply will take a lot of pie tins.

12

Herbs for Cooking, Canning, Freezing, and Drying

Fresh herbs bring a flavor to canned foods—or fresh foods for that matter—that herbs you buy in the store rarely offer. If you grow your own, you can toss out last year's leftovers and put up a new supply each fall—and you should. Even better, if you grow your own, you can blanch and freeze many of them for winter use. Though they won't have the texture of fresh-picked herbs, they retain most of the flavor.

One to three plants of each of your favorite herbs is usually enough for use fresh, for putting up, and for winter cooking. Grow them in the open garden, in a window box, in the flower garden, in containers on terraces or patios or porches, on a roof top, in a sunny window, or on a small balcony. The perennial herbs make good houseplants, since most come from hot, dry countries where the climate resembles that brought on by central heating. A few that fade in winter indoors can be brought back by refrigerating.

HERBS IN FORMAL SPACES

A formal herb garden is a delight, if you have space for it, and easy to care for once established. Design well-defined spaces for your herbs, as they are nearly all rather straggly and will look like weeds unless groomed. Easy ways to outline herbs include between the spokes of an old cartwheel and between the rungs of a ladder. Divide each area in your herb garden with sunken boards, or corrugated or plastic boards. Many of the herbs spread by means of underground runners and the dividers will keep them in bounds. Formal herb gardens often have a central motif—a small sundial or a bird bath are suitable. The shape can be a square or a pair of squares, a rectangle, a circle or a pair of half circles, or a long oval or a pair of long ovals.

Mark out the formal bed with strings and stakes, and section off well-defined patterns (squares, circles, free-flowing swatches) and plan which herb will go in which. Tall herbs should go at the back of the bed. Give the bed a low edging—such as parsley, an herb you want lots of—or outline it with dwarf lavender, a perennial that can be clipped each year to provide fragrant materials for the makings of potpourris. Include some flowers to brighten the herbal sea of green—geraniums that bloom all summer (use scent-leaved types, which can be added to jams) or nasturtiums, whose leaves and flowers you can use in salads.

WHEN TO PLANT

In colder areas many of the perennial and biennial herbs are treated as annuals and planted early. Many herbs germinate slowly; start these indoors, which speeds the process. Or buy started plants or root-tip cuttings in early spring or late summer from a neighbor's planting. Instructions for starting seeds indoors are given in Chapter 5.

Potted seedlings and herb seeds are planted in the open garden in mid-spring after the weather has warmed. You can sow biennials and perennials in midsummer, as long as there are two full months of warm growing weather ahead.

HARVESTING AND USING HERBS

For Daily Use

When herb plants are established and growing vigorously, you can begin to pick tips of branches as needed. Picking tips is a form of pruning that improves the plant shape and production. You won't

Anise	Basil	Borage
Caraway	Chervil	Chives
Coriander	Dill	Fennel
Lavender	Marjoram	Mint
Parsley	Rosemary	Sage
Savory	Sesame	Sorrel
Tarragon	Thyme	Verbena

Seedlings of herbs

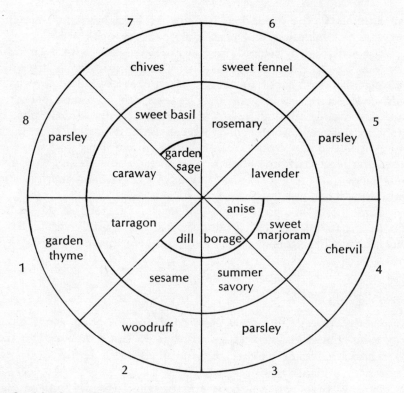

Cartwheel herb garden

harm the plant unless you strip it of more than one-third of its foliage.

The fragrance in herbs is in the essential oils the leaves contain. These oils become windborne when the sun vaporizes them. The leaves are richest in oils before the sun comes up, and easiest to dry, for instance, after the dew has dried. So harvest in midmorning on a warm, dry day.

For Drying

Harvest the herb leaves for drying through the summer, any time the plants seem especially full and fragrant. Pick 3- to 6-inch tip ends that look fresh and healthy. Toward the end of the season, pot up the foliage herbs, those you want to try indoors as houseplants.

Cut annuals to the ground and break off branches long enough for hanging. Cut biennials and perennials back by one-third.

Discard spoiled foliage, rinse away dirt lightly with a sink spray (I prefer not to rinse them unless they really are dusty), dry quickly between sheets of paper toweling, spread over a window screen lined with cheesecloth, or sprinkle over cheesecloth in a reed basket. Set in a dry, well-ventilated, warm, dark room to dry. Herbs picked in branches long enough for hanging can be tied loosely together and hung upside down from a clothesline. In ten days to two weeks, when the leaves are crackling dry, strip from the stems, pack whole into large jars for teas and lotions, or in small, tightly capped jars for kitchen use and giving.

Some herbs are used ground or crushed instead of whole. Herb mixtures usually call for ground herbs. To crush your herbs, rub them in bunches against a sieve and put them through a large pepper mill.

For Freezing

Raw herbs frozen will stay in good condition for about eight months, just time enough for new crops to begin to come in. You can freeze your herbs in small batches, a handful of fresh sprigs every week or so as the plants bush out.

Pick 3- to 6-inch tip ends for freezing, remove any damaged foliage, rinse the herbs quickly under cold water, drain, and dry well. Don't combine herbs; blanch each in its own kettle of water. Bring a 2- or 3-quart kettle filled with hot water to a full, rolling boil. Clean the sink and fill it full of cold water. Add ice to the water. Wrap each herb into a cheesecloth envelope, knotted at one end, loose at the other. Place a dozen sprigs in each envelope. Place the envelopes in a colander or a sieve and lower them into the boiling water. Leave them there for 30 seconds exactly. Remove at once and plunge all the bundles into the ice water in the sink. Leave them there 30 seconds, then drain them, unwrap each bundle, spread the twigs on paper towels, and pat dry.

Wrap each sprig in a twist of clear plastic film, or wrap groups of sprigs of a size you usually use in your recipe. Pack all the twists together into small plastic bags closed with tie twists.

Place the bags in the coldest part of the freezing compartment. When frozen, store in the freezer. When you need a sprig of parsley or basil, open the bag, remove one sprig, reseal the bag.

Frozen herbs are used in the same quantity as fresh, whereas dried herbs are used in half quantities.

Herb Seeds

Most herb flower stalks begin to dry late in the summer, and this is the time to gather their seeds. Line a basket with old cotton sheeting or linen and snip the seed heads into the basket. Spread the seed heads to dry on linen-lined screens in a dark, warm, dry, well-ventilated place. In about five days the flower heads will have dried. Thresh the seeds by rubbing them between your palms over a large bowl, in a light breeze outdoors on a porch or close to a fan indoors. The wind will blow the chaff away and the seeds will drop into the bowl. Spread the seeds to dry for another ten days on their linen-lined screens, then store in tightly capped jars. If the jars show any signs of moisture in the next few days, redry the seeds for two hours in an oven at 250 degrees Fahrenheit; then rebottle.

THE CULTURE OF HERBS

Anise

An annual, 2 to 3 feet at maturity. Start seed indoors in individual pots and transplant to light soil with lots of sand after the weather warms. Gather seed heads just before stems dry; harvest fine leaves to use fresh, or scald fresh leaves 30 seconds and freeze. Or dry the leaves. Two or three plants are enough for a family.

Basil

For flavoring, grow sweet basil rather than Dark Opal, a variety that is more ornamental but not as good for cooking. Basil is 1 to 2 feet tall at maturity. Start basil indoors in individual pots and set out after the ground has warmed. Pinch often to encourage bushiness. Gather fresh leaves at will for kitchen use or freeze or dry the leaves. If you do a lot of Italian cooking, plant four or five basils.

Borage

An annual, 1½ to 2 feet tall at maturity, used in salads and for pickling. Start indoors in individual pots or sow as seeds. Set in full sun in sandy, not too fertile soil. Harvest leaves at will for freezing, drying, or fresh use.

Caraway

A biennial, to 2 feet tall at maturity, it often self-sows and rarely needs to be replanted as do other annuals and biennials. Set plants in full sun in neutral sandy soil. Harvest seed heads as stems begin to dry. Dry and store. Three plants should be enough.

Catnip

A hardy perennial that tends to go wild in the garden. Contain it in empty-ended tin cans when planting. It reaches 2 to 3 feet at maturity in rich soil. Sow seeds in mid-spring. It germinates in about 10 days. Or plant root divisions or rooted stem cuttings from mature plants in midsummer. Cut for drying when the first flowers buds begin to appear.

Chervil

A gourmet's parsley 6 inches to 1 foot tall at maturity, this is an annual that self-sows and so acts as a perennial. Sow seeds in mid-spring, broadcast, and tamp firmly. They'll germinate in about 7 days. Chervil likes rich soil and will succeed in partial shade or in sun. Harvest side branches at will after plants are well established, but don't strip any one plant. At the season's end, allow one plant to go to seed so it can sow next year's crop. About three to six plants will supply all the leaves you need for fresh use and for freezing or drying.

Chives

One of the most useful herbs to grow, chives develop from little clumps of tiny onionlike bulblets, and go on for years either in the open garden or in containers. They are 12 to 15 inches in height at maturity and are hardy to about 35 degrees Fahrenheit. Set out started plants in early spring in rich, moist soil in sun or partial sun. Cut snips of the reedlike stems at will for fresh use. Cut back the plant by a third every few weeks when it becomes overgrown, and freeze. About three to four plants will supply one family abundantly.

Coriander

An annual about 18 inches tall at maturity. Coriander seeds are harvested from the ripe heads at the end of the season. The leaves are used like parsley, fresh, and in Chinese cooking. Start seeds indoors in individual pots or sow seed directly in the garden. Coriander doesn't transplant well. Germination takes about 7 days. Plant in moderately rich soil. In cool areas set in full sun; in hot areas set in partial shade. Harvest leaves as soon as the plant is well established for fresh use or for freezing or drying. Harvest seeds from drying flower heads at season's end and store. About six coriander plants will supply the average family. Coriander will self-sow if some seeds are allowed to ripen on the plant.

Cumin

An annual to about 6 inches tall. Grow cumin for its seed, which is used in Oriental cooking and in dishes tarragon might flavor. Sow seed outdoors in early spring in full sun, in well-drained ordinary loam. Sow where it is to stay—it doesn't transplant well. If you start it indoors, plant it in individual peat pots and transplant pot and all to the garden. Gather seed heads when the stalks begin to dry at the end of the season. About three plants will supply lots of seed for Indian cooking and to make your own curries.

Dill

An annual 12 to 15 inches tall. Dill is used heavily in pickling, either fresh or dried. It germinates in about 7 days and grows easily any-where—under lights indoors, in a window box, or the open garden. It transplants badly. If you start seed indoors, start them in individual peat pots and transplant pots to the garden when the weather warms. Plant dill in full sun in well-drained, rather rich garden soil and keep weeds down until the plant is well established. Snip dill leaves as needed for fresh use or to freeze. Snip leaves from sides of plants so flowers heads can develop at the tops. When the heads begin to show seed and turn to gold, remove and dry the seeds. Cut all re-maining foliage and freeze for winter use. Half a dozen dill plants supply the average family. You can use frozen dill leaves and branches for pickling.

Fennel

Fennel seeds and the feather foliage are used in cooking Mediterranean dishes, and sometimes in pickling. *Foeniculum vulgare* is the type to plant. It is a perennial that grows to 5 feet tall. Sow seed in light, well-drained soil in full sun. Use side leaves for flavoring salads and for freezing, and allow the center to grow seed heads to harvest just before the stalks dry. Three fennel plants supply the average family, unless Italian cooking is a specialty of the house.

Garlic

See Chapter 6, where Garlic is listed alphabetically.

Ginger

This is fun to grow indoors under lights. Buy fresh roots with shiny skin in shops specializing in Oriental foods, and plant them in regular indoor potting soil just beneath the surface of moist soil. Ginger will grow in a sunny window but does better under fluorescent lights. When the roots fill the pot, cut several 2- to 3-inch pieces to start new pots, and candy the rest or freeze it for use in cooking.

Lavender

Lavender is an herb used to make dry perfumes and moth bags, not for cooking, but no real herb garden is without it. The plants are perennials, set out as seedlings purchased from catalogs or nurseries. The most highly scented is the English species, *Lavandula officinalis*, also often listed as *L. spica*, a plant that reaches about 3 feet at maturity. There are dwarfs, Hidcote and Munstead, for growing in small containers on the patio—about 18 inches tall. You can also start lavender from seed in peat pots indoors as it is slow to germinate and takes some coddling. Lavender prefers rich, alkaline soils on the sandy side. Harvest the buds just before they open. You will need a dozen lavender plants to make moth bags annually. Buy three and multiply your holding by rooting tip cuttings of semi-new wood in damp sand in early spring.

Marjoram

Marjoram is a perennial in mild climates but is planted as an annual in cool regions. It grows to about 12 inches tall. Sow seed indoors in spring in individual pots. Germination takes 10 to 15 days. Set out when the weather warms in sweet, well-drained soil in full sun. Water well during dry spells. Harvest the leaves for fresh use or to freeze. At the end of the season, pot up marjoram and bring it indoors as a houseplant. One or two plants supply the average family needs.

Mint

Mints are perennials that multiply easily via underground runners. They are hardy to about 20 degrees. Dig a portion of a friend's plant or buy a small started mint plant, set it in a large can open at both ends, and plant it in the open garden or in a container. It spreads beyond the number of plants you are likely to use. It is most successful in semishade in humusy soil. There are many attractive varieties, but the best for cooking use and to make mint teas are spearmint or peppermint. You can propagate the mints by rooting tip cuttings in moist sand or in water in a sunny window. One plant to start with is all you need.

Oregano

Oregano is a perennial, hardy to about 25 degrees, 24 to 30 inches tall at maturity. Start seed or cuttings rooted in spring and plant in full sun in ordinary garden soil. It can stand the hottest spot you have. Keep it clipped and use the clippings fresh or freeze them. Or dry them for winter use. Potted in fall, oregano makes a fairly good houseplant. One plant is all you need to start with.

Parsley

Parsley is probably the most useful of the kitchen herbs and I grow at least half a dozen plants each year. It's a biennial about 6 to 12 inches tall that will come back the second year but will quickly go to seed. Start this year's plants from seed. Soak them overnight in warm water to speed germination. It takes 10 to 15 days to germinate indoors and 3 weeks outdoors. Next year, plant a new set of seeds near the old bed so that when the old plants begin to bolt, the new ones will be ready for picking. Pick leaves at will to use fresh or to freeze. I find dried parsley tasteless. Parsley does well in sun or partial shade, in moderately rich soil.

Rosemary

Rosemary is a perennial hardy only to freezing point. About 2 feet tall in cool climates, it can reach to 6 feet in warm areas. It grows well in sandy, even poor, soil as long as the soil is sweet and there is lots of sun. Start seeds indoors as they are slow to germinate, or start as root tip cuttings in damp sand in spring and transplant when the weather warms. Harvest the leaves for fresh use or to dry as needed. Or bring your rosemary indoors and use it fresh all winter; it makes a fairly good houseplant. One plant is enough for most families.

Sage

Salvia officinalis, Mammoth Sage, is considered one of the best sages for flavoring. It is a straggly plant; keep it picked and trimmed or it will take over the garden. It is a perennial, hardy to about 30 degrees. Sow seeds indoors in March, where germination takes about 14 days; or sow outdoors in late spring, where germination takes 21 to 30 days. Or start plants from cuttings taken in spring and rooted in sand. Left year after year in the open garden, it will ground-layer and root new plants by itself. One or two sage plants is all you are likely to need. Take leaves at will for fresh use and to freeze or dry for winter use.

Savory

Summer savory, an annual, is the milder type. Winter savory, a perennial, hardy to about 20 degrees, is stronger in flavor. Sow seed in the open garden in mid-spring. Germination takes about 7 days. Summer savory prefers light soil with lots of humus; winter savory needs a well-drained soil and requires less moisture than the summer type. Both thrive in full sun. Winter savory also makes a good house-plant if trimmed often. One or two savories of either type are all the average family needs.

Shallots

This is a small herb, like a cross between a tiny onion and a clove of garlic, with a flavor that resembles both. Seedsmen and catalogs sell planting heads, which are divided into cloves to be planted broad base down in very rich soil. Plant shallots when the frost has left the ground, in holes 1 inch deep; cover with ½ inch of soil. Like chives or onions, shallots grow tall, tubelike stems that bear round seed heads. When a few seed heads have fallen over, bend them all over and dig the bulbs 8 to 10 days later. Leave them to dry for 2 or 3 days in the open garden, then braid them by the stem ends or remove the stem ends and store in a cool, dry place in a mesh bag for winter use. A quarter pound of shallots will supply the average family with enough shallot sets to plant a 25-foot row—plenty for winter use.

Tarragon

Tarragon is a perennial that grows 6 to 8 inches tall and is hardy to about 10 degrees. It should be grown from root division, as good tarragon seed is hard to come by. Once you have a tarragon of a good type, you can increase your plants by taking tip cuttings in August and rooting them in moist sand. Set the plants out in mid-spring, in moderately rich soil in semishade or full sun. Use leaves fresh as needed or freeze sprigs. Tarragon will grow for some time indoors on a sunny window sill as a potted plant. If it begins to fail, putting it in the refrigerator for a month or so is supposed to bring it back.

Thyme

Thyme is a perennial hardy to about 20 degrees, and about 6 to 12 inches tall. The best variety for flavoring is *Thymus vulgaris*. Good seed is hard to come by and takes 15 to 21 days to germinate, so buy started plants if you can. Plant in mid-spring in dry, sandy soil in full sunlight. You can pot up thyme and bring it indoors for winter. Keep the plants clipped to encourage bushiness. Pick leaves or sprigs as needed for fresh use and to freeze or dry. One or two plants will supply the needs of the average family.

HERB RECIPES

BASIL VINEGAR

Preparation: Follow recipe for Caraway Vinegar, but replace caraway seeds with basil, leaving sprigs whole.

CARAWAY VINEGAR

Preparation: To make 1 pint of caraway vinegar, you will need 2 tablespoons of dried caraway seeds and 2 cups of white-wine vinegar. In a small glass bowl mash the seeds. Heat the vinegar to the boiling point but don't boil. Pour the vinegar over the seeds, stirring and mashing as you pour. Pour into a pint jar, cover, and let stand in a warm room for 10 days. Shake the jar daily. At the end of the 10 days taste. If the flavor isn't strong enough, strain out the old sediment and start all over again with 2 more tablespoons of caraway seeds, mashed. When it has macerated for another 10 days, strain through wet doubled cheesecloth, cap, and keep in the refrigerator.

CORIANDER CURRY POWDER

Preparation: For each ¼ cup of coriander seeds, you will need 2 tablespoons saffron threads, 1 tablespoon cumin seed, 1 tablespoon mustard seed, ½ tablespoon crushed red pepper, and 1 tablespoon poppy seed. Grind together in a pepper mill, mix well, and bottle tightly.

GARLIC BUTTER

Preparation: For each 6 cloves of garlic, you will need ½ cup of soft butter, salt and pepper to taste, 2 tablespoons finely minced fresh parsley, and 1 cup boiling water. Set the unpeeled cloves in the boiling water. Bring back to a boil and boil for 5 minutes. Drain, peel, and rinse under cold water. Return to the boiling water and allow the water to boil up once. Drain the garlic again, and pound it with the salt and pepper to a smooth paste in the bottom of a small bowl. Beat the butter into the garlic and combine with the parsley. Store in refrigerator or freeze. Serve 1 teaspoonful with broiled or boiled white fish, hamburgers, steaks, boiled potatoes, and to enrich sauces made with drippings from roasts.

CANDIED FRESH GINGER

Preparation: For each pound of fresh gingerroot, you will need 2 cups granulated sugar, 1 cup water, 1 cup superfine sugar. Pare the fresh gingerroot and cut into thin slices across the grain. Cover with cold water in a saucepan and heat to boiling. Simmer 5 minutes. Drain ginger. Cover with cold water. Heat to boiling, simmer 5 minutes, drain, and dry on paper towels. Combine granulated sugar and 1 cup water in heavy kettle and boil 10 minutes. Add ginger.

Cook but do not boil, stirring until all syrup is absorbed, about 40 minutes. Remove ginger from kettle and place on wire racks to dry. Roll ginger in superfine sugar sprinkled on waxed paper and let ginger stand in sugar until it crystallizes. Spoon into cold sterilized jars and seal.

HERB MIXTURE FOR PORK

Preparation: In a small bowl, crush 3 tablespoons each of dried summer savory (or 2 tablespoons of winter savory), dried sweet basil, dried sage, and dried rosemary. Mix thoroughly, and put up in a small bottle with a tight stopper. Use 1 teaspoonful to flavor 4 to 6 portions of pork chops, or a pork casserole.

HERB MIXTURE FOR BEEF

Preparation: Mix 3 tablespoons each of the dried crushed leaves of summer savory, basil, sweet marjoram, parsley, and chervil. Test it, then change the emphasis to suit yourself and mix in larger batches for storing.

LAVENDER POTPOURRI

Preparation: For each 3 cups of dried lavender flowers you will need 2 tablespoons each of dried lemon peel, dried sweet basil, and dried rosemary; 4 tablespoons each of orrisroot powder and dried spearmint leaves, 1 teaspoon of benzoic acid powder, and 6 drops of oil of lavender. Combine all the ingredients except the oil. Add the oil a drop at a time, tossing as you add. Seal and store in a dark, dry, warm place for 6 weeks, shaking daily. Pack into a glass container with a tight stopper.

FRESH MINT SAUCE

Preparation: For each ⅓ cup of finely chopped mint leaves, you will need 3 tablespoons cold water, 1½ teaspoons confectioner's sugar, and ⅓ cup strong vinegar. In a small saucepan, combine water and sugar, and over low heat stir until the sugar is dissolved. Add mint leaves and vinegar, mix well, and allow to marinate 30 minutes before serving. The sauce can be stored in the refrigerator.

MOTH REPELLENT FROM KITCHEN HERBS

Preparation: Knot into a nylon stocking end, or into a square of muslin or cheesecloth, herbs in the proportions of 1 cup each of dried rosemary, thyme, and mint to ½ cup of ground cloves.

FRESH PARSLEY SALAD

Preparation: You will need 1 large iceberg lettuce head, torn, 6 tablespoons vegetable oil, 1½ tablespoons vinegar, ⅛ teaspoon dry mustard, ¼ teaspoon granulated sugar, 1 teaspoon salt, ⅛ teaspoon black pepper, ½ cup very finely minced parsley. Mix all ingredients but parsley and lettuce in the blender for 1 minute at low speed. Chill. Wash the lettuce, tear to bite-size pieces, and chill. Just before serving, toss the lettuce in the chilled dressing until thoroughly mixed, then toss lightly with the parsley.

MOTH REPELLENT WITH ROSEMARY

Preparation: The simple moth repellent below combines rosemary and lavender. The recipe for Rubbing Lotion can be used as well. Bruise together in a small bowl 2 cups each of dried lavender and dried rosemary, 1 tablespoon of crushed cloves, and the dried peel of a lemon. Tie into cloth muslin bags.

ROSEMARY HERB PILLOWS

Preparation: You will need 4 cups dried rosemary, 4 cups dried lavender, and 8 cups dry pine needles. Crush the ingredients together and fill small bags to put under sleeping pillows or with nightclothes in a drawer.

RUBBING LOTIONS

Preparation: Pick 1 cup of leaves from your thyme, lavender, verbena, mint, marjoram, or rosemary plants and crush with a pestle in the bottom of a 1-quart glass jar. Pour rubbing alcohol over the crushed leaves, cap tightly, let stand 2 weeks, shaking daily. Strain through a fine cloth, bottle, and cap tightly. Use after baths.

FRESH SAGE STUFFING FOR PORK OR FISH

Preparation: You will need 2 tablespoons butter, ¾ cups minced onion, 2 cups bread crumbs, ¼ cup beef bouillon, 1 clove garlic, mashed, 2 teaspoons fresh or 1 teaspoon ground sage, ¼ cup minced parsley, ⅛ teaspoon allspice, ½ teaspoon salt, ⅛ teaspoon pepper, and 1 whole egg. In a medium saucepan melt the butter and simmer the onions until translucent. Remove from the heat. In a large mixing bowl combine onions and pan juices with the remaining ingredients and mix well. Spread the stuffing along the cut between the ribs and the boney back of a pork rib roast, and tie the roast back together with a clean string. Cook ½ hour longer than usual.

SAGE BATH MIX

Preparation: You will need 1 cup each of camomile, spearmint, sage, rosemary, and thyme. Bruise the ingredients together in a large bowl, then sew into little cheesecloth bags. Drop into the bath when you turn on the water.

FRESH SHALLOT BUTTER

This butter recipe and the next one are made with shallots and are typical of gourmet uses of this wonderful herb.

Preparation: You will need ½ cup butter, 3 tablespoons minced shallots, and 2 tablespoons minced parsley. Cream the butter in a small bowl and crush the minced shallots into the butter. Beat with the parsley into the butter. Chill. Put 2 teaspoons of shallot butter on broiling steaks or fish 3 minutes before the end of the cooking. Store in refrigerator or freezer.

BUTTER FOR SNAILS

Preparation: You will need ½ cup butter; 2 tablespoons minced, peeled shallots; 2 cloves garlic, peeled and minced; 2 tablespoons minced parsley; and salt and pepper. Whip the butter soft. Crush the shallots and the garlic into the butter and beat together with the parsley. Add salt and pepper to taste.

Use this butter to stuff snail shells after you have inserted canned snails into clean shells. Broil the snails until the butter melts completely and they are sizzling hot. Or put 1 teaspoonful on each fish fillet 5 minutes before it is served. Store in refrigerator or freezer.

TARRAGON VINEGAR

Preparation: You will need 1 cup of tightly packed fresh leafy tarragon tips and 1 quart of white-wine vinegar. Bruise the leaves in the bottom of a bowl, then press them into a 1-quart canning jar. Bring the vinegar to a boiling point but do not boil. Pour at once over the herbs, leaving 2 inches of headroom in the jar. Cap the jar tightly and let the contents marinate for 10 days in a warm room. Shake the jar vigorously daily. A the end of the 10 days taste the vinegar. If you want the flavor to taste more strongly of tarragon, strain out the herbs, pick and crush a new cupful of tarragon tips, and pour the vinegar over it. Leave 10 days more. Strain the vinegar through clean cheesecloth, and pour into an appropriate bottle. Scald a 4-inch sprig of fresh tarragon for 15 seconds in rapidly boiling water, dry quickly on paper towels, and press into the tarragon vinegar. Cap the bottle tightly.

VINAIGRETTE SAUCE WITH CHIVES

Preparation: To make ⅓ cup you will need 2 cloves garlic, peeled; 1 teaspoon salt; ⅛ teaspoon pepper; 1 cup olive or vegetable oil; ½ teaspoon dry mustard; 2 tablespoons white-wine vinegar; 2 tablespoons Tarragon Vinegar; 1 shallot, peeled, or 1 slice of onion; 3 tablespoons minced chives; and 2 tablespoons minced parsley. In the blender process all the ingredients for 2 minutes. Store covered in the refrigerator until ready to serve.

APPENDIX A: WHERE TO ORDER

GARDENING CATALOGS

Here's a listing of some of the important mail order suppliers of seeds for food plants; there are many others with fine seeds and plants to offer.

F. W. Bolgiana Seed & Plant Company, Inc.
411 New York Avenue, N.E.
Washington, D.C. 20002

D. V. Burrell Seed Growers Company
Box 150
Rocky Ford, Colorado 81067

Burgess Seed & Plant Company
Box 2000
Galesburg, Michigan 49053

W. Atlee Burpee Co.
Philadelphia, Pennsylvania 19132

Comstock, Ferre & Company
Wethersfield, Connecticut 06109

Earl May Seed & Nursery Company
6032 Elm Street
Shenandoah, Iowa 51601

Farmer Seed & Nursery Company
Faribault, Minnesota 55021

Henry Field Seed and Nursey Company
407 Sycamore Street
Shenandoah, Iowa 51601

Gurney Seed & Nursery Company
1448 Page Street
Yankton, South Dakota 57078

Joseph Harris Company
Moreton Farm
Rochester, New York 14624

H. G. Hastings Company
Box 4088
Atlanta, Georgia 30302

Jackson & Perkins Company
Medford, Oregon 97501

J. W. Jung Seed Company
Station 8
Randolph, Wisconsin 53956

D. Landreth Seed Company
2700 Wilmarco Avenue
Baltimore, Maryland 21223

Nichols Garden Nursery
1190 North Pacific Highway
Albany, Oregon 97321

Robert Nichols Seed Company
Box 15487
Dallas, Texas 75215

L. L. Olds Seed Company
2901 Packers Avenue
Box 1069
Madison, Wisconsin 53701

George W. Park Seed Company, Inc.
Greenwood, South Carolina 29646

Reuter Seed Company, Inc.
New Orleans, Louisiana 70119

Seedway
Hall, New York 14463

Harry E. Saier
Dimondale, Michigan 48821

R. H. Shumway Seedsman
628 Cedar Street
Rockford, Illinois 61101

Stark Brothers Nurseries
Louisiana, Missouri 63353

Otis S. Twilley Seed Company
Salisbury, Maryland 21801

George Tait & Sons, Inc.
900 Tidewater Drive
Norfolk, Virginia 23504

The Wetsel Seed Company, Inc.
Box 791
Harrisonburg, Virginia 22801

APPENDIX B: LIST OF

GOVERNMENT EXTENSION SERVICES

A gardener's best friend can be his local Agriculture Extension Service. The Service will test your soil, in most states for a nominal charge, and give good advice on varieties most likely to be successful in your area. It will recommend possible solutions for any trouble that besets you. The Service is not, as is often supposed, interested in helping only the professional farmer; it is also designed to help you, the tax-paying home gardener. Look below for the address of the Extension Service nearest you.

Alabama Polytechnic Institute, Auburn, Alabama
University of Alaska, College, Alaska
University of Arizona, Tucson, Arizona
College of Agriculture, University of Arkansas, Fayetteville, Arkansas
College of Agriculture, University of California, Berkeley, California
Colorado State University, Fort Collins, Colorado
College of Agriculture, University of Connecticut, Storrs, Connecticut
Connecticut Agricultural Experiment Station, New Haven, Connecticut
School of Agriculture, University of Delaware, Newark, Delaware
University of Florida, Gainesville, Florida
College of Agriculture, University of Georgia, Athens, Georgia

University of Hawaii, Honolulu, Hawaii
University of Idaho, Moscow, Idaho
College of Agriculture, University of Illinois, Urbana, Illinois
Purdue University, Lafayette, Indiana
Iowa State College of Agriculture, Ames, Iowa
Kansas State College of Agriculture, Manhattan, Kansas
College of Agriculture, University of Kentucky, Lexington, Kentucky
Agricultural College, Louisiana State University, Baton Rouge, Louisiana
College of Agriculture, University of Maine, Orono, Maine
University of Maryland, College Park, Maryland
College of Agriculture, University of Massachusetts, Amherst, Massachusetts
College of Agriculture, Michigan State University, East Lansing, Michigan
Institute of Agriculture, University of Minnesota, St. Paul, Minnesota
Mississippi State College, State College, Mississippi
College of Agriculture, University of Missouri, Columbia, Missouri
Montana State College, Bozeman, Montana
College of Agriculture, University of Nebraska, Lincoln, Nebraska
College of Agriculture, University of Nevada, Reno, Nevada
University of New Hampshire, Durham, New Hampshire
Rutgers University, New Brunswick, New Jersey
College of Agriculture, State College, New Mexico
College of Agriculture, Cornell University, Ithaca, New York
State College of Agriculture, University of North Carolina, Raleigh, North Carolina
State Agricultural College, Fargo, North Dakota
College of Agriculture, Ohio State University, Columbus, Ohio
Oklahoma A. and M. College, Stillwater, Oklahoma
Oregon State College, Corvallis, Oregon
Pennsylvania State University, University Park, Pennsylvania
University of Puerto Rico, Box 607, Río Piedras, Puerto Rico
University of Rhode Island, Kingston, Rhode Island
Clemson Agricultural College, Clemson, South Carolina
South Dakota State College, College Station, South Dakota
College of Agriculture, University of Tennessee, Knoxville, Tennessee
Texas A. and M. College, College Station, Texas
College of Agriculture, Utah State University, Logan, Utah
State Agricultural College, University of Vermont, Burlington, Vermont
Virginia Polytechnic Institute, Blacksburg, Virginia

State College of Washington, Pullman, Washington
West Virginia University, Morgantown, West Virginia
College of Agriculture, University of Wisconsin, Madison, Wisconsin
College of Agriculture, University of Wyoming, Laramie, Wyoming

APPENDIX C: WHEN TO PLANT VEGETABLES

Early Spring

As soon as the ground can be worked *

VEGETABLE	PLANTS 50' ROW	YIELD 50' ROW	SPACE BETWEEN ROWS	SPACE BETWEEN PLANTS	DEPTH TO PLANT	APPROXIMATE DAYS TO MATURITY
Asparagus (perennial)	35 plants	25 lbs.	4'	18"	5"-6"	second season
Beets	½ oz.	1 bushel	12"-18"	2"-3"	½"	early, 45 days; late, 65 days
Broccoli	25 plants (1 pk. seed)	25-40 heads	20"-24"	18"	¼"-½"	plants, 50-60 days; seed, 80-100 days
Brussels sprouts	25 plants (1 pk. seed)	1-2 bushels	20"-24"	18"	½"	plants, 60-70 days; seed, 95 days
Cabbage	25 plants (1 pk. seed)	25 heads	20"-30"	18"	½"	early, 40-50 days; late, 70-90 days
Carrots	¼ oz.	1 bushel	20"	1"-2"	¼"	75-80 days
Cauliflower	25 plants (1 pk. seed)	25 heads	20"-30"	18"	½"	plants, 65-75 days; seed, 80-100 days
Chard, Swiss	½ oz.	2 bushels	18"	4"-6"	¼"	55 days
Chicory	½ pk.	30 lbs.	12"	4"	¼"	112 days
Cress, Garden	1 pk.	20 lbs.	24"	12"	¼"	20 days
Garlic (cloves)	½ lb.	¾ bushel	8"	3"	1¼"	125 days
Horseradish (perennial)	25 roots	¾ bushel	24"	15"	12"	120 days
Kale	½ pk.	125 lbs.	12"-18"	10"	½"	56-75 days

Leeks	2 pk.	100 plants	10"–12"	2"–3" later 6"	1/4"	130 days
Lettuce	1 pk.	50 lbs.	12"	2"–3"	1/4"	40–90 days
Onion sets	1/2 lb.	1 bushel	12"	8"	1"	110 days
Parsnips	2 pk.	1 1/2 bushels	12"	3"–4"	1/2"–1 1/4"	95–150 days
Peas	1/2 lb.	1 bushel	20"–30"	3"	1"–2"	early, 58 days / late, 80 days
Potatoes, Irish	2–3 lbs.	2 bushels	2'–3'	18"	trench 4"–6" cover 2"	80–100 days
Radishes	2 pk.	50 bunches	12"	1"–2"	1/4"	early, 20 days / late, 60 days
Rhubarb (perennial)	17 roots	too much	3'	3'	10"	second season
Spinach	1/2 oz.	1 bushel	12"	4"	1/4"–1/2"	40–50 days
Strawberries (perennial)	35 plants	1/2–1 quart	4'	18"	1 1/2"	second season
Turnips	1 pk.	1 bushel	18"	6"	1/2"	early, 35 days / late, 60 days

* "As soon as the ground can be worked" means as soon as a handful of soil squeezed into a ball in your fist crumbles readily under pressure from your thumb.

Mid-Spring

As soon as the ground has warmed *

VEGETABLE	PLANTS 50′ ROW	YIELD 50′ ROW	SPACE BETWEEN ROWS	SPACE BETWEEN PLANTS	DEPTH TO PLANT	APPROXIMATE DAYS TO MATURITY
Artichokes (perennial)	17 plants	2 bushels	36″	36″	5″–6″	second season
Beans						
bush, snap	¼ lb.	25 quarts	20″–30″	3″–5″	1″–1½″	55–65 days
pole	¼ lb.	2 bushels	30″–36″	4–6 per pole	1″	65 days
limas, bush	¼ lb.	7 quarts	30″–36″	4″	1″–1½″	75 days
limas, pole	½ lb.	10 quarts	30″–36″	4–6 per pole	1″	12–14 weeks
Celeriac	¼ pk.	100 roots	20″	6″	¼″	120 days
Celery	¼ pk.	100	20″–24″	6″	¼″	120 days
Corn						
sweet	¼ lb.	75 ears	36″	8″	½″–1″	75 days
Indian	¼ lb.	75 ears	24″–36″	10″–12″	½″–1″	105 days
popcorn	¼ lb.	12–15 lbs.	24″–36″	10″–12″	½″–1″	90–105 days
Cucumbers	½ pk.	75 lbs.	48″	4″–6″	½″ in peat pot	50 days
Gourds	½ pk.	Too much	36″	5′	1″ in peat pot	100 days
Kohlrabi	¼ oz.	30 lbs.	18″	6″–8″	½″–1″	48–60 days
Parsley (biennial)	½ pk.	25 lbs.	18″	6″–8″	¼″	120 days
Peppers	35 plants	2 bushels	20″–24″	18″	¼″	60–80 days
Pumpkins	½ pk.	150 lbs.	5′	5′	1″	100–120 days

	PLANTS 50' ROW	YIELD 50' ROW	SPACE BETWEEN ROWS	SPACE BETWEEN PLANTS	DEPTH TO PLANT	APPROXIMATE DAYS TO MATURITY
Rutabaga	1 pk.	1 bushel	18"	8"	½"	85–90 days
Salsify	2 pk.	1 bushel	12"	3"–4"	¼"–½"	120 days
Shallots	½ lb.	½ bushel	12"	3"	1"	80–100 days
Spinach, New Zealand	½ oz.	1 bushel	18"	6"	¼"–½"	70 days
Squash						
summer	½ pk.	60–70 lbs.	24"–36"	6"	1"	45–50 days
winter	½ pk.	150 lbs.	6'	5'	1"	90–110 days
Tomatoes	17 plants	75 pounds	3'–4'	2'–3'	¼"–½"	70–80 days

* "As soon as the ground has warmed" is about three to four weeks after the ground has become workable.

Late Spring

When the temperature stays above 70 degrees

VEGETABLE	PLANTS 50' ROW	YIELD 50' ROW	SPACE BETWEEN ROWS	SPACE BETWEEN PLANTS	DEPTH TO PLANT	APPROXIMATE DAYS TO MATURITY
Eggplant	½ pk.	150 fruit	20"–30"	18"	½"	60–75 days
Melons						
cantaloupe	½ pk.	40–60 fruit	4'	8"–10"	1" in peat pot	70 days
watermelon	1 pk.	150 lbs.	6'	3'	1"	70–85 days
Okra	2 pk.	30 quarts	20"	15"–24"	½"	56 days
Sweet potatoes	2–3 lbs.	2 bushels	24"–36"	18"	5"	120–150 days

209

VEGETABLE	WHAT IT LOOKS LIKE	WHAT IT PROBABLY IS	HOW TO CONTROL OR PREVENT
Asparagus	Ferns yellow, have spiky look.	Rust	Plant resistant varieties.
	New shoots eaten.	Beetle	Rotenone during harvest; Methoxychlor after the harvest.
Beans	Round, dark, sunken areas on pods, pink in center.	Anthracnose	Use Western seed. Do not touch plants when moist.
	Brown area on leaves, red-brown spots on pods.	Bacterial blight	As above.
	Yellow mottling of leaves; stunted plants.	Mosaics	Plant resistant varieties. Control aphids that spread disease with Malathion.
	Skeletonized leaves.	Mexican bean beetle	Control with rotenone dust.
	Round holes in dried, stored beans.	Bean weevil	Use treated seed.
Lima beans	White mold on pods.	Downy mildew	Treat weekly with Maneb or Zineb.
Beets	Brown spots that dry and leave holes.	Leaf spot	Bordeaux mixture; Ziram or Zineb.
	Small green lice on leaves, which become dwarfed.	Aphids	Nicotine dust or spray.
Brassicas cabbage cauliflower	Plants yellow, brown, then die.	Black rot	Use 4-year crop rotation.
Brussels sprouts	Plants wilt; roots are malformed.	Club root	As above. Keep soil pH between 6.0 and 7.0.

Crop	Symptom	Trouble	Control
Broccoli	Plant dwarfed; yellowed lower leaves drop.	Yellows	Plant resistant varieties.
	Foliage eaten by green caterpillar.	Cabbage worms	Rotenone.
	Stems of seedlings eaten by pale brown caterpillar.	Cutworms	Use prepared poison bait.
Carrot	Yellow or brown spots on leaves. Top may die.	Leaf blight	Maneb or Zineb, 4 to 5 times at 10-day intervals, starting when plants are 6" tall.
	Yellowing of center leaves.	Yellows	Control leafhopper that spreads disease with Malathion or Carbaryl.
Celery	Leaves show small yellow spots that turn gray.	Early blight	Use treated seed. Use Maneb or Zineb every 7 days.
	Older leaves have small brown spots that develop black dots.	Late blight	As above.
	Stalks eaten by mottled brown bug.	Tarnished plant bug	Control with Malathion or rotenone.
Corn	Plants show silver or gray swellings that puff black spores at maturity.	Corn smut	Burn swellings before maturity. Use 3-year crop rotation, and resistant varieties.
	Light green or yellow streaks on leaves. Plant stunted or wilted.	Bacterial wilt	Control flea beetles that spread disease with Carbaryl before seedling appears. Use resistant varieties.
	Holes bored into ears.	Corn borer	Use Carbaryl when half the tassel can be seen.
	Silk and tips eaten.	Corn earworm	Treat emerging silk with Carbaryl. Repeat 3 times at 2-day intervals.

211

Vegetable Troubles and What to Do (*Continued*)

VEGETABLE	WHAT IT LOOKS LIKE	WHAT IT PROBABLY IS	HOW TO CONTROL OR PREVENT
Cucurbits cucumber squash melons	Sunken spots on fruit, pink at first, then black.	Anthracnose	Use treated seed. Rotate crops. Use Captan or Maneb at 7- to 10-day intervals starting when plants appear.
	Grayish purple fungus on underside of leaves.	Downy mildew	Use resistant varieties. Treat at 7- to 10-day intervals with Maneb.
	Powdery gray-white growth on leaves. Defoliation.	Powdery mildew	Spray with Karathane when mildew appears. Repeat 10 days later.
	Leaves turn dull green and wilt; plant dies.	Bacterial wilt	Rotenone dust.
	Foliage devoured.	Striped cucumber beetle	Control with Carbaryl, Malathion or Methoxychlor.
Eggplant	Leaves turn yellow, then brown; plants stunted.	Verticillium wilt	If garden is infected, change location.
	Young plants covered with brown spots.	Phomopsis blight	Use treated seed. Use Maneb or Captan weekly.
	Seedlings rot at soil level, and die. Tiny holes in leaves.	Flea beetle	Use Carbaryl or rotenone at weekly intervals.
Lettuce	Rot at plant base spreads to top.	Bottom rot, drop rot	Change planting to well-drained location. Use 4-year crop rotation. Omit mulch.
	Chewed leaves. Badly formed heads.	Leafhoppers	Use Carbaryl, Malathion, or Methoxychlor as soon as seedlings appear.

212

Melons	See Cucurbits.		
Onions	Pink root	Plants stunted, then die. Roots turn pink, then black.	Use resistant varieties. Do not plant onions where disease exists.
	Downy mildew	Plants turn yellow; tops of leaves have pale green spots.	Maneb or Zineb.
	Thrips	Leaves at neck of bulb eaten.	Several applications of Malathion.
Parsley	Crown rot	Soft rot that spreads.	Crop rotation.
Peas	Root rot	Stems decay; plant dies.	Resistant varieties. Crop rotation; plant only in well-drained soil.
	Aphids	Dwarfed leaves: small green lice.	Nicotine dust.
	Ascochyta blight	Gray areas, with brown dot, on pods and leaves.	Resistant varieties. Crop rotation.
Peppers	Bacterial leaf spot	Raised yellow spots on leaves.	Use treated seed. Control disease with fixed copper spray.
	Phoma rot	Water-soaked areas which enlarge and blacken.	Crop rotation.
	Blossom end rot	Dark brown sunken area on fruit bottom.	Avoid excessive use of nitrogen fertilizer. Maintain even moisture supply.
	Aphids	Soft-bodied insects on undersides of leaves.	Malathion.
	Mites or red spider	Small white spots on leaves where minute pale or reddish insects have fed.	Malathion.

Vegetable Troubles and What to Do (*Continued*)

VEGETABLE	WHAT IT LOOKS LIKE	WHAT IT PROBABLY IS	HOW TO CONTROL OR PREVENT
Potato	Dark brown circular spots on foliage.	Early blight	Zineb; plant only healthy tubers.
	Water-soaked areas.	Late blight	As above.
	Dark fungus on tuber.	Rhizoctonia	Use disease-free seed.
	Scabs with corky ridge on tuber.	Scab	Plant only in soil with acid pH.
	Reddish larvae on leaves; striped beetles with brown markings.	Potato beetle	Rotenone.
Pumpkin	See Cucurbits.		
Spinach	Yellow spots on leaf tops, gray mold on underside.	Downy mildew	Meneb or Zineb; several applications.
	Mottled yellow on inner leaves spreading to outer foliage.	Yellows	Control aphids which spread disease with Malathion.
Squash	See Cucurbits.		
Tomato	Dark brown sunken area on fruit bottom.	Blossom end rot	Avoid excessive use of nitrogen fertilizer. Maintain even moisture.
	Lower leaves wilt, yellow and die.	Fusarium wilt	Plant resistant varieties. Use 5-year crop rotation.
	Rolling of leaves.	Leaf roll	Does not affect yield.

214

Abnormal fruit formation at lower end. Cause unknown.	Catface	Grow locally recommended varieties.
Brown irregular target-pattern spots.	Early blight	Maneb every 5 to 7 days during growing season.
Dark, water-soaked greenish-black blotches.	Late blight	As above.
Round water-soaked spots on fruit.	Anthracnose	Stake plants. Apply Maneb weekly, starting when plants bloom.
Leaves and fruit eaten by large hideous green caterpillar.	Horn worm	Control with Carbaryl; or pick off by hand.
Small white spots on leaves.	Mites or red spiders	Apply Malathion to underside of leaves.
Tiny holes in leaves.	Flea beetle	Carbaryl or rotenone at weekly intervals.

Report troubles hard to identify to your Agricultural Extension Service.

APPENDIX E: FRUIT PLANTING AND SPRAYING

FRUIT	PER PLANT YIELD	HEIGHT	DISTANCE BETWEEN ROWS	DISTANCE BETWEEN PLANTS	POLLINATION	USE COMBINATION SPRAY
Dwarf Apple	1-2 bushels	8'-10'		Allow 10' x 10'	Cross-pollination required.	1. When buds show pink but before blossoms open.
Semi-dwarf Apple	2-3 bushels	12'-15'		Allow 10' x 20'	As above.	2. As soon as petals have fallen. 3. Ten days later.
Dwarf Pear	1-2 bushels	8'-10'		Allow 10' x 10'	Cross-pollination required.	4. Two weeks later.
Semi-dwarf Pear	2-3 bushels	12'-15'		Allow 10' x 20'	As above.	5. Two weeks later (omit for early varieties). 6. Two weeks later.
Dwarf Peach	1-2 bushels	8'-10'		Allow 10' x 10'	Most are self-pollinators.	1. In very early spring while plant is still dormant.
Semi-dwarf Peach	2-3 bushels	12'-15'		Allow 10' x 20'	As above.	2. As soon as petals have fallen. 3. Ten days later.
Nectarine and apricot	As above.			As above.	As above.	4. One week later. 5. Two weeks later. 6. Six weeks later (omit for early varieties).
Semi-dwarf Plum	1-2 bushels	12'-15'		Allow 10' x 20'	Most require cross-pollination.	1. As soon as petals have fallen.
Standard Plum	2-4 bushels	20'-25'		Allow 16' x 16'	As above.	2. Ten days later.
Standard Sour Cherry	1-2 bushels	20'-25'		Allow 16' x 16'	All are self-pollinators.	3. One week later.

216

Semi-dwarf Sweet Cherry	1–2 bushels	12'–15'	Allow 10' x 20'		Cross-pollination required.	4. Two weeks later (omit for early varieties of cherry).
Strawberry	½–1 qt.	6"	3'–4'	18"	A few require cross-pollination.	Protect from birds with netting.
Raspberry	1½ qt.	6'–8'	6'–7'	3'		As above.
Blackberry	1¼ qt.	6'–7'	6'–7'	3'		As above.
Blueberry	4 qt.	10'–15'	8'–10'	4'–5'	Cross-pollination improves yield.	As above.
Grapes	15–30 pounds	up to 50'	7'	7'	Some require cross-pollination.	1. When new growth is 12' long. 2. When shoots are 12". 3. One week after bloom. 4. Three weeks later. 5. Four weeks before harvest.

217

APPENDIX F

HERB PLANTING AND USE

HERB	HEIGHT	PROPAGATION METHOD	REMARKS AND USES
Anise (annual)	2'–3'	Seed	Licorice flavor; fresh leaves in salads; seed in breads; cakes; dried leaves for teas; powdered flower flavors wine or alcohol.
Basil, sweet (annual)	1'–2'	Seed; seedlings	Keep top pinched out; fresh leaves for vinegar, soup, salad, tomatoes.
Borage (annual)	18"–2'	Seed	Attracts bees. Won't transplant. Cucumber flavor. Fresh leaf in cool drinks, salads, pickles.
Caraway (biennial)	2'	Seed	Harvest seeds second season. Sows itself. Use seeds in breads, sauerkraut, with cheese.
Catnip (perennial)	2'–3'	Seed; root division	Cut for drying when first flower buds appear.
Chervil (annual)	6"–12"	Seed	Flavor like fine parsley. Use fresh leaf in sorrel salad, spinach soup, egg dishes, salads. Dry for winter.
Chives (perennial)	10"–12"	Seed; bulbs	Mild onion flavor. Use fresh in soups, salads, cheese, fish and meat sauces.
Coriander (annual)	18"	Seed	Won't transplant. Ripe seeds are fragrant. Dried powdery seeds in breads, baking, with baked apples, vinegar. Crush seeds for demi-tasse.
Cumin (annual)	6'	Seed	Gather seeds for use in Oriental cooking and curries.
Dill (annual)	2'–3'	Seed	Won't transplant; prefers rich soil. Use fern fresh in salads, with vegetables, meats. Dried seed for winter. Dried seed head for pickles.
Fennel, sweet (annual)	6"–10"	Seed	Faint licorice flavor. Use as celery, raw or cooked.

218

HERB	HEIGHT	PROPAGATION METHOD	REMARKS AND USES
Ginger (perennial)	———	———	Grow as a potted plant indoors.
Lavender (perennial)	2'–3'	Seed; root cutting; root division	Very slow to germinate. Keep top pinched out first year. Harvest second season. Dig in wood ashes in fall. Moth deterrent, insect repellent; lovely scent.
Marjoram, sweet (annual)	1½'	Seed; cuttings	Bring indoors in cold climates. Fresh leaf in vinegar, soups, salads, meats, stock, egg dishes, vegetables. Dry for winter.
Mint (perennial)	2'–3'	Root cuttings	Apple and orange mints are most delicate; pineapple is the prettiest. Contain the root, it spreads like a weed. Leaf fresh or dried for teas, lamb sauces, pea soup, jellies, vinegar.
Oregano (perennial)	24"–30"	Seed; cuttings	Use fresh or dried in Italian cooking; notably pizza.
Parsley (biennial)	8"–12"	Seed	Fresh or dried in salads, vegetables, soups, stocks. Dry for winter.
Rosemary	3'–6'	Seed; cuttings	Slow to germinate. Bring indoors for winter. Leaf in stews, soup, Italian recipes. Add to deep fat for frying potatoes.
Sage, garden (perennial)	2'–3'	Seed; cuttings	Replant every 3 to 4 years. Dried leaf for tea, stuffings, soft cheese.
Savory, summer (annual)	12"–18"	Seed	Likes rich soil. Fresh leaf in salads, sauces, meats, stuffings. Dry for winter. Fresh crushed leaf relieves bee sting. Nice in baths.
Tarragon (perennial)	3'	Cuttings	Winterkills easily. Fresh leaves with steaks, chops, salads, fish sauces, mustard, mayonnaise, pickles. Dry for winter.
Thyme (perennial)	6"–8"	Seed; cuttings	Very slow to germinate. Fresh leaves in vinegar, meats and fish stocks, chowders. Dry for winter. Dried leaves in sachets to deter moths.

Index *

* Page numbers in bold face indicate recipes.

221